SECOND EDITION

Full Range Leadership Development

SECOND EDITION

Full Range Leadership Development

Bruce J. Avolio

Executive Director, Center for Leadership & Strategic Thinking
Foster School of Business
University of Washington

Los Angeles | London | New Delhi
Singapore | Washington DC

For information:

SAGE Publications, Inc.
2455 Teller Road
Thousand Oaks, California 91320
E-mail: order@sagepub.com

SAGE Publications India Pvt. Ltd.
B 1/I 1 Mohan Cooperative Industrial Area
Mathura Road, New Delhi 110 044
India

SAGE Publications Ltd.
1 Oliver's Yard
55 City Road
London EC1Y 1SP
United Kingdom

SAGE Publications Asia-Pacific Pte. Ltd.
33 Pekin Street #02-01
Far East Square
Singapore 048763

Printed in the United States of America

Library of Congress Cataloging-in-Publication Data

Full range leadership development/Bruce J. Avolio. — 2nd ed.
    p. cm.
Rev. ed. of: Full leadership development. 1999.
Includes bibliographical references and index.
ISBN 978-1-4129-7475-2 (pbk.)
    1. Leadership. I. Avolio, Bruce J. II. Avolio, Bruce J. Full leadership development.

HD57.7.A95 2011
658.4′092—dc22   2010016009

This book is printed on acid-free paper.

10 11 12 13 14 10 9 8 7 6 5 4 3 2 1

Acquisitions Editor:	Lisa Cuevas Shaw
Editorial Assistant:	MaryAnn Vail
Production Editor:	Libby Larson
Copy Editor:	Heidi Crossman
Typesetter:	C&M Digitals (P) Ltd.
Proofreader:	Wendy Jo Dymond
Indexer:	Wendy Allex
Cover Designer:	Candice Harman
Marketing Manager:	Helen Salmon

CONTENTS

PREFACE

"It's never too late to be what you might have been."

George Eliot

A great deal of my work on leadership over the last decade has made me realize how important it is to step back from what you are doing to envision what might be one of the many desired alternative future states. Now, after this book has been in print for 10 years, I have been asked to do the same with what I said to readers back in 1999, and yes, it does seem like a century ago to me. What I hope to accomplish with this new edition is to share with you what I have learned over the last decade from the mountains of research that has been completed by colleagues around the globe on full range leadership, how leadership development has evolved in practice, and most importantly what it all means to anyone's leadership development. I also intend to add to this book where I hope the field of leadership may head next.

In all the discussions I had about leadership prior to writing the first edition and now the second, one issue repeatedly came up. The issue involves discussing leadership as a systemic process, as a person, or as a combination of both. When discussed as a system and process, we can explore the context in which leadership occurs, the characteristics of followers, the timing of events, the history in which leadership is embedded, and so forth. When discussed as persons, we get into names, personality characteristics, values (whether they are born versus made), experience, how intelligence plays a role in successes and failures, and so forth.

My goal in writing the initial version of this book was to help leaders to begin thinking about leadership as a system, one that has a very broad range and depth. I refer to the range as a "full range of leadership" potential. To think about leadership as a system, one needs to consider the *inputs,* which for now we can say are the people, timing, and resources; the *process,* which we can describe as the system or context in which these people and resources interact over time; and the *outcomes,* which are the levels of motivation and performance we expect to achieve after optimizing the full potential of the leadership system. By optimizing the total leadership system, we intend to enhance each individual's vital force and, in turn, the collective force of the group or organization. At the same time, I remain interested in exploring leadership at individual, team, and organizational levels in order to fully understand how one can effectively lead an entire organizational system.

A core organizing concept used in the first edition of this book is called *vital forces*. The concept of vital forces comes from African humanistic philosophy.[1] One's vital force is either enhanced or diminished by the relationships one has with others.[2] Each of us has our own force and energy that are enhanced (and sometimes diminished) by our relationships with others. How was your vital force when you worked in an organization where every relationship was politically motivated? Full range leadership development works to enhance the individual and collective vital forces in groups and organizations.

According to African humanistic philosophy, in one's family, the grandfather's vital force is seen to be greater than the father's and the son's, given the grandfather's proximity to the family's ancestors. Yet, each family member derives a share of this vital force because of her or his unique relationship with other members and because of the unique talents they each represent. In some ways, the vital force is a perfect blend of collectivism and individualism, which for many people, especially current leaders, would seem quite paradoxical. I will have more to say on this collective-individualism distinction shortly.[3]

Leaders, followers, and peers are enriched in terms of what they can accomplish through the quality of relationships they have developed with each other. If we examine the quality of each relationship in an organization and continuously work to improve those relationships, the probability is reasonably high that the organization will achieve its full potential. I say probability because many other factors effect the success or failure of an organization's leadership system, including timing, resources, and luck.

I believe that, by fully understanding what is going on in the relationship between a leader and his or her followers, a much deeper appreciation can be developed for what constitutes a highly effective and more fully developed leadership system. Being added to the current discussion here is the idea of looking at this relationship along what I call a full range of leadership development potential and how that contributes to one's individual and collective vital forces.[4]

People derive their vital forces through the relationships they have with each other at all levels of an organization, including the culture and climate of that organization. Relationships built on trust provide the basis for building the vital force that differentiates the average team from the highly developed one,[5] the average organization from the market leader, and the exemplary leader from one who simply gets a job done. The task we now have before us is to provide a clear idea of how to build relationships between leaders and followers that can enhance the vital forces in each to achieve their highest aspirations and potential. So, it does not matter whether you are a leader, a follower, or both. In fact, in any one day, it is rare that most people are not both leader and follower, and it is in the optional exchanging of these roles that the best organizational systems and teams are built.[6]

I am pleased to say that the full range model of leadership that guided the development of the original version of this book and my focus on leadership development for 2 decades has been nearly completely supported and validated. I say nearly, because there are always some shortcomings in terms of what is missing or how we measured something or in regard to predictions we made during the very early stages of our work. Asking you to develop to higher levels along the full range of leadership, such as embracing the four Is of transformational leadership discussed later in this book, has been so strongly endorsed in the accumulated research that the original message to develop to the highest end of the range remains firmly in place.

Yet, there have been many important nuances, variations, build outs, and applications that were not yet born prior to 1999 that have enriched what we consider the full range of leadership and its development. I have highlighted below 10 concepts that I did not place enough emphasis on back when this book was first written. I use hindsight to weave these now into the revised version of this book. My top 10 include:

1. We are all validated once we achieve certain personal goals. This form of validation then raises more confidence so we can lead ourselves and others. This learning may occur on our own naturally, by receiving feedback from others, or through some combination of both. Validation through science helps us determine what we said was true is true. Validation is a central organizing concept for developing leadership and what we might call our *authentic leader self.* It helps each of us determine if what we think is true about our self is indeed true.

2. I have come to realize how important taking ownership is to the core of what makes leaders successful. To have followers that fully own their roles and responsibilities in a way that readies them to lead is an extraordinary accomplishment of leadership. In fact, I think it is the central outcome of transforming leadership and why followers choose to become leaders in terms of formal or informal roles.

3. So much of the field of leadership has focused on leadership as a one-way street—top down. Of course, I should not be surprised that we are still using the terms *boss* and *subordinate* in everyday conversations in 2010, but I am. What we do not use enough is leading up, nor is it promoted enough. I ask myself the question, and of you as well, how do transformational followers lead up?

4. I have come to realize that someone can be a pretty effective leader by just being authentic. One could be a very effective, authentic transactional leader who is respected and someone who consistently achieves expected performance. Becoming authentic is, in my view, the ultimate human journey, which I never fully appreciated back in 1999.

5. Although the work on transformational leadership was clearly geared toward positive forms of leadership, I never fully realized how central positivity was to the work we were promoting. This insight has driven nearly a decade's worth of work on what constitutes something that got labeled *psychological capital*—hope, optimism, resiliency, and efficacy.

6. Transparency. And that is all I have to say about it. More seriously, this is one of those slippery concepts that you think you have understood until one day someone says, "You think you are transparent, and I think you are just rude." With transparency, we are all smarter and faster in terms of enhancing what we know and do not know.

7. Although not completely off my radar screen 10 years ago, I never realized how customized leadership development needed to be in order to optimize development for each individual leader's potential. This has led me to explore how the developmental readiness of each individual factors into accelerating his or her leadership development and the readiness of the organization.

8. Ten years later, shared leadership still mystifies me. What is it? How is it created and sustained? Why is it important? And how can we develop it, if indeed I believe my own rhetoric that all leadership is shared, which I frequently say it is?

9. Distributed strategic leadership has become a core interest area of mine, as I have learned through my practice that leaders at all levels struggle with disseminating the strategic intent they have or, even more complicated, that their organization possesses. How can leaders take the kernel of strategic intent at the top and translate it down and across throughout a complex, geographically distributed organization frequently spanning multiple

cultures? This was only marginally covered in the writings done on indirect leadership in the first version of this book. I will only be able to minimally address this issue in this version as well, as there is relatively little work on the topic thus far.

10. Leadership in the extreme is likely not exactly the same as leadership in the broad range of normal challenges. There are people who must lead and follow in the most extraordinary circumstances—repeatedly. These circumstances usually put their lives at risk, our lives at risk, or both. How do they do it? How do they prepare to do it? What can we do to help? Ironically, one might argue that the genesis of transformational leadership is oftentimes in the cauldron of dramatic changes and crises, yet it was not until recently that I began to consider how these extreme contexts impact leadership and its development.

BOX 0.1 Does Leadership Intervention Work Matter

Avolio, Reichard, Hannah, Walumbwa, and Chan (2009) conducted what is called a meta-analysis of the past 100 years of research on leadership interventions. (A *meta-analysis* is a study of studies, wherein the researchers aggregate the effects of all studies to produce the average relationship.) To be a leadership intervention required that by using such things as training or experimentation, the researchers were trying to change leadership. The findings from this extensive, quantitative review of the literature affirmed that experimental/quasi-experimental leadership interventions had a positive impact across a broad array of interventions, organization types, leadership levels, theories, levels of quality of research, and outcomes. The authors reported moderately positive effects when they examined leadership interventions. In terms of utility, participants in the leadership treatment condition, broadly defined, had on average a 66% chance of positive outcomes compared to only a 34% chance of success for the comparison group for the data set corrected for outliers (50–50 would be random). These authors showed that leadership interventions do make a positive difference.

Assuming this is your second pass through this book, here we go again, traversing through the full range of leadership and its development. If it is your first pass, no worries; you will get the insights I left out last time and the essential points that have stood the test of time. For those of you who did read the original version, I do not know how far you have developed in the past decade—that has always been something you must own. What I expect to do here is trigger some new ideas and ways of pursuing them that can add to what I hope has been a rewarding leadership-development journey. This time around, I would like to start focused more on you first and then address our relationship, which was previously Chapter 1 back in 1999. I begin with the concept of validation as it centers all of the work I do as a researcher, practitioner, leader, and follower.

In sum, so again, for whom is this revised book written? The same group as last time, but now it is a decade later. It was written for any level of leader, follower, and team member in any organization large or small that is operating in any culture. The principles associated with a full range of leadership potential are expected to be universal across levels, organizations, and cultures.[7]

ACKNOWLEDGMENTS

I wanted to thank Linda Hietbrink, Latia Lau, and Khanh Nguyen who work with me at the University of Washington's Center for Leadership & Strategic Thinking for their help in preparing the final manuscript for this book. Their work is always exemplary, on time, and supportive of what I do. I also wanted to thank my copy editor Heidi Crossman, who made the words, the sentences, the structure of the sentences, and their meaning much better than I could have done on my own in revising the final manuscript that went into press. Finally, let me thank every single leader, follower, and peer that provided me with a life's worth of experiences that I enjoyed the first time around in my life stream, the second time around in the first edition of this book, and now the third time with this revision.

Hello, Dolly, / this is Louis, Dolly, / we're so glad to have you back where you belong. / You're lookin' swell, Dolly, / I can tell, Dolly, / you keep glowing, you're still growing, you're still going strong.

(From Louis Armstrong's rendition of "Hello, Dolly")

For my mother, Esther Greenspan, or Dolly to her friends and family, who taught me as her son that the most vulnerable people in this world often possess the greatest strength in their ability to love others with all their heart and with little expectation for any return. I have come back to where I started, realizing how important your kindness has been to my development. Every year of my life, your light is much brighter for me than the last, and today I add ten more years to my life stream versus the last time I published this book. I am forever your follower in both my mind and heart.

CHAPTER 1

VALIDATION

Give your difference, welcome my difference, unify all differences in the larger whole—such is the law of growth. The unifying of difference is the eternal process of life—the creative synthesis, the highest act of creation.

Mary Parker Follett

I was just starting a new position charged with developing a center at the University of Washington's Foster School of Business. In my first month on the job, I was asked to coordinate a session titled Leaders to Legends, to which we invited alumni and business leaders to attend a luncheon to hear about new developments in leadership. The leader who was speaking was a senior vice president of marketing at Starbucks. She and I had agreed to set up the session where I would lead off with some comments about the goals of the session, and then we would talk about her life stream of events that had brought her to her current position in life and at work. Just prior to the session commencing, I asked her to tell me about a trigger moment in her life or career that had shaped her views of herself as a leader. Over the past decade, I have asked many leaders the same question, usually adding a positive trigger event. She looked at me and within a minute or two said, "Got it."

When we started the session and got to that point, she told the story that went back to when she had just started working at Starbucks. She had a meeting with the then-CEO of Starbucks. She indicated that he called her into his office and proceeded to tell her all of the leadership qualities he saw in her that needed to be nurtured, and he wanted to take on the responsibility of helping her rise in the Starbucks' leadership hierarchy. She was quite stunned at his remarks but left his office feeling (as she said, for the first time) *validated* as a leader. I think she would later add "initially validated."

If I asked you to think about someone in your life who triggered in you such validation, would you have someone in mind? Usually people do, especially when they have been fortunate enough to have key individuals who recognized in them something they did not recognize in themselves. In fact, it is almost a principle or law of leadership development that when people talk about feeling validated in their leadership, they typically add, "And you know, I didn't see that in myself." Why? Because it is at the foundation of where we might say leadership development and personal development emerges. It is called self-awareness.

Now, what is actually being validated? It appears it is one of the selves that make up who we are as individuals. Yes, I did mean *selves* as is, in plural. For instance, in the example above, we could say it is the *leader self* or self-image that was validated by the CEO in that early career meeting. However, beyond the part that makes up who she is, there is also a *parent self,* a *peer self*, and a *community citizen self-concept.* What we are learning is that there are multiple selves that make up the composite of who we are and more importantly who we are becoming. Validating one of those selves provides assurance that we are becoming whatever roles go along with that self. Thinking about multiple selves also helps us unpack what constitutes one's self-awareness. Specifically, we have to ask, which self in the larger or total *self* are we referring to in terms of validation?

The sort of validation that occurred above with a senior leader can also occur with peers, followers, individuals we know outside our organizational lives, and even our own natural learning from events. In terms of learning from events, the idea that leadership development occurs through natural learning processes is something that is gathering steam in organizations around the globe. What I mean by *natural learning* is deriving messages, learning, and validation from events you live through at work or outside of work—typically unplanned. For example, a number of authors talk about the work and life challenges that shape leadership development as being events like assuming a new position, taking on a transition in roles, working in a different culture, managing significant change, and dealing with a major new initiative. You will notice that I did not mention traditional training or in-classroom development.

Interestingly enough, the evidence we have now collected certainly supports short training interventions can have a positive impact on leader development. Indeed, when my colleagues and I went back to review the past 100 years of research referred to in Box 0.1, we found that even a few hours of training could have a positive impact on one's leadership development. However, most would now agree that the big bang for the buck is taking advantage of real challenges to facilitate leadership development. The real challenges are what I referred to above as natural learning events.[8,9]

It may be helpful to further examine what is meant by natural learning. Have you had a challenge in your work or a significant transition in life over the past 3 months? For me, the transition challenge was moving from Omaha, Nebraska, to Seattle, Washington, going from a maturing leadership center to building a brand-new one. As I looked forward at this transition, I thought in advance of what I hoped to accomplish, what the school needed, who my stakeholders were, how I would resource the center, where I would start on boarding others, and so forth. I was self-aware enough to see the new position as not only a job, but also a leadership transition challenge for myself. This level of leader self-awareness came about as this was my third center start-up, so I was much more aware of what a center was and what my role would be in building the new center, including having to be one of its leaders. These reflections even led me to pick my personal leadership goal: to assume positive intent in others. I chose this goal, as I thought it was the best way to onboard others and to accelerate our center's development. This goal can be sourced to the work I have been engaged in over the past 7 years examining how leader positivity, or what Fred Luthans has called *psychological capital,* predicts motivation and performance. My goal was to see if leaders' positivity could trump plowing forward to get what I wanted done. I have some more to say on this later.

So if you have had a role transition, what did it mean for yourself as a leader? How did it challenge what you knew? How did it challenge what you needed to know? How have you done so far in addressing the transition? Have you learned anything about your leadership that has challenged you to think about areas you need to develop? If so, what are those areas? Maybe you have been luckier than I, and in addressing your challenge you have been validated? Transitions are really fertile events for naturally promoting leadership development, especially if you are mindful of how the event may be used to foster your development.[10]

In order to take advantage of transitions or natural learning challenges, you must be mindful of three things: First, your current leader self—What makes you effective, and what might hinder your ability to succeed in this new transition? Second, the possible leader self you want to become—How might you change how you think about leadership, how you act in your role as leader or follower, and how you use the means available to lead in this new transition? Third, your goal regarding your leader self—What is the end goal of what you want to achieve as a leader in order to maintain the positive energy to stay the course? Have you considered these three issues with the last transition or challenge you went through at work or outside of work? If so, how have you evolved as a leader? What did you learn? By the way, you can ask these questions and use the reference of follower, peer, or even parent.

You might be taking from my comments above, that one does not just become validated and can say, "Been there and done that." In fact, as we go through the challenges we confront in life, as leaders, we must continually go through revalidation. What is interesting is that is also true of things in science that we say are validated. For example, you can validate a measure of leadership in 100 different samples around the globe. Yet, it is not appropriate to say you have a *valid measure of leadership*. Why? In the 101st sample, the measure may not predict what it was designed to predict, and thus we would consider that measure invalid for that sample, although the probability of that happening is not high.

Each time we move to a different level of understanding ourselves, truly understanding ourselves, we can say we have gone through another stage of validation. It is when we are not mindful of this validation process that we tend to lose perspective on who are, who we are becoming, and what we can do. There are many leaders we might describe as not being in touch with his or her leader self. In some instances, the individual has so little confidence in his leadership he simply cannot see himself as being validated. I am not saying the individual cannot be validated, but he may not be ready to be validated, a concept I will take up later in this book.

At the other extreme are my "favorite" leaders, the ones who have too much hubris to be concerned about validation. Why should anyone have to validate them, or they themselves? They are born to be leaders. These types of leaders can be very surprised when their self-ratings of leadership do not match those of their followers when completing 360 surveys. The ratings they give to themselves are oftentimes way over what others have seen in their leadership. This gap in and of itself may be a wake-up call for prompting some individuals to do further reflection on their leadership. It may also lead them to reject what others have to say, moving them forward without passing the validation checkpoint.

So let us turn these events into a developmental lesson. Validation will occur or not occur to some degree regardless of what you chose to do in terms of your leadership development. What I mean is that serendipity may have its way, and events may come along or not that can shape your development leading to validation. However, you can also stack the deck in favor of further validation by using two strategies. First, be mindful that life and work both trigger events regardless of what you do. The more mindful you are of their potential, the less likely you will miss them passing by in your life stream.

Second, you can choose different life streams to explore what will increase the probability of a trigger event occurring that has some potential validation attached to the event. I have personally found that moving three times over the past 7 years has triggered a number of events associated with our living and career transitions that has shaped my development. Consequently, as the literature might suggest, taking on challenging new assignments, living abroad, and trying to change the way you impact others can each trigger your development, again, if you are mindful of the possibilities. Thus, it is not just the event, but your readiness to learn from the event that potentially triggers development.

Do you have a trigger moment that you can identify that led to some form of validation for you? What was the situation? Who was the source? How did it impact the way you lead?

BOX 1.1 Trigger Moments and Validation

A total of 74 interviews between 2006 and 2007 were conducted with top CEOs from Singapore, Bangalore, Hong Kong, Mumbai, Shanghai, and Beijing. We completed a minimum of 9 interviews and a maximum of 23 from top management leaders from the respective cities noted above to examine how their leadership developed (23, 12, 9, 10, 11, and 9, respectively). Interviews were conducted one-on-one, going through a list of standardized questions used for all interviewees. Interviews in Singapore and Bangalore were conducted face-to-face, while interviews in Beijing were primarily conducted by phone. The CEOs interviewed tended to believe that leadership was both made and born/heritable, as I have found in similar samples in the United States and elsewhere around the globe. Most of the Asian leaders said they never planned to be in such a prominent leadership role, which led me to label them *accidental leaders*. The three most common responses to why they ended up in leadership roles were either because it "just happened" (accidental) in terms of right place/right time; they were simply seeking to do well in their current position and, as a result, increasingly had leadership opportunities presented to them (incremental); or they had a desire to have an impact through being a leader (impact). Many of the CEOs said their most important leadership development experiences occurred outside of formal educational/ training. Their comments coincided with earlier work reviewed by Avolio (2005) that revealed exemplary leadership as typically developed in natural learning contexts such as one's home, school, or workplace.

SOME THINGS WORTH REPEATING AND REFLECTING ON

To recap, one of the fundamental processes that fuels leadership development is being validated. Validation typically occurs when another respected individual sees in you something you do not yet recognize in yourself. Over time, as you gain experience via development, self-validation is certainly possible.

Natural learning events shape the course of our development, and the more developmentally ready we are to address, the higher the likelihood that we will extract out the type of meaning from those events that can accelerate our leadership development.

A SHORT EXERCISE

At the end of each chapter, there will be one short exercise that will take no longer than 5 minutes to do.

Think back now over the past 3 months and identify any situation where you felt you were validated as a leader.

- What did the individual or individuals do to help you feel you had been validated?
- What impact did such validation have on your model of leadership, your behavior, and your treatment of others?
- When is the last time you validated someone, and how did you do that?

CHAPTER 2

RELATIONSHIPS

How an entity becomes constitutes what that actual entity is ... It's being constituted by its becoming.

Alfred North Whitehead

Many books have been written on the subject of what constitutes effective leadership. I can almost guarantee you that, in running training programs around the world, one will get asked the question, "What does it take to be an effective leader?" Of course, this question typically follows the debate on the differences between a leader and manager, which are usually more about processes and roles than about differences between persons. "How can one be a manager and also a leader?" is the typical question being asked. I leave this debate for others to work out and instead concentrate on those individuals or groups who engage in taking ownership in the process of leadership, whether they are first-line managers, CEOs, project leaders, teammates, teachers, coaches, parents, siblings, shop stewards, or counselors. Let me add, for emphasis, *especially parents.* The most important leader in any society is the parent or significant other who raises you, next the teacher, and coming in a close third are the manager and the administrator. What the parent or significant other does not develop, the teacher handles, and what the teacher falls short on becomes the responsibility of the manager to develop in his or her followers. And if the manager fails, the developing leader goes to trainers and coaches.

Please take a moment and think about the type of ownership good parenting takes for developing children in order for them to take ownership for their actions. If you are a parent, or the recipient of parenting, how was ownership transferred to you or others? Now, generalize that level of ownership to developing your best follower. I describe taking ownership for developing one's followers as a case example for assuming ownership and how it informs leadership development.

Level 1: Accountability—Minimally, good leadership requires setting very clear standards for personal accountability and establishing what is expected from the individual. Accountability, where standards are set and clearly enforced in terms of the expected goals to be achieved, falls within the range of what is called transactional leadership. Taking accountability should involve leaders and followers using a simple set of rules, easily recalled and enforced, that can hold everyone accountable. The transactional arrangement should be simple enough for leaders to consistently role model and provide feedback to help followers make adjustments toward achieving desired goals. For example, dealing with conflict by treating others unfairly or ignoring their needs does not solve conflicts or address the root of the problem. Holding individuals accountable for understanding and appreciating the needs of others can be a simple rule to adhere to, whether you are a parent or a manager when addressing conflict. Another simple rule is to assume positive intent of those you work with and for in an organization. Assuming positive intent, you can avoid rushing to judgment until all of the facts are in to be deliberated. Do you have a set of simple rules to hold yourself and others accountable?

Level 2: Efficacy—To move from compliance levels of accountability to commitments, one has to feel a sense of efficacy that control can be obtained and whatever challenges or tasks that must be addressed can be done successfully. It is incumbent upon leaders to help those they lead feel they have the required agency to get the task done. Frequently, people choose not to engage in tasks because they feel the probability of success is so low it is not worth it. To the extent that we describe people as human agents that impact how they live and flourish, this is an agency with low potential. This may explain why some people seem to take on one leadership experience after another and others seem to avoid them throughout life and career. I would suggest that the ones who continually take on increasingly more challenging leadership experiences are the ones who, later on, we say are born versus made.

The roots of these choices may lie in the efficacy or agency the person feels he or she can succeed. So, to the degree that a leader role models for followers how to successfully influence others, he is inevitably boosting his follower's agency or efficacy to lead. Providing feedback and recognition even when attempts to lead result in failure should still promote greater efficacy and a higher likelihood of individuals taking ownership for similar leadership roles in the future. If you look back in your own life stream, how did your parents or significant others in your life develop your efficacy to influence others, especially after you may have tried and failed at leading? If you are a parent, how are you developing the efficacy of your children to step up and lead right now?

Level 3: Sense of Belonging—The more accountable we feel and the more efficacious we feel, the higher the likelihood we will conclude that we belong in the role or position. In parenting, we want children to feel comfortable that they are central to the family even when they do not hold up their agreements in terms of accountability. The same is true in our organizations, where leaders want members to feel a sense of belonging to their team, unit, division, or organization. By developing this sense of belonging built on higher efficacy and taking greater accountability, we can expect individuals to step up and do what is needed and sometimes anticipate and do something that will be needed and not yet recognized by either the parent or leader in our example. Did your current or last manager develop a sense of belonging in you? What impact did that have on what you did and would do for your organization, your fellow employees, and your leader?

Level 4: Identification—One of the highest levels of ownership is feeling that you totally identify with what you are asked to do for someone else. In the context of work, you see your organization and its mission and values as synonymous with your own. Ask firefighters about their work, and you will frequently see that they cannot separate their life role from the job role. When they are introduced to others they are firefighters and then something else. I find the same is true with exemplary elementary school teachers. When leading others, you want to strive for the same level of identification to occur with your values and the values you want to represent your organization. To the extent individuals identify with your organization, the higher the likelihood they will take ownership for doing what is determined the right thing to do.

You may notice that, as we transcend from Level 1 to Level 4 ownership, the controls for how things get done move from the outside in terms of being *compliant* and *accountable* to the inside where it is what individuals *commit* to doing because it validates who they are and the organization to which they belong. A New York City fireman told me that you do not have to hold firefighters accountable for not leaving a burning building if a civilian is still above them. If they have fully developed their identity as a firefighter, they would not hesitate to go up when all of the signals say to leave the burning building, as the ethos of their profession is to not leave other firefighters or civilians behind.[11]

The same type of ownership can be seen in many military organizations that refer to it as the *warrior ethos,* which entails not leaving a fellow soldier behind. This type of ownership puts members' lives at risk and sets a very high bar for ownership and identification not seen, or likely needed, in most organizations. However, it might be interesting to ask yourself, how many of your fellow coworkers or leaders would not leave you behind if it came down to them sacrificing something that was very important to them.[12]

WHAT IS OWNERSHIP FOR THE LEADERSHIP PROCESS?

Most of what we are now learning about leadership development is that the highest impact events are those that are genuine or authentic. Specifically, what moves people up in terms of developing their leadership capacity and potential is experiencing real or virtually real events that change the way the individual views himself or herself (back to the leader selves) and how they choose to behave as a leader going forward.

It is important to point out that there are many facets to leadership that at least include the leader, follower, and situation. There are also many facets that contribute to the leadership development process, not least of which are the person many authors have labeled *the follower*. Here, I attempt to broaden the focus regarding leadership to go beyond the figure—the leader—to also include the background—the follower and the context in which both are embedded over time. Adding time brings into focus a very critical fourth dimension: *We cannot examine leadership development at one point in time.*

We have to be willing to watch and evaluate how leadership evolves over time, and for some leadership concepts, it could take years and for others minutes. Let me explain. The development of one's higher moral and ethical base takes years to emerge, if it ever does. However, learning how to get feedback on a specific goal may take a relatively short amount of time to master because the processes underlying it are less complex. It is, therefore, critical to put in your mind's eye that each individual leader who is developing has an individual trajectory that follows its own course over time that will vary based on the individual's readiness to develop at the starting point, the challenges that arise, the support received, and how mindful the individual is in terms of being disciplined to stick to his or her development plan.

Complicating matters, but long overdue, is the increasing focus that needs to be placed on the follower as a key component of the leadership and leadership development process. However, why focus on the follower now? Lorraine Matusek,[13] in her book *Finding Your Voice,* suggests that "leaders should think of themselves as individuals surrounded by mirrors of many kinds." What they say and do is often reflected back to them in the behavior of their followers.

Nearly 100 years ago, Mary Parker Follett, a very famous management writer in the early part of the 20th century, basically said the same thing, but for years we neglected the important role a follower plays in leaders being successful and developing successfully. She said, "Leadership is not defined by the exercise of power but by the capacity to increase the sense of power among those led. The most essential work of the leader is to create more leaders" (Follett, 1924, p. 3).

Now imagine a situation where you are unable to meet with a particular leader of some large organization but are given the opportunity to meet with the person who reports to that leader, someone we might call the *second in command*. What can you learn from this meeting to help you understand the leadership system and dynamics in this organization? Could you possibly learn everything you need to know about the leader's role in the leadership process by just talking with the leader's follower? I believe that the answer to this question is often yes, but in reality, it is also great to talk with both because each will add something unique to describing the leadership process that is quite valuable—his or her own perspective.

In the spirit of being provocative, however, let us set a standard that if we were to talk with the second in command, we would learn everything we needed to know about the leadership system in that particular organization that you would have learned from the leader. If you are in a leadership role right now and that were the case with your leadership, how would you accomplish that objective?

Several things you might consider before addressing that question. First, I suspect that the less the follower has to guess, the more likely there is a higher degree of transparency in your relationship with him or her. Second, you have probably taken a lot of time to get to know your follower's needs, challenges, and strengths, and in doing so, your follower has gotten to know what you value. Third, you have probably been very clear on what your ethical standards of conduct are and likely have been a role model consistently reflecting the execution of those standards. Consequently, if the follower can speak for you in terms of your leadership, you have likely done what most great leaders do—you have transferred leadership and ownership for it to your follower. If you have done all of the above, your followers can describe your leadership (and their leadership) quite accurately.

One realization that usually takes emerging leaders some time to understand is that those who are following them observe their leadership typically much more than they realize. I say *observe leadership* here because I realize that you are watching exactly what I'm saying, even perhaps more than would typically occur with the average leader–follower interaction since you can go back and reread what I just said. In real life, we hear it, interpret it, recall it, and then judge what is said to us—a process potentially fraught with errors of transmission and reception.

By the way, I, too, do not always know what you are thinking, whether you are reflecting on what I have just said, whether you are annoyed, bewildered, concerned, or inspired. Like many leaders, I am trying to keep in mind that if I do not get my messages through to you, then subsequent interactions you have with others will be neither positively nor negatively affected by my influence on you. Simply put, to fully lead, I cannot do it without your engagement. No leader leads without followers. And almost all leaders must shift between being a follower and a leader on a daily basis and, in some cases, on an hourly basis. This is even more true today with trends toward flattened, networked organizations that are establishing shared leadership systems and with the rapid emergence of social networking that requires a great deal of leadership by the crowd.[14,15]

To develop, leaders would benefit by being aware of the roles they serve in and what they enter those roles with in terms of their self-concept, their expectations, and how they think they are impacting others. Most importantly, leaders must always try to keep in mind their vulnerabilities. Being aware of the way one follows and leads will, to a large extent, determine the way one's followers lead and follow. This is true because followers model leaders they respect, and in doing so, they reflect those leaders' missions, values, and behaviors. Perhaps this is what Laing (1981) meant when he said, "The range of what we think and do is limited by what we fail to notice. And because we fail to notice that we fail to notice, there is little we can do to change until we notice how failing to notice shapes our thoughts and deeds" (p. 377).

The failure to notice is one of the biggest nuggets you can take away from this discussion. You do not fail to notice if you are mindful of your interactions. To be mindful, you have to decide what to focus on in your interactions and in your relationships with others. For example, going back to our discussion of ownership, if you are mindful of developing accountability with your followers, then you will be able to focus on how you set them up to take more ownership, how you convey your desires, and how you support and evaluate how well they have taken up ownership. Being mindful requires that you focus attention and where you miss something you seek feedback. Setting up mechanisms for feedback with followers is a way of helping them develop their understanding of your leadership and what you expect of them.

At the outset of building any leadership relationship and broader system of leadership development, we must establish a framework for working together, and part of that framework is building a sense of ownership that transcends Levels 1 to 4. This requires that we discuss the parameters we must establish for our relationship to enhance its ultimate effectiveness, or what I have referred to in earlier work as our *vital forces*. If we can agree to examine leadership as a process, then at the core of this process we must examine how relationships are built that involve leaders and followers. For example, as a basis for our relationship, from time to time I will ask you to give further consideration to what I have said and how you might apply it to your own leadership development with your second in command, peers, or supervisor. Without such discussion and agreements, leaders are even more vulnerable than normal, as they do not know what you know and do not know, and this puts their execution of tasks at risk.

Let me state up front one of my basic leadership principles in terms of my work with followers: I would never be satisfied with a passive follower. This would be inconsistent with the basic philosophy expressed throughout this book and the research used to support the full range model of leadership. Being accepting of a passive and dependent follower is inadequate and inconsistent with what my colleagues and I have described countless times as more effective, if not exemplary, leadership. At its core, leadership and the systems it is a part of involve development, or helping people grow to their full potential where they can then effectively lead themselves.[16] Stated another way, the legacy of any great leader is typically observed in the ability of his or her second, third, and fourth in command to assume the responsibilities of the first—and that is, of course, to lead in new directions. In today's world, the turnover of responsibility between the first and second level and so on down the line occurs almost on a daily basis through delegation, empowerment, and shared leadership processes emerging in teams. We must learn ways to efficiently accelerate this process.[17,18]

When I was asked to draw a metaphor of my conception of a follower more than a decade ago, I immediately drew a person in a cape with a tight blue outfit and boots. Taking into consideration my artistic limitations, it resembled my image of a hero. I consider the best followers my heroes. They have helped me fly much higher in my work as a consequence of their efforts, and that represents one basic aspect of my philosophy of leadership. What better reflection of oneself as leader than someone who is an exemplary follower?

Today, I am not so sure that I would dress followers up as heroes. Part of my reasoning for not doing so is that once we dress anyone up as a hero, we then proceed to find ways to destroy them. I think I would prefer my followers to be dressed as dancers who are each dependent on the others to produce the most fantastic production. And I am just one of those dancers.

Regardless of the context, whether it is at work or otherwise, to develop others to their full potential requires continuous input, and where the input is filtered and poorly edited, the leader is placed in a position of greater vulnerability. Not knowing what one does not know makes any leader extremely vulnerable in a negative sense. Thus, if this book is to have any real impact on your development, input is required from you for each of us to be optimally effective. It is no different in any other leader–follower interaction, so I hope to practice what I preach within this context, while fully realizing that I have to lead you at a distance with a larger span of control than I have been used to in the past and in an environment that is constantly changing, depending on whom I am working with at any one point in time. Does this sound familiar?

Rest assured that I do have some idea what your questions might be because many a great follower before you has taught me about what it takes to be an exemplary leader even if I have not behaved as such. Let me add that I can typically describe what needs to be done, but perhaps like yourself, I still personally have a lot of work to do to achieve what will be described here as exemplary leadership.

BOX 2.1   Outcomes of Team Development Programs

Salas, Mullen, Rozell, and Driskell (1997) completed a meta-analysis of research testing the effects of team building on team development. Team-building efforts that emphasized role clarification were more likely to enhance performance and team development. Emphasis on building a base on how the team was to transact with itself seemed to be an important contributor to team development. *It is not what you tell them; it is what they understand is required of them, that really counts.*

Because we are unable to sit down across from each other and talk, we will each have to rely on our inner voices to communicate, using some anticipation and, whenever necessary, what we will call *strategic redundancy* to catch our communication disconnects and mistakes. When I think about this issue with communication, I have always tried to keep in mind the philosophy expressed by coach Red Auerbach of the Boston Celtics that it is not really what you say to people, but it is what they hear. This is a very important principle for anyone assuming the role of a leader. Why? How you transmit a message and through which channel (verbal, nonverbal, e-mail, and so forth) makes a huge difference in how it is received and interpreted. Just think of the last time someone said to you, "I did not realize that was what you meant in the meeting, your e-mail, or based on our last conversation, and now I do after hearing you further." Yet, when mistakes in communication occur—and they certainly will occur, given the fragile nature of our communication systems—let us try to pick them up along the way, to learn from them, and to resolve them so that we both can benefit from our exchange.

The best way to assure the accuracy of the communication is to keep it as simple as possible, but not simpler than the message needs to be to convey your intentions. Be sure to repeat the message in as many different ways as you can. Make sure you have communicated the most important message through many different channels with examples appropriate to the audience. Whenever possible, tell your message using stories and visualizations because people remember that more than words. Lastly, make sure there are redundant ways to get feedback. I say redundant as usually one channel for feedback is one too few for critical messages.

Perhaps it is time to tell you my goals for writing this book. To be specific, one of my challenges writing this book was to engage you in the process of leadership development in parallel with writing about the processes of leadership. I guess you could call it *just in time application*. Engagement represents an active involvement on your part to learn and apply what is being discussed and to challenge it when it does not make any sense to you. If you are willing to consider such a role (notice that I have not assumed you would, nor even required that you do), then perhaps we can start building a full range of leadership potential and the vital forces in you and I that result. All along the way, when we talk about leadership development, we should also be trying to practice it through its description and in our own philosophy and behavior. Frankly, my personal and perhaps self-interested view in writing this book was to make myself a better leader, peer, and follower. Rewriting this book has made me reflect on instances I have experienced and the work of many colleagues and, in the end, reconsider how I have influenced others. My hopes are that it will do some of the same for you as well.

You may have noticed in Box 2.1 where I present a brief review of a study conducted by Salas et al. (1997). Throughout the book, I refer to leadership research that either directly or indirectly supports the points I raise in the text. I have tried to place similar boxed summaries at points in the book where I hope you will reflect on my message and find that some research out there corroborates what is being said here. I said *may* because one research study only provides evidence that we *may* or *may not* be correct. Once you implement what I have suggested, however, you will know whether it is correct or valid. Also, by threading in the research, I want to convey another message. This is not your average self-help book. I hope the messages in this book are relevant to you, but they also must meet my own standard of being rigorous. I mean to say that underlying what is being discussed here is the accumulation of leadership research that has validated what I am suggesting.

SOME THINGS WORTH REPEATING AND REFLECTING ON

- My goal is to demonstrate that the principles contained in this book can also be demonstrated in parallel in helping each of us develop as we work through this material together.
- At the outset, we use a full range framework to examine leadership as a total system, with particular emphasis on the situations in which leaders and followers interact over time.
- Although often neglected in prior discussions of leadership, the follower will play a more prominent role in how we examine and develop the vital forces contained in a *total* leadership system, with our second in command being a reflection of the first.
- Consider the following: "There are two types of organizations: those that see the cliff coming, and those that don't" (Mike Walsh, former CEO of Tenneco). I would like to make you part of the former organization.
- I briefly summarize research findings that are directly and indirectly related to our discussions of a full range view of leadership. I highlight research throughout this book, acting as a translator to convey to you what we have learned about what works and what does not work in terms of leadership and its development. Also, I believe that what we recommend for leadership development should be seen as relevant and based on rigor.
- Are you ready to be an active follower reader?

BOX 2.2   Psychological Ownership

Avey, Avolio, Crossley, and Luthans (2008) were interested in examining the effects of transformational leadership of supervisors with the role of promotion-oriented, psychological ownership (helping followers to assume ownership in terms of identity, efficacy, sense of belongingness, and accountability) and individual-level follower outcomes of empowerment and performance. Participants in this study included 283 full-time employees of a metallic plating manufacturing organization. Transformational leadership of supervisors in a large

(Continued)

(Continued)

manufacturing plant was positively related to ratings of psychological ownership by followers. Results also revealed a positive association between followers' psychological ownership and empowerment while demonstrating negative relationships with territorial ownership. Lastly, empowerment mediated the relationship between psychological ownership and follower performance, thus providing support for all the hypothesized relationships in the study.

Psychological Ownership Measure (www.mindgarden.com). Psychological ownership was measured in the above study using a 16-item psychological ownership measure (Avey, Avolio, Crossley, & Luthans, 2008). Example items are

- (territoriality; α = .83) *I feel I need to protect my ideas from being used by others in my organization.*
- (efficacy; α = .89) *I am confident in my ability to contribute to my organization's success.*
- (accountability; α = .86) *I would challenge anyone in my organization if I thought something was done wrong.*
- (belongingness; α = .92) *I feel I belong in this organization.*
- (identity; α = .80) *I feel being a member in this organization helps define who I am.*

The overall promotion-oriented psychological ownership measure demonstrated favorable reliability (α =.91).

A SHORT EXERCISE

Think about a person who had a profoundly positive impact on your taking ownership for leading someone else. What role did he or she play in your life or just at work? What were the top three attributes of this person that immediately come to mind? Please discuss your leader with someone else, and ask that person to do the same with you. Look for commonalities in your description and then see if these attributes, later on, map to what constitutes transformational leadership.

Attributes:

_____

_____

_____

How do you aspire to be like the leader you have described above? How can that help you develop ownership in others?

CHAPTER 3

INTERCONNECTED

There are many objects of great value to man which cannot be attained by unconnected individuals, but must be attained, if at all, by association.

Daniel Webster

To engage you as an exemplary follower, we both will need to clarify what we expect from our relationship. That is a very important first step that works well both with individuals and teams.[19] I call this our *compact of understanding,* which will form the basis for a later chapter on building shared leadership in teams. This will become an evolving document of sorts that details what we expect from each other to maximize the full potential of our development and performance. Keep in mind that what derails many relationships, including those between leaders and followers, is missed expectations.

Contained in the philosophy of African humanistic thinking are two sayings that capture what I view as being the essence of really working together: "Together each of us accomplishes more successes" and "We are all together on the inside." Let me propose that we set a standard for ourselves to engage in a *knowledge-generating partnership* from which both of us should benefit over time. If we continue to generate new and interesting knowledge, then we have a good chance of renewing our relationship and of achieving the full potential of the leadership dynamic being created here.

The main reason for developing a compact of understanding between us is that leadership is a process that typically requires at least two individuals, one typically enabling the other to achieve an objective or goal that is meaningful. I do realize that people can also lead themselves out of difficult situations, and this has been called *self-leadership* by some of our colleagues.[20] I will not ignore the process of self-leadership in this book by any means. To the contrary, sometimes the best leader and follower are actually you in rapid succession. In fact, in a high-performing team, organization, or community, you need to frequently be both, and the ability to shift back and forth between one and the other is crucial not only to your own success but also to the success in building an effective and sustainable leadership system.[21]

Taking the situation I raised in Chapter 2 regarding the absent leader, if we talk with the second in command, who is accustomed to assuming the first in command's roles and responsibilities, then how much would we be missing by talking with the second about his or her leader's leadership? Very little indeed, I believe, suggesting as I did in Chapter 2 that the follower can be a mirror image of effective leadership depending on the relationship that is built between the leader and follower. The mirror can also be cracked under circumstances representing less exemplary leadership where followers have no clue what the leader's intentions are or why the leader does what he or she does. The low levels of transparency in many leader–follower relationships and corresponding mistrust would make it difficult for the follower to know who the leader is in terms of ideals, values, or beliefs or why the leader does what he or she does.

The term *understanding* in the compact assumes that you will not be a passive follower in the process of learning more about the leadership relationship. To understand requires active engagement, challenge, and self-reflection. If you say to me, "You're the expert; tell me the best ways to lead. Come on, I have 5 minutes here, so let's get on with it," my response will be, "Please read another book, one that does not require your active involvement in the process of your own leadership development." To have someone disengaged in the process of learning about leadership is just not good leadership; it is not even good followership.

Consequently, for us to be successful, you must ask questions of yourself, and you will need to spend time reflecting on those questions throughout this book. In some sense, the process of reflection is the basis I have used in selecting what is included in, and now excluded from, this revised book. You will use reflection to determine what you think is worth pulling out from this book for future reference and perhaps what you think was missing. Paraphrasing Laing (1981), there are likely to be many instances where I failed to notice what I did not notice and should have noticed. If you take on the role of an exemplary follower, however, those areas I neglected can be captured in your feedback to me, enhancing my *noticed quotient* at bavolio@uw.edu.

My first specific request of you is that you allocate 300 seconds of your time every day, anytime, anywhere. If you do not have 5 minutes right now in your life to invest for some mindful or focused self-reflection, please wait to read this book at some future point in time. Much greater sacrifices than allocating 5 minutes will be asked of you as you fully engage in the process of leadership development. I, therefore, strongly recommend that you embrace the leadership development process when you have the time and are ready developmentally.

To be developmentally ready, you have to have some motivation to lead and to learn. These are two concepts that form part of what my colleague Sean Hannah and I call *developmental readiness.*[22] Someone who is developmentally ready to engage in leadership would have more energy for wanting to influence others toward a particular goal—including the leader. They would also be motivated to learn how to best go about influencing others and would understand that failing initially is part of the learning process. We refer to this third facet of developmental readiness as one's *learning goal orientation.* People who have a *performance goal orientation* tend to be more task focused and want to avoid failure. Learning leadership will require some false starts and mistakes, so shifting your thinking to more of a learning goal orientation will help make you more developmentally ready to lead.

A fourth component of developmental readiness is referred to by cognitive psychologists as *self-concept clarity.* You will recall that I mentioned that we all have multiple selves to figure out and understand as we traverse our life streams. My selves include being a father, professor, and mentor, among other selves. The more clarity I have with the roles associated with those unique selves, the more able I am to question them, take feedback, and point to areas for improvement.

Some authors also refer to the self-concept in terms of its complexity.[23] They suggest that a sufficient level of complexity is required to incorporate new aspects into the self. For example, as my leadership roles become more expansive, how I lead up close *and* at a distance both matter to my effectiveness. Early on, I might have thought about leadership as something you do directly with one's followers. However, if I have 100 people working for me, the dynamics of leadership changes, as does the complexity. If I continue to think that leadership is something you do just face-to-face with a limited set of followers, I would be restricting my development in terms of leading large groups at a distance, oftentimes across unique divisions and cultures.

One of the challenges I see in developing leadership is getting you to be open to enhancing the complexity through which you view yourself in a leadership role. Many people in technical roles start out as project leaders, and their view of leadership is what happens in face-to-face interactions. When technical people have to lead in the more abstract and ambiguous world of strategic leadership, they oftentimes have a difficult time adjusting their self-concept. Why? Most engineers want to know what are the analytics and calculus of the processes they engage in at work. When the process of leadership becomes more strategic, the calculus changes, and it is difficult for them to understand that the calculus largely includes how they view their role as a leader, changing from direct to indirect or even to more abstract using symbolic leadership. For example, how leaders behave in public can be interpreted as providing cues to their intentions. If a leader spends more time with a particular group or unit, he or she may be seen as preferring to work with that group. It is in the transition to how to lead both indirectly and symbolically that we see the need for greater self-concept complexity in order to incorporate these new roles and, at the same time, to work toward greater self-concept clarity.

BOX 3.1   Developmental Readiness

Early theory-building (Avolio & Hannah, 2008) and empirical testing suggest that leaders' developmental readiness is a function of at least two general areas: leaders' *motivation* and *ability* to develop. Avolio and Hannah (2008) define leader developmental readiness (DR) as "the ability and motivation to attend to, make meaning of, and appropriate new leader KSAAs (knowledge, skills, abilities, and attributes) into knowledge structures along with concomitant changes in identity to employ those KSAAs" (p. 5). Prior research has now tested the effects of three of the DR constructs in predicting the acceleration of leader development: learning goal orientation, metacognitive ability, and self-concept clarity. Two longitudinal field studies with military cadets concluded these DR variables significantly moderated development of transformational leadership, authentic leadership, and leadership efficacy over 6 months. DR also predicted subsequent leader performance (Avolio & Hannah, 2008).

Okay, so do you have 5 minutes to allocate to reflect on points raised in this book? If you do, that gives us 1,800 seconds of quality time per week to dedicate to reflecting on how you perform as a leader. You see, I am trying to be reasonable. I could have asked for the full 2,100 seconds! And those 1,800 seconds will contribute to the 10,080 minutes per week that I would expect you to be in your leadership role.

In terms of indirect leadership, consider that leadership comes from who you are, what you do, and how it affects people's ability to achieve their full potential. The *how it affects* part is, of course, in large part up to the follower and how he or she perceives your leadership behavior. You can get some idea of what I mean by examining the research in Box 3.2 below on the Pygmalion effect.

BOX 3.2   The Power of the Voice: Pygmalion Effects on Performance

Eden (1990) has confirmed numerous times, in both laboratory and field settings, that what we say to ourselves or to others can become self-fulfilling prophesies. When they are positively set expectations, they can represent positive improvements in performance. Negative effects, however, have also been observed in performance when the expectations were not positive in the form of Golem effects. Let's work on your inner voice and its potential impact on you and others.

Gully, Incalcaterra, Joshi, and Beaubian (2005) summarized the results of their meta-analytic findings looking at a form of team expectations referred to as *team-efficacy*. Their results indicated that team-efficacy (meaning the team's collective judgment about their team) was strongly and positively related to performance, with an estimated true-score correlation of .41. The authors noted that values were similar to but stronger than the relationship between cohesion and performance. The authors also reported in this study that interdependence moderated the relationship between team efficacy and performance, such that the optimal levels of performance were achieved where teams had high interdependence and high levels of team efficacy. Consequently, like individuals, the extent to which teams believe in themselves can become self-fulfilling.

Returning to the formation our relationship, let me be very specific here because, in the formation of relationships, one major failing that occurs is a lack of clarity in what is initially expected from each person. (This is one conclusion we can take away from the team research I cited in Box 3.2.) I would like to avoid this common trap and assume that what happens early in the formation of our relationship really matters. Consequently, I am asking that as you work your way through this book, you write down a question or questions you think are important enough to reflect on and to give deeper consideration to for your own development as a leader or follower. Our compact of understanding is that you agree to allocate, minimally, 5 minutes each day for some deep reflection on these questions. (I am obviously making an assumption here about our agreement, which we can test out as we work together over time.) These 300 seconds will constitute your personal debriefing time in active engagement with your inner voice.[24] Your inner voice will walk you through what you did, how you did it, how you could have done it, what the consequences were, and how you felt about your choices, decisions, and actions. Like most things applied to leadership, some people's inner voices can be real task masters or screamers, whereas others are very quiet, if not all too reserved. We are going to work on the tone of your inner voice, as well as on the content in terms of your full leadership development. Recall that what you say to yourself can potentially be seen in your own actions over time, as well as be reflected in the behavior of others, who might end up mirroring you.

My fondest hope is that you will find the issues, incidents, or observations you jotted down to be important enough to discuss with someone else for her or his feedback and reflection. My compact with you is that I expect a minimum of one provocative question per chapter and of 5 minutes a day to reflect on each of those questions. The questions will form the basis for your engagement in a process that most famous leaders in history have engaged in, and those current ones we say are the real deal: *they really reflected on what is important.* Honestly, would you respect a leader who would not spend 5 minutes contemplating your most significant problem at work?

Thus far, the compact represents a preliminary basis for engaging you and me in some specific actions that lead to your reflecting on issues, examples, and crucial points being raised and then your considering, through reflection, how it has affected your perspective about the leadership process and system you are attempting to build over time. What I am asking you to do represents a very important aspect of your leadership development, summarized in the following statement:

To lead means to step back before moving forward.

As you read on, at certain places in this book, I refer you to additional points to include in our compact of understanding. Also, by working together, we should try to anticipate, as often occurs in the process of leadership, something you might not understand by offering current examples, a story, a parable, a historical moment, or—and I hesitate to say this, knowing the reaction of many managers—research evidence. To make it easy on you, I present research evidence in boxes or at the ends of chapters so that you can read on if you think you already understand the main points being made or that you are not interested in research. You will notice that I have already slipped in some research along the way. I also use these boxes to highlight other messages along the way.

Again, consistent with one aspect of what we will now call a *full range* model of leadership, I attempt throughout this book not to address the average needs of readers but rather to address the individual needs, with the goal of enhancing each individual's full potential. So, for some readers, the research evidence will provide further reassurance and comfort concerning what I am suggesting for you to consider in your own leadership development. For others, it may be unnecessary, and I would simply say, read on. Ultimately, my goal is to provide information that grows on and with the learner.

My internal voice also indicates that research evidence reassures me that what I am suggesting as a personal intervention has some support that your efforts will ultimately be productive. So, as a follower, bear in mind my needs as well. My need for research support as a basis for helping you achieve your full potential is, in my mind, similar to any situation where a treatment is being recommended. In leadership development, the treatment is a suggestion to change some aspect of the way you think or your perspective and some aspect of what you do as a leader, a follower, or both. We can also suggest a need to change the context. In another context where treatments are frequently considered, could you imagine an official from the U.S. Food and Drug Administration (FDA) saying, "Why don't you try this particular drug? It is blue and a very nice color. Our chemists have made its taste very enjoyable, and I *think* it will have the impact you desire"? Okay, raise your hand if you would take the drug. What, no hands? Having seen no hands raised, I would like, with your permission, to refer from time to time to the broad research literature that forms the basis for many recommendations contained in this book. So, if the leadership pill is blue and tastes good, it actually has some proof that it works.

I would also like to add that I have consciously selected research that supports the recommendations made in this book. I intentionally make a strong inference here because I believe that what I am suggesting will work for you and will provide what I consider supportive evidence for my recommendations.

BOX 3.3   Leadership at the Base of Leadership Effectiveness

The bulk of research on establishing positive transactions and exchanges between leaders and followers indicates that followers who work with leaders who set clearly defined expectations and agreed-on levels of performance are more likely to achieve these goals than are followers who work with leaders who do not clearly define goals and expectations. Positive transactions in the form of contingent reward leadership positively relates to follower satisfaction and performance (see, for example, Bass & Bass, 2008; Bass & Riggio, 2006; Dumdum, Lowe, & Avolio, 2002; Judge & Piccolo, 2004; Podsakoff, Todor, Grover, & Huber, 1984). Effective transactional leadership can create the conditions on which deeper levels of trust are formed.

Let's revisit what I am asking of you. (This is my way of demonstrating strategic redundancy.) First, I need your active engagement in the process of developing leadership potential. Second, to gain that active involvement, we are building a compact of understanding that delineates a framework and agenda for establishing our mutual expectations. And at least for the moment, these expectations are quite simple: Ask a question and step back and reflect on it for *no more than 5 minutes per day.* That is it. I said for the moment these expectations were rather straightforward; however, as any relationship evolves and develops, one's expectations may become more complex, yet still doable if they are in line with one's developmental trajectory and potential. If they are impossible or too simple, they will not be very good expectations.

A significant aspect of developing leadership potential requires knowing the expectations one should have of others and stretching them when an individual or group of individuals is prepared to be stretched (see Box 3.3). Stated another way, development of your full potential as a leader has some building blocks, including, first and foremost, an articulation of the expectations you have of yourself and of others you are attempting to influence over time. Through your expectations and your collective achievements, identification and trust are built.[25] This is a connection often missed by newcomers to leadership development who are beginning to explore and learn the leadership development process, an issue we take up in much more detail throughout this book because, without trust, you can never achieve the full potential of your leadership or the vital force. Yes, I meant to say *never.*

In this chapter, we have discussed the importance of developing a set of mutual expectations with a goal of clarifying our understanding of what underlies those expectations and their impact on relationships over time. If you extend this process with your own followers, peers, or supervisor, the development of expectations clarifies what you seek from each other. As a leader in this process, it also tells you something about the developmental level of the people who work with you over time. Some expect a lot of direction and support and clarify those levels for you through their expectations, suggesting a less mature level of development. Others want more discretion and will require or expect more self-direction, indicating a more mature level of development or that their expectations exceed their abilities. It is perhaps obvious, but worth restating, that the second in command, third, forth, and so on are quite varied in their needs, expectations, and capabilities, which also change for each group over time. This makes the establishment of expectations both informative and instructive for relationship-building purposes—your relationship with others. It also makes it necessary to repeat this process as new followers become involved.

Investing in the development of effective transactions with others will pay off to a great extent later in the relationship-building process as we move from simple transactions based on agreements and contracts to trust being the internal basis for our expectations of each other. It is important to understand that if you consistently honor your expectations with others, you build the conditions for trust, and trust is the credit in the bank that leaders acquire and use in situations where they do not have the time to clarify the rationale for their choices.[26] Simply put, they expect and hope that they have the trust to do what is required.

You must build identification (high-level ownership) with your main purposes and trust in every calm moment because, when a crisis occurs, you have to hope that enough time is available to reflect before acting. Frequently, however, there is not enough time, and everyone, including yourself, has to *trust* that you are heading in the right direction. Why would anyone do so? Because he or she identifies with you as a leader, and identification breeds trust, and trust gets people to work much harder than compliance.

To summarize, for many years, my colleagues and I have argued that transactional leadership was the basis for developing transformational leadership.[27,28,29] This, in part, explains the high correlation between the transformational and transactional leadership ratings often found when people report their results using the Multifactor Leadership Questionnaire (MLQ)[30] (see Box 3.4). The relationship between these two leadership orientations is discussed throughout this book. Here, we introduce the concepts to underscore that both are important to achieving the maximum potential along the full range of leadership development. Without the transactional base, expectations are often unclear, direction is ill defined, and the goals you are working toward are too ambiguous. It is certainly possible, however, to get people inspired in this context, but it is difficult to align them around what their focus should be and who does what when. Transactions clearly in place form the base for more mature interactions between leaders and followers over time.

BOX 3.4   Exchange Tactics and Transformational Leadership

Tepper (1993) had followers of managers in a financial institution rate the leadership of their managers. Those leaders who were seen as more transactional tended to employ exchange and pressure tactics to influence followers, whereas those leaders who were rated as more transformational frequently employed legitimating tactics that resulted in higher levels of follower identification and internalization of values.

In terms of reflection, consider your most successful attempt at building people's identification with what you were striving to accomplish at some point in your life, going back as far as you can recall. What was the first thing you did? What did you do next? And what made this particular situation stand out in your mind?

SOME THINGS WORTH REPEATING AND REFLECTING ON

- A compact provides the basis for building a clear sense of what each of us wants to derive from our relationship.
- The compact is a living document that must be revisited periodically to determine whether it is still relevant.
- Transactions are the basis for building trust and identification and for launching a sustainable full range leadership system.
- There is no stronger force toward compliance than identification (see Box 3.5).

BOX 3.5   Taking More Responsibility—Maybe Call It Empowerment

Empowerment may be viewed as a psychological mind-set, according to Conger and Kanungo (1988). Relevant to anyone asking you to take responsibility for your own development, you will feel more empowered to the extent that you see meaning in what the person is suggesting and have a clear idea of the direction and ability to achieve what has been asked of you. People we will call transformational leaders attempt to make the challenges meaningful for you, ones you feel capable of handling and encouraged to persist at until you have been successful. Generally, underlying this process is a form of identification where followers come to see the mission and goals as something tied to their future self or self-concept as generally known.

BOX 3.6   Team Performance and Leadership

The long-term success of firms can be attributed to a significant extent in the combined capacity of the members of top management teams (TMTs; Carpenter, Geletkanycz, & Sanders, 2004). Leadership can play a critical role in leveraging top management team talent as noted in the following quote by Bass (1998a), who concluded that "transformational leadership at the top of the organization is likely to be needed for commitment to extend to the organization as a whole" (p. 19). Supporting this claim, Colbert, Kristof-Brown, Bradley, and Barrick (2008) reported that CEO transformational leadership was positively related to organizational performance. More recently, Peterson and Zhang (in press) reported results studying 67 top management teams, which showed that teams led by more transformational leaders collectively exhibited what Luthans, Youssef, and Avolio (2007) refer to as psychological capital (PsyCap) and higher business unit performance. PsyCap is characterized by four psychological resources: task-specific self-efficacy (confidence to take on and put in the necessary effort to succeed at specific tasks), hope (one's ability to persevere toward a goal considering multiple pathways), optimism (a positive expectation about succeeding), and resilience (sustaining and bouncing back to attain success when beset by problems and adversity; Luthans et al., 2007). Transformational leadership positively predicted the collective PsyCap of these TMTs, which in turn predicted business unit performance.

A SHORT EXERCISE

Oftentimes what you do during the very first moments of a relationship can impact the course of that relationship's development for many years. Please think back to the first moments that you started working in your current position.

- What specifically did you do to build trust with the people you work with and for? Consider your first conversation, meeting, or e-mail.

If you do not recall any specific actions, please go back and reset what you could have done, and think about how you would do it now, using one of the 4 factors of transformational leadership. Which factor did you choose to develop trust, and why? How could you use transactional leadership to build trust?

CHAPTER 4

LEVELS

The most useful thing I learned was to be humble and listen.

Larry Bossidy, CEO of Allied Signal

Effective leadership is not limited to the heads of organizations or to one best way of leading.[31] Recall that we are talking about a process of influence and building a relationship that can include anyone, at any level, and in any organization. I came across an elementary school teacher who exemplifies many aspects of what might be considered on anyone's scale exemplary leadership and followership. I discuss her style of leadership in some detail because of the importance elementary school teachers have to the future development of leaders in any society.

Stacey (a fictitious name) is an elementary school teacher who taught second graders. Her capabilities as a teacher were well known not only to her colleagues, her students, and the parents in her district but also to the state examiners who assigned her the best teacher award. She was also known to the federal examiners who evaluated her as one of the runners-up for the best teacher award in the United States. A little more about Stacey being a runner-up for this prestigious award later.

On the last day of school one year, a stream of fifth graders who were leaving for the middle school stopped by to wish Stacey a great summer. Many students had been in Stacey's class several years earlier, and they were leaving for the middle school and wanted to wish her well. It was especially interesting to observe the boys coming up to her and embracing her before leaving.

What makes Stacey so different from other teachers? She constantly searches with her students for what might be an avenue to help them achieve their full potential. When you talk to Stacey, you quickly get the feeling there is a development plan in her head that usually ignites the fire inside each student to learn to his or her potential. Having asked many managers around the world whether they have such plans for each of their followers, I can tell you this is a rare situation indeed. Although I should add that I learned from an interview with Steven Kerr,

Vice President for Corporate Leadership Development at GE, that when Jack Welch was CEO, he kept track of nearly 1,000 managers at all levels of GE in terms of how they were progressing in their careers, often asking very specific questions about one particular individual's progress and status.[32] Stacey's plan includes each student as an active participant in his or her own development. It is clearly not seen as a one-way street or as being just Stacey's responsibility to develop students. (I do hope you see some parallels to our emphasis in developing a compact of understanding.)

It is evident from her behavior that Stacey respects her students, values their opinions, seeks out their views on tough issues, and follows up when she is unsure how they feel or when students appear not to understand something they should have learned the first, second, third, or fourth time. She truly believes in her students and inspires them to believe in themselves. In a final letter sent home at the end of the year, she closed the letter by saying, "Please remember the times I asked you to repeat, 'I am the best, therefore I will do my best.' . . . I believe you are the best, and I hope you do, too!" This is what I referred to above as the Pygmalion effect in action.

Stacey is both demanding and fair, and often she structures her class so that more controls for behavior reside in the children, and what eventually becomes their own control system, they own individually and collectively. I called this *ownership* earlier, where she is transferring and reinforcing who is accountable for development. By the way, I find that such enablement is a very common characteristic among exemplary teachers who are highly respected by students.

One example of taking ownership is her infamous jar of beads. On the left-hand side of her desk sits a jar filled with beads. On the right-hand side sits an empty jar. Generally, by the end of the day, the right-hand jar has gained some advantage, and on a really difficult day, it is brimming with beads. The right-hand jar is a visual way of showing the challenges the class faced that day in terms of poor behavior. The goal, of course, is to have the right-hand jar remain empty.

At the beginning of each year, Stacey repeatedly clarifies her expectations of students, as they do of each other and of her. The jar is there to remind everyone when expectations were or were not met. A full jar on the right is one clear indicator of missed expectations, and a near-empty one is something to celebrate because the expectations that were set were met and typically benefited everyone in class. She provides positive recognition (see Box 4.1) for achieving a very skimpy right-hand jar of beads.

On the surface, Stacey's approach appears to be a simple behavioral reinforcement strategy that one might observe in some other classroom or in a work setting where certain rules for safety are set and the organization keeps track of how many days the rules have not been violated. Her approach is similar to any sports team, which must work within the expectations and rules set for its members' behavior. Indeed, I have recommended to several companies that if they really want to use the sports analogy for building teams, which many do, then they should place a referee in the hallway, calling rule violations. For example, let's say that you had a really bad meeting with someone. Why not call in a referee to throw a flag for roughing the leader? Why do we think we can build teams any more effectively than sports organizations do, usually without the aid of experienced coaches, referees, and rules—very clear rules?

And now, back to Stacey. Some core lessons for building a leadership system underlie her constructive approach to dealing with aberrant or unexpected behavior in class. Stacey's focus goes beyond simple reinforcement toward building internal control and accountability for one's actions, as well as learning and support through feedback. We can identify three clear components of the leadership system that are external to Stacey. On the *inputs* side are the students and Stacey working on the establishment of the rules and expectations. In terms of *process* are the behaviors exhibited by the class and Stacey and how they relate to the rules. On the *outcomes* side are the consequences associated with behavior. A feedback mechanism is also very clear in terms of the jar of beads, a simple system that appears to work quite well over time in helping develop students to their full potential.

BOX 4.1   Recognition From Employees

In an article, "The Magnificent Seven" (1994), which refers to the top seven CEOs in the United States, Butler describes Mary Kay Ash's philosophy on providing recognition—that from the moment of birth onward, the one constant that most people look for in life and at work is to get attention and recognition. Much of Mary Kay Ash's success as a business leader has been attributed to her constant attention to providing employees with recognition.

Over time, we can observe in Stacey's class, students giving each other feedback to avoid a situation where another bead "bites the dust." Through this and many other clever systems, Stacey builds a structure or process for her class that is considerate of their needs yet provides a framework concerning what is and is not considered appropriate behavior. As noted above, we are again back to setting clear expectations. By clarifying and honoring my expectations, I can eventually build trust with you. It is a very fair system, with clear redlines and recognition established for behavior. The expectations set are clearly expressed, mutually agreed to over time and, most importantly, quickly owned by the entire class, including by Stacey. This is evident when you see the class work together on a really good bead day, to beat the all-time low in terms of the number of beads transferred to the right.

Interestingly, a recent large-scale analysis of the past 30 years of research on team building, noted in Box 2.1, would support Stacey's approach. Eduardo Salas and his colleagues found that the most important effect in the early development of teams was learning how to structure roles and expectations. This was seen as the foundation for building effective teams and could apply to any classroom, battlefield, or workplace.

Until the early 1980s, what was described above may have been the end of the story for many of us on what constitutes effective leadership. The leader or group creates a structure in which expectations are then clarified. The needs of the group are considered and folded into those expectations, and from there it is all about implementation, consistency, feedback, and in some cases rewards or recognition for achieving expectations. A large amount of what constituted leadership was achieving effective exchanges. With a system of consistent, effective exchanges in place throughout an organization, we should be able to reduce the level of cynicism in their workforce? How? It is not uncommon for leaders to fail at clarifying their expectations or, worse yet, violate the ones specified, resulting in disengaged and cynical followers. Over time, these types of inconsistencies can lead to many bad interactions and intentions that can limit a team or organization from achieving its full potential.[33,34] So, getting the transactions right consistently, in what we have labeled transactional leadership, is essential to becoming an effective leader, follower, and team.[35]

However, Stacey has actually demonstrated much more in her leadership style and perspective than simply exhibiting effective transactional leadership using clear expectations. Her frame of reference on how to treat students is not simply to get students to meet *her* expectations. The leadership system at its most basic level is there for students to build respect and commitment with each other, to take the initiative to do the right thing, and ultimately to offer the second in command an increased share of responsibility for achieving the objectives for the class. Students learn to be active, responsible followers and leaders. Very early in the school year, the necessity to point out missed expectations has fallen into the hands of the second in command, whom we can call students. They are in command of monitoring expectations they have agreed to for their class. Control goes where it belongs and will do the most good—on the inside of student's thinking, looking out in terms of setting accountability.

What also is taking place within Stacey's leadership system is that students are feeling more validated in their work. How? First, they are feeling validated because their teacher respects them enough to ask them to be accountable for their own behavior and, more importantly, the behavior of others. Second, Stacey has put them all into leadership roles, and thus, through practice, they are also validating themselves as leaders. And finally, Stacey has provided them some space to lead up, as sometimes it is her behavior that deserves a bead placed in the jar.

One question you might have is, "Are we talking about leadership here, followership, peer influence, or something else?" For the moment, let's just say we are talking about all of them and that each is a component of the leadership system taking shape in this classroom. This leadership system can parallel the formation process that goes on each time a group gets together and decides, either consciously or not, to form a team by using the development of each other's expectations as a foundation. Let me add here that if we are talking about developing a leadership system, then by definition we must discuss both leading and following, especially when it applies to the same person across time and different situations and challenges.

As you may have already concluded, Stacey is highly respected by her colleagues and trusted by her students. People who know her often describe her in idealized terms. She demonstrates a true passion for learning and a commitment to teaching her students to achieve their full potential. As I indicated at the outset of this story, Stacey had won the best teacher award in her school district and was in the running for the national award. During the evaluation process, however, she suddenly pulled herself out of competition. During her interview with the board of examiners, she was asked how she planned to spend the 50% of her time teaching other colleagues around the country her methods of instruction. Up to that point, Stacey was unaware she would have to travel so often during the school year, which was a newly established requirement for the award. On hearing this, she politely finished the interview, excused herself, and told the head examiner on her way out that she was removing herself from the competition.

There was no way Stacey would begin the school year with a new class of students, telling them that they should expect her to be around only 50% of the time because of her travel schedule. This was a tremendous sacrifice for her. Yet, she did not appear to have a moment's hesitation on making the right decision, nor apparently any regrets. If not for the principal of her school and a close friend who was involved in the selection of the best teacher award recipient, no one would have known about her decision to excuse herself from the competition. Her perspective on which decisions she should make appears to come from an internal set of standards, which represent a compass for taking what she considers the right course[36] (see Box 4.2).

Some say in leadership that the very best leaders know the difference between choosing something that is *right* versus *less right*. You may have heard the expression "the leader's moral compass." This expression is exemplified in Stacey's choice. She knew what she needed to do upon brief reflection, and the criterion for that decision was not a set of external standards or expectations like the one described above for her class. It was a much higher set of standards that makes a significant difference in both a leader and follower's accomplishments over time. It is their core beliefs, which are often shown in the expectations they set and are reinforced through numerous interactions, that led them to conclude, "Now this is the right course of action to take."

Although Stacey did not win the national award for teaching, later in the year she was nominated for and won the opportunity to carry the Olympic torch in the summer Olympics. Consistent with her style, she decided that this privilege should not be given to just one individual. She started a contest in school: Any student who read a certain number of books would be eligible to sign the sneakers she would use to run with the torch. The sneakers would be put in the school's trophy display cabinet to celebrate how they all had carried the Olympic torch a little closer to Atlanta. By the time Stacey ran with the torch, very little white space was left on her sneakers for additional signatures. She had moved the honor of running with the Olympic torch from an individual level of recognition to a collective level—that is what great leaders seem to do.

At the end of each year, Stacey approaches several parents and asks whether it would be okay for their children to meet with her periodically over the summer. Her objective is to continue with some of the work she has begun with those students to help them ascend to their next level of development. These are students who are dealing with a very broad range of issues, from being able to organize themselves in their work to difficulties with concentration, reading, or comprehension. It is not a planned summer program, nor do all parents know about this offer. Those who do, however, know that Stacey is simply trying to continue her work with children to help them achieve their full potential and that, for her, the end of the school year is merely an arbitrary and temporary point of closure in this process. Stacey spends her summer continuing her work with children in a very individualized way. If students or their parents do not wish to meet with her, then that is as far as the offer goes.

You can see in Stacey's behavior that she also demonstrates a very high level of ownership herself that we call *identification*. In Stacey's case, she identifies with the full role of being a teacher. By *full role* I mean she sees the complete development of her students as her responsibility. It is not sufficient for her students to simply learn the material in her course; rather, she is intent on growing her students to their full potential. This is part of her identity, whereas with other teachers, they simply identify with getting the job done. And the job for them is to make sure students are competent with the material, no more and no less.

BOX 4.2   High Moral Compasses and Transformational Leadership

Lucius and Kuhnert (1997) examined the moral development levels of 32 cadets at a large military institute, using Jerome Kegan's interview procedure (Lahey, Souvaine, Kegan, Goodman, & Felix, 1991). This procedure is based on constructive-developmental theory, which indicates that as people mature, they go from making decisions based on external standards (for example, Will I be punished?) to higher internal standards (for example, How do my actions affect the welfare of people I work with here?). Lucius and Kuhnert reported that those cadets who rated higher on transformational leadership by their peers were also evaluated as having higher perspective-taking capacity and moral development as measured by interviews and James Rest's Defining Issues Test (Rest, 1986). Further work linking moral perspective-taking capacity and transformational leadership is reported in both Avolio (2005) and Bass and Riggio (2006). For example, Turner, Barling, and Epitropki (2002) found a positive relationship between the leaders' rated transformational leadership and their perspective-taking/moral capacity level.

My inner voice asks, "What parent in his or her right mind would turn down such an offer?" Well, some parents do because they themselves are not ready to appreciate her extra effort, do not see the need for it, and may not be unwilling to sacrifice *their* time. They are perhaps not developmentally ready for this type of leadership behavior in their teachers. In some cases, the students choose not to meet with her. The varied reactions of either parents or students are not unlike what one typically observes in any leadership context.[37] Clearly, there are some parents who are indebted to her for offering this option. Some do not see it positively at all; they may even see it as a negative regarding her ability to accomplish in the year what she should have accomplished. This very straightforward gesture on Stacey's part, and the range of reactions it receives is a very important lesson about leadership that you may want to allocate 5 minutes to reflect on today.

The true and most accurate interpretation of leadership always rests in the eye of the beholder. We say that people are *meaning makers*. What we *mean* by that is that they construct what they observe, not simply observe it. So, for some parents, they see Stacey's offer as being altruistic, while for others, they see it as not fully meeting expectations during the year. This is a very important outcome of leading that you need to fully understand as you progress with your own leadership development. If you understand that it is not the behavior that impacts others, but their interpretation of that behavior and meaning assigned to it, you will have learned a very important principle about leadership.

The only way for you to learn how people make meaning is to get to know them, to get feedback, and to sometimes be redundant with the message. By *being redundant,*

I mean presenting a message in a lot of ways so it triangulates for others around the meaning you intend to convey. You can convey your messages very powerfully through the consistency of your actions and words, the stories you convey and how you react to what others say to you. Think about whether these suggestions characterize leaders you fully understand and have respected.

So, let me repeat what I said in a slightly different way. What constitutes the accuracy in terms of how a message is received is based on each individual's perception of leadership, and using the term *leadership* suggests that perceptions are based on what the leader does and how the follower interprets the leader's actions or, in some cases, inaction within a particular context over time.[38]

When leaders are asked to evaluate how they come across to their followers, we usually find that their followers typically do not agree on their evaluations about how the leader behaved. The reason for the disagreement is that both the leader and follower are meaning makers. And if they create meaning in different ways or weigh information differently, then it is likely they will not be in agreement on many things including how the leader has behaved.

Going back to Stacey, one last point about her behavior relates to her interactions with peers. Typically, she meets with teachers who will be working with students from her class during the next academic year: She briefs them on the individualized plans she has developed, activities that worked well with each child, options to avoid, and in special cases, detailed plans regarding where Stacey and the student left off in their work together. It is not her way simply to throw students "over the wall" to the next class, captured in the phrase, "Hey, it's not my department!"

I cannot say that this is a typical behavior I have observed in many companies around the world but one that is clearly necessary for building a learning-centered culture based on ownership and collaboration. The more common occurrence is at the lowest end of ownership, which I have referred to as *territorial*. Why should Stacey inform other teachers? Is that really her job? Well, Stacey views her job in a much more expansive way and has stretched it to include the hand-offs she makes to other teachers, working with parents and teachers during the summer and taking responsibility for the full development of her students.

I hope that by not using a typical corporate example, I can convey to your inner perspective and voice that leadership can occur in all the right places (see Box 4.3). Like many other leaders I will discuss with you, and their followers, Stacey exhibits four essential ingredients to exemplary leadership, whether it occurs with individuals, groups, or organization level's culture. Those four components are what my colleagues and I refer to as the four Is of transformational leadership: *idealized influence, inspirational motivation, intellectual stimulation,* and *individualized consideration.*[39]

Stacey is *idealized* in her efforts to build trust through her consistent expression of positive values, *inspiring* in the degree to which she is willing to sacrifice her own time for the good of others, *stimulating* in the way she challenges students to be actively engaged in creating their expectations, taking ownership and the creative use of beads, and *individualized* in her constant attention to what each student most needs and desires to develop to full potential including during summers and in other classes.[40]

I wonder whether you have thought of a parent in the role of leader. Have you thought of the family as a high-performing team? I suspect that we all have thought about children as followers, willing or otherwise, and sometimes even exemplary. I think, too often, that many parents create a dependent followership until around age 13. Then a battle occurs for who will set expectations and take ownership, and the conflict that ensues is not always adaptive[41] (see Box 4.4). This statement presupposes that conflict can be very productive, so productive that it is actually developmental. Although more complicated than the average team working on NASA's space shuttles, the transference of authority and accountability in families is very much the same challenge that one observes in high-performing teams. If the challenge is ignored, the team and the child both suffer in their mutual potential and development. There is not a point where ownership must be transferred, there is a series of points where you begin to transfer ownership, and over time, the individual, in this instance child, takes full ownership.

BOX 4.3   Transformational Leadership and School Performance

Silins (1992) examined the relationship between transformational and transactional leadership and its effects on schools, teachers, students, and programs in a sample of 256 elementary schools in British Columbia undergoing reform. Results indicated that transformational leadership had a more significant and positive relationship with school effects than transactional leadership, supporting the full range model of leadership. Transformational leadership in school systems has been shown also to have a positive impact on levels of trust, commitment, citizenship behavior, and satisfaction levels of teachers (Koh, 1990). Most significant about Koh's study was that transformational leadership augmented transactional leadership in predicting levels of commitment, trust, and satisfaction, which, in turn, predicted hard measures of school performance in a large sample study of Singaporean principals. Additional results reported by Philbin (1997) in secondary schools showed a strong and positive relationship among the transformational leadership of the principal and how effective he or she was perceived to be, satisfaction with his or her leadership, and the willingness among teachers to put in extra effort. Transformational leadership was shown to have a greater impact among more capable students in terms of their overall scholastic performance, something we can also see in Stacey's work with students.

Think about the aspects of Stacey's leadership that differentiate her from other teachers. Now, think about the aspects of any leader in your life that has represented what Stacey's does with her students. How committed were you to that leader and your work? Why?

BOX 4.4   CEO Leadership

Zhu, Chew, and Spangler (2005) demonstrated that CEO transformational leadership was mediated in its impact on organizational performance by the level of commitment they engendered in followers. By doing so, they can connect followers to the mission and vision of the organization providing them with a greater sense of the importance of the work they are doing for the organization and, in turn, linking the work to how followers view themselves (Bono & Judge, 2003).

SOME THINGS WORTH REPEATING AND REFLECTING ON

- Leadership can be observed in almost any meaningful role including teachers and parents.
- A job is like a rubber band: It is elastic and stretchable to include the best one can do.
- Leadership builds accountability through effective transactions that can lay the foundation for transformations in individuals, groups, and organizations.
- By reaching out to others, we lay the foundation for developing up.

A SHORT EXERCISE

Providing employees with authentic recognition is one of the more powerful ways to motivate effective performance. Go back and take a look at your last recognition moment—where you offered recognition to someone you were leading. Ask yourself:

- What did I know about that individual's likes and dislikes?
- How timely was my recognition?
- What were the consequences of providing recognition?
- How can I apply recognition moments more effectively to develop my follower's motivation using individualized consideration?
- How did providing recognition to someone else make you feel and perform? Why?

CHAPTER 5

ADAPTIVE CONFLICT

Conflict is only uncivil when it is either hidden or unnecessarily blown out of proportion.

M. S. Peck, *A World Waiting to Be Born*[42]

Adaptive conflict represents the highest order of human interaction and the essential basis on which truly profound insights are generated and deployed. Unless there is some degree of tension, which conflict generally creates, there are no insights. Part of what constitutes effective leadership is coming to know how to hold tension with others in order to achieve insight.

Elliott Lehman, former cochairman and founder of FelPro, Inc., one of America's most well-respected companies, approaches this issue in the following manner with his employees: "There is only one silly question, the one you don't ask. There is only one silly comment, the one you don't make." Questions and comments will inevitably create tension in organizations with leaders and followers who truly want to have continuous learning and improvement. And not asking the "wrong" question can be disastrous for an organization.

Now, to create tension for tension sake is not helpful either. So, leaders have to choose what are the appropriate tension points and time for doing so. For example, if a follower is highly stressed out, just creating tension does not help form insight. Indeed, by including some degree of positive perspective, balanced with the creation of tension, you cannot only enhance the level of inquiry shown by those you lead but also the nature of insights.

BOX 5.1   Conflict as the Basis for Profound Transformation

Ron Heifetz, in his 1994 book *Leadership Without Any Easy Answers*, views the creation of adaptive conflict or challenge as being central to the leadership process. He advocates creating the dilemma for leaders and followers and keeping the level of distress at a tolerable level to clarify the issues and to move toward a new level of understanding and, ultimately, resolutions. Heifetz suggests that, without contradictory impressions, there appears to be little to awaken reflection. The adaptive part of the challenge is that we learn from conflict if handled properly, which allows us to move to higher levels of understanding and perspective.

Kegan and Lahey (2009) go further and describe what they call an organization's as well as a leader's *immunity to change*. The basic thesis of their book is that individuals and organizations develop mind-sets that become very immune to change. Part of the immunity to change comes about from the mismatch between the increasing complexity of the world and how we construe the world as being simpler than it appears in line with our mental models. In what the authors call the *socialized mind*, we find individuals who are wonderful conformists, loyal to the cause, even when things seem to have changed dramatically, warranting a very different course of thinking and action. The self-authoring mind and leader represents someone who has set an inner course based on principles and values that may likely end up in conflict with the common conception of what needs to be done, but nevertheless, the leader will pursue against others if needed. At this level, self-initiative characterizes the nature of the way the leader thinks, believes, and instills principles and values in those around him or her. So, do not be the good soldier following the wrong mission—question, challenge, and adapt. The adaptive challenges may require a very different mind-set that is completely in conflict with the one you had that worked in the past. Getting followers who support the current state to question what they are doing and not doing is critical to change. Immune systems reject things they do not understand. The very holy grail of change then is seeing the limits of our current way of knowing what is the right and wrong thing to do in a particular circumstance. The optimal conflict is between the ways you know and the ways you need to know to adapt and change. The authors suggest that to change, leaders must hold conflictual, challenging, and often intense, uncomfortable conversations.

As you consider how far to push people and the type of tension to create, you also have to learn where people are in terms of their development. A hard truth is that some people are damaged by their parents' actions or the parents' absence and require a great deal of recovery before effective leadership development can actually begin. Others have already had exemplary leadership training from a parent or parents or significant other, and often I personally think, as a developer, that I am simply reaffirming and extending what they already know and do in their roles as leaders or followers.

To put a label on a methodology in use, they have already been developed from the *inside out*, and my role is to refine the style and enhance their perspective even further, often by creating tensions, adaptive challenges, and conflict. This goes along with General Colin Powell's comments about leaders having the gut instinct (which I see as being nurtured) that we end up honing and shaping through training. At the other end of development, the foundation work on the person's perspective of how to relate to others must first be developed. Stylistic considerations come later in the "life" training program.

One interesting leader that was not fully developed was Warren Buffett, the top financial investor in the world, who lives in Omaha, Nebraska. In a recent biography of his life, the author discusses how Warren was afraid to come home from school before his father returned because his mother would go for years being very kind and caring, and then one day she would go nuts. She was very unpredictable. One thing that really seems to screw up leaders-in-the-making is having an unpredictable, if not whacked out, mother. For Warren, his mother was a wild card, and his first wife Susie recognized this when she first met him. She observed how difficult it was for Warren to be around others. This generally is described as a form of being unattached, or lacking in the ability to attach to others. We see in the biography, titled *Snow Ball*, that personal attachments were difficult for Warren with not only acquaintances but also his family. Susie set as her goal to replace what Warren had missed in terms of the unconditional love that mothers can give to their children. Having met Warren Buffett, I can say she has done a very effective job. Susie entered Warren's life stream early enough to make a real difference in who he was becoming.

BOX 5.2 How Well Attached Are Your Leaders? Attachment Level and Leadership Development

Bowlby (1969, 1973) posits that humans have a survival need to be attached to caregivers who can provide security. Attachment is a lifelong need characterized by individual differences in the level of security that people require in their relationships with significant others. Micha Popper recently reported that securely attached leaders were also rated by their followers as more transformational. Such securely attached leaders have the ability to attend to another person's needs because they are not so consumed by their own. Those people classified as *insecure-avoidant* were not evaluated as transformational. Following along the same line of research, other researchers have also reported that most implicit models of ideal leaders and followers were affected by their level of attachment. What you see as ideal is based, in part, on your own foundation and development (Berson & Yammarino, 1997; Popper, Mayseless, & Castelnovo, 1998).

THE LIFE STREAM WE TRAVEL IN

Something I find helpful in my own work on leadership development that may be of some help to you is a metaphor I call the *life stream*. When I meet a group of people for the first time in a leadership development workshop, I try to visualize a life stream for each person. For some, the stream is very narrow, straight, and perhaps shallow. For others, it is quite turbulent, dramatic, and circuitous. For the remaining members, the streams have their waterfalls, but for the most part they are not so unique or all that dramatic. By using this metaphor, I realize that I am just one point in their life streams, charged with building on the *in vivo* leadership training they have already received from a parent, coach, teacher, former manager, or friend (see Box 5.3). Now, we are engaging in *in vitro* training, and I must build on what they have developed thus far to help them understand the process of developing themselves and others to their full potential.[43],[44] In the best instances, we can add value to the established base, which comes along in the life stream. In the worst case, we may not have a clue of how much anxiety or damage we caused in their development. Perhaps you can see how important it is to the development of Stacey's students that she is meeting them early in the life stream, making her downstream impact from everyone's account enormous.

I suggest that you now may want to take a step back and look at your own life stream. How fast has it brought you to this point in time, and how far downstream can you see? What have you learned that was fundamental to developing your perspective about how you treat others, including yourself, and your life in general? Are there particular trigger moments perhaps associated with adaptive conflict that have occurred in your steam that continue to impact you? For example, I met Marilyn Nelson Carlson who ran The Carlson Group a while back, and she told us a story about her father and her. She recounted a drive home from Sunday school as a teenager where she decided to tell her parents that she was not going back to Sunday school again. She explained to them how it was chaotic and she learned nothing there. At that moment her father pulled the car over and turned to her and said, pointing his finger at her, "If you don't like it, fix it." That was it—the beginning of a trigger moment that I would characterize as *adaptive conflict*.

On Monday they went to meet the minister, and Marilyn was asked to describe her disappointments plus what she thought might fix it. The minister listened patiently and committed to working with her and others to make it a better Sunday school. Marilyn said that experience over 50 years earlier was a very significant trigger event in her life that has shaped the way she leads others. She frequently tells her employees, "If you don't like it, fix it"—perhaps without pointing a stubby finger at them.

BOX 5.3   Early Antecedents to Leadership Development

Gibbons (1986) compared the life history profiles of senior managers at a Fortune 100, high-technology company on the basis of the following leadership ratings breakdown: high transformational and transactional, high transformational, high transactional, and high laissez-faire leadership. These leaders also completed the Personal Orientation Inventory, which measures a person's degree of self-actualization. Gibbons found that transformational leaders tended to be more self-actualized, but not significantly so. The high-high leader group had significantly higher scores on Self-Regard and Capacity for Intimate Contact than all other groups.

As children, transformational leaders were expected to be the best and to do the best, with moderately high levels of responsibility given to them by parents. These individuals were stretched, but in a balanced way. These individuals learned how to deal with conflict, stress, and disappointment, which positioned them to turn conflict into adaptive conflict. The best leaders had a pattern of many prior leadership experiences that they reflected on over time to improve themselves. They had a very strong desire to engage in development work, and it was so much a part of them that it was seen as automatic. Role models, workshops, and training were all incorporated into improving the personal development of these leaders. They had a very strong tendency toward self-reflective learning and to integrate what they had learned to improve themselves.

Exemplary leadership is a process whereby we continuously develop ourselves and others to our full potential. To do so, we must be very conscious of the past, but not so tightly bound to it that we cannot move in new directions with equally new challenges. We must know where we want to go, which may take time and some data collection. What I mean here is that we have to know how much tension we can create for individuals to move them forward. This requires getting to know the people you influence in a way that you can take them up the trajectory of tension but not so far that it becomes maladaptive.

Knowing the depth of the stream and course you have entered, its speed, and the points where it might flood over if given too much pressure are crucial issues for developing all people, or as Ron Heifetz (1994) alluded, creating adaptive versus maladaptive challenges or conflict. And perhaps most crucial is for you to know what you intend to leave behind.

I have no doubt that Stacey would understand the metaphor of a life stream in her work with students. They come back to thank her because the intervention she made in each of their life streams caused them to change course, to deepen their positions, to address the waterfalls, and to do so with the intent of building perspective about who they are and what they can accomplish. Knowing oneself at each stage along the life stream is the absolute basis for knowing others (see Box 5.4). You develop yourself in order to develop others; therefore, you must jump into your own stream before attempting to change others. Actually, this statement is based on Confucius' view on leadership development, which is to first take care of developing who you are and then developing others.

BOX 5.4   The Power of Observation for Leadership Development

We need to train others to observe how they observe themselves and others. We learn to observe by distinguishing certain information from its background. We make it distinctive and often create stories to capture and summarize our observations. Learning is the act of learning new distinctions that we otherwise would not notice. "Water is fluid, soft and yielding, but water will wear away rock, which is rigid and cannot yield. As a rule, whatever is fluid, soft, and yielding will overcome whatever is rigid and hard . . . what is soft and strong" (Lae-tzu, cited in Matusek, 1997, p. 127).

In the study of Asian leaders cited in Chapter 1, the CEOs also described learning early in their careers that if they listened before acting in groups, oftentimes they were sought out for their leadership. Initially, many said they wanted to jump in and take charge of a group at school and found the group resistant to them doing so. These leaders learned early in life that it was important to earn leadership from others by first listening. This insight typically came from both being self-aware and a role model or mentor in their lives. Others also said that they were very organized and process oriented and that members of groups would often look to them to get the process started and, therefore, lead.

Unfortunately, not all great leaders had the wisdom or the belief system to either know or understand what they were leaving behind or even creating as they moved down their own life streams. They did not consider how they were affecting the life streams of individuals and, in some cases, entire societies. So, when someone asks you whether Hitler, Mussolini, Pol Pot, and Stalin were great leaders, you might simply answer with a resounding, "NO! They were *not* great leaders." Why? The legacy they left behind was much worse than the conditions in which they started their leadership journeys. Among many things, their followers were no closer to achieving their full potential than they were before those individuals came into power. Usually, such leaders leave a vacuum that must be filled again with leadership development. The followers of these leaders are largely destroyed, but with less extreme leadership situations, followers not only do not develop but also do not achieve their full potential. Indeed, they typically were much farther away, having been completely suppressed by these leaders in terms of personal development.[45,46]

Ralph Waldo Emerson once wrote, "An institution is the lengthened shadow of one man [or woman]." (I will keep adding *woman* to somewhat outdated quotes.)

It is the criterion I always keep in mind when judging the full leadership potential of people, and with leaders like Stacey, the conclusion on her leadership legacy is very clear to me. Her shadow will be long and deep and reflected positively in the lives of many children who will become more effective adults over time as a consequence of her efforts. Some trainers will feel and sense her shadow if, years from now, they ask participants who had her as a teacher to identify leaders in their lives who had a profound impact on their development. No doubt, her shadow will emerge on the flip charts and through the perspectives demonstrated by those people as they work to influence others.

It is easy to spend a lot of time talking about quality people like Stacey. Now let me tell you about another leader I met in a very unusual setting. I met Sam, a technology supervisor in the Canadian Correctional Services, back in the early 1980s when I first went out to train transformational leadership. At that time, books on the topic by Tichy and Devanna,[47] Bass,[48] and Bennis and Nanus[49] had just appeared in the literature. To a large extent, these books talked about transformational leadership among senior executives in a very broad range of organizations. I do not think any included prisons. In this period, and in meeting people like Sam, I discovered that transformational leadership was much more pervasive than my colleagues had noted in their excellent books. I found it occurring in many strange places, such as in Sam's shop and in the correctional services root cellar.

Sam's unit in the correctional services had one of the lowest recidivism rates in the country. I believe there is an inverse relationship between the adaptive conflict that is created by a leader with followers and whether they revert backward to maladaptive behavior or, in this instance, return to prison. Let me say just a few words about Sam, and then I will add more about him later in this book.

Sam worked with inmates in a metal-working shop, a shop filled with very sharp devices. He was a very short man in his late 50s or early 60s. I recall walking into his shop for the first time and seeing a large group of men standing around a machine. I could hear someone in the middle of the group talking but could not see who it was at first. Sam was in the middle of the circle and was instructing the group how to operate a particular machine. They all had tools in their hands, really sharp ones. With his back to the group, he described the process of working on the machine. Because this was a maximum security prison, the inmates were there for often very brutal crimes. I was nervous, and they had their backs to me.

While Sam was talking, I noticed on the wall four pieces of metal. One was a raw piece of metal. The second was severely scratched and bent. The third looked a little better. The last one had a high-gloss finish and was perfectly cut to specs. After the group left the room, I had some time to talk with Sam alone. I asked him about the metal art on the wall. He explained that he needed a way to convey to his students what they could do in Months 1, 2, 3, and 4 if they were willing to work with him and trust his directives. He laughed and then said, "A limited vision of sorts." Because many of his students were illiterate, Sam needed some visual indicator of future potential and progress that could be achieved by his followers. A vision statement pasted on the wall would not have worked. This is one of many examples Sam used to frame what he was trying to accomplish with people. He treated his followers with respect and dignity, and they, in turn, did the same with him. Of course, the ones who did not were handled by the group, so to speak. Sam had the best protection in the correctional facility: He had the full commitment and trust of his closest "employees"—big, strong employees.

Sam would use adaptive conflict in rather subtle ways. For example, many of his employees had been abused in their life streams, from sexual abuse to other forms of physical and psychological abuse. So, the last thing he wanted to do was to break them down. Rather, the adaptive conflict was sourced from what has been, what is, and what could be. To someone in prison, they must feel that they have choices. If they lose that, they lose everything, including hope. Sam worked hard to expand what they saw as their choices.

I can say with some degree of confidence that neither Sam nor Stacey would describe themselves as leaders; in fact, Sam said this to me at one point in our conversation. It suggests the problems we have with the term *leadership* (see Box 5.5) because, without a doubt, both were not only leaders but also exemplary in their leadership styles and the impact they had on their followers. They were the best of leaders in the sense that they really knew who they were and what their real work was all about. They had built a set of internal standards and perspectives that helped guide them through their work with others. What may have started at some point in their life streams as a set of external expectations had clearly become internal standards and principles that guided their actions and behaviors. I will go further: They were not just leaders; they were transformational.

In *Lightning Bolt,* Storm (yes, I know what you are thinking) suggests that we battle in life to reduce self-ignorance in that ignorant individuals cannot see the truth as it applies to themselves. This type of ignorance about the self increases the propensity to conform.[50]

BOX 5.5 Training Transformational Leadership

Crookall (1989) conducted a training impact study of prison shop supervisors, comparing the impact of transformational leadership training to situational leadership training on inmate performance. Three groups of supervisors were involved: Group 1 received situational leadership training; Group 2 received transformational leadership training; and Group 3 received no training. Measures were taken on work group productivity and inmates' personal growth for a 3-month period before the onset of training and after the close of the training intervention. Both trained groups improved on an order of 10% to 50%, depending on the measures. Although both training programs had a positive impact on performance and personal growth, the transformational training had a more significant effect on personal growth and development, whereas situational leadership training had greater effects on productivity levels. Transformational leadership significantly improved inmates' respect for their managers, potential skills, and good citizenship behavior as rated by case managers in the correctional services.

Barling, Weber, and Kelloway (1996) examined the impact of transformational leadership training in a true field experiment. The study was conducted with bank branch managers who received individual coaching and training in transformational leadership that was extended over time with booster sessions. Barling et al. reported significant differences in ratings of intellectual stimulation in the experimental versus the comparison group. Significant effects were also shown with the performance of bank branches comparing the two groups.

Dvir, Eden, Avolio and Shamir (2002) set out to do a true field experiment comparing the best transformational training to a newer and more refined focus on transformational leadership development. Using Israeli platoon officers, who assumed command of a new platoon that had no history, the platoon commanders in the new experimental training group performed better on objective measures of performance collected during months of basic training. The soldiers in these experimentally trained platoons also had more positive attitudes (in line with their noncommissioned officers), perceived themselves to be more similar to their leaders, and showed more collectivistic orientation and active engagement.[51]

BOX 5.6 Asian CEO Leadership

From the interviews done with CEOs in Asia cited in Chapter 1, we coded the CEO responses to questions regarding the type of life events that shaped their leadership development using a coding scheme from the life stories literature. Each type of event based on the individual's life narrative (originating event) was a turning point signifying change or an anchoring point that became a basis of a personal philosophy. Additional options included *redemptive events* (initially negative, but came to be viewed as positive), *triggering events* (resulted in changes for the positive or negative), *analogous events* (repeated or reenforced earlier life events), or *contaminating events* (demeaning or insulting). The overall results of our coding showed that anchoring events were the most commonly described as having an impact on leadership development, followed by positive triggers, redemption events, and originating events.

(Continued)

(Continued)

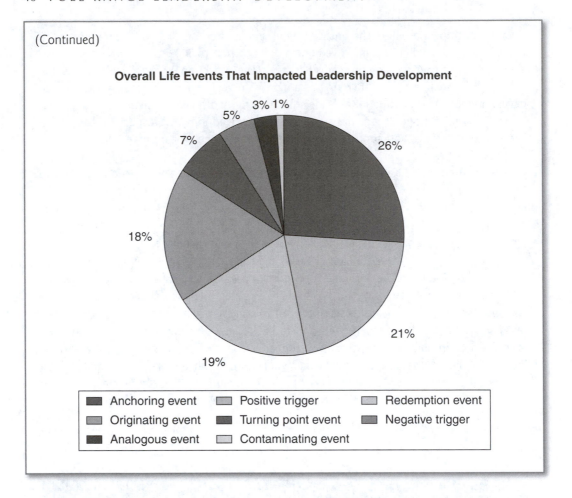

Overall Life Events That Impacted Leadership Development

Legend:
- ■ Anchoring event
- ▨ Positive trigger
- ▨ Redemption event
- ▨ Originating event
- ■ Turning point event
- ▨ Negative trigger
- ■ Analogous event
- □ Contaminating event

BOX 5.7   Self-Other Ratings

Atwater and Yammarino (1997) addressed a crucial area in leadership development; it concerns the growing popularity of using upward and 360-degree feedback for leadership development. The controversy stems from the fact that the agreement between self- and other ratings is often rather low. The gap between self- and other ratings has implications for effective leadership specifically. Atwater and Yammarino (1992) demonstrated that self-other agreement was a predictor of the leadership performance relationship. Research evidence indicates that over- and underestimators of their own leadership styles vary in terms of how effective supervisors rate their leadership potential and performance. Atwater, Ostroff, Yammarino, and Fleenor (1998) demonstrated that simultaneous consideration of self-ratings, other ratings, and their gap was important to predicting leadership effectiveness.

Let's leave this chapter with one question for you to consider. Look back over the past several months and ask yourself, What have I done in my interactions with others to create adaptive conflict that might impact them well into their life stream?

SOME THINGS WORTH REPEATING AND REFLECTING ON

- Get to know your own life stream as well as triggers and those of others to help focus you on the individual needs of others.
- Think about your leadership legacy now so that it can fruitfully unfold during the course of your life span. It is never too early.
- Transformational leaders can be found at all organizational levels and in all cultures, so do not worry about the role so much as who you are and how you enable others to excellence.

A SHORT EXERCISE

I want you to think about the type of legacy you have either left behind or may leave behind in the future depending where you are in your leadership life stream.

- As you have moved from one leadership role to another, what was the plan you had in mind going in that determined the type of leadership legacy you left behind?
- If you did not have a plan, can you describe the outcomes of your avoidant leadership in this instance?
- Now, if you are currently engaged in leadership, how would you construct your legacy thinking about what you want to leave behind in terms of follower ownership and the qualities of the culture in your unit and organization?
- What will you have to do starting now to develop that legacy?
- You are receiving a final toast to your leadership at your farewell recognition ceremony. What is the last line that you would like for that person to say about you and your legacy?

CHAPTER 6

FULL RANGE LEADERSHIP

Some cause happiness wherever they go; others, whenever they go.

Oscar Wilde

In the preface of this book, I referred to the overwhelming amount of research that has supported our claims that transformational leadership is a consistently highly effective form of leadership at all organizational levels and across all organizations. We have seen over the past decade's worth of research that people want to stay with transformational leaders. People have a greater sense of ownership at the highest levels in terms of identification and are willing to provide the extra effort needed to succeed. People are more committed to their work, more highly engaged, and more satisfied. In return, they produce more. This supports working hard to be more transformational at the highest end of the full range of leadership.[52,53]

Yet, although transformational leadership across time, organizations, cultures, and individuals seems to be the most effective form of leadership, it is important to reemphasize that without the more positive forms of transactional leadership such as setting expectations and goals, as well as monitoring performance, leaders and those led would be limited in their ability to succeed. Indeed, what has been most interesting is to see how transformational leadership adds to transactional in predicting performance. What I mean here is that being transactional will move the meter positively in the right direction in terms of a very broad range of performance outcomes. Transactional leaders at the top of their game will not achieve the same level of performance, however, without transformational leadership. Let me unpack this a bit as it has relevance to what we will discuss in the remainder of this chapter.[54]

There are situations where being transactional will achieve exactly the performance you expect, and that may be high performance. Yet, if you continue to be purely transactional in the way we define this leadership style in the current chapter, you would never inspire followers, never fully develop them, never challenge them to come up with breakthrough insights, and never embed your highest moral values and standards in their behavior and actions. Indeed, going back to our earlier discussion of the second in command, we would find that if the purely transactional leader was pulled from the scene, the individuals they have worked with would likely be less prepared to lead on their own. Why? Transactional leaders can get the job done, but they do not focus like transformational leaders in developing followers to lead. Their attention to performance is very important to optimizing existing performance systems but not to optimizing change and development.

What we have clearly learned is that leaders who can balance transactional and transformational leadership across time, situations, and challenges are the most effective.[55,56,57] The difficulty is that most transactional leaders do not know what it means to be transformational and, therefore, cannot shift their balance of attention and effort up the range to transformational leadership. The way they define leadership is confined to a transactional quid pro quo framework. So, how do you conceive of the highest end of the range of your own leadership? What occupies that space in terms of your thinking about leadership and your behavior? How much of what you do in a leadership role involves executing the task versus developing potential, setting an example for high ethical conduct, and challenging ways of thinking that create totally new insights?

Where we deviated 10 years ago from the field of leadership was in describing that it takes two very different mind-sets to lead as a transactional versus transformational leader. What this means is that you actually think differently when you have the transactional leadership mind-set versus the transformational, and there is now research to support these differences from both the cognitive science and neuroscience literature. Where the brain processes information according to an MRI varies if you are transactional or transformational in your leadership orientation. Consequently, to develop you to traverse the range, we have to promote not only changes in your behavior but also changes in the way you think.

Let me give an example to help illustrate the points above.

You are given a specific task to meet some challenging customer requirements in terms of both quality and time of delivery. Taking a purely transactional perspective, you would proceed by making sure you have the appropriate resources to achieve expectations. Likely, you would focus on scoping the project and setting goals and objectives that would assure you are successful, including in your analysis appropriate contingencies and support systems. People working with you would have a clear idea of the goals set, the means available to achieve them, and the rewards for satisfying the goals.

Someone who is higher up on the full range of leadership could do everything described above under the rubric of transactional leadership. However, transformational leaders might also do the following:

- Highlight the importance and long-term meaning in meeting the customer's expectations and requirements. They often would go beyond simply the immediate goal, placing the challenge in a larger context in terms of relevance to the organization, customers, and employees.
- They could think about how to use this challenging situation as a way of providing development for some of the high-potential employees. They might create leadership roles to allow those employees to stretch their leadership capabilities with support from them.
- As part of the scoping process, they may challenge some basic assumptions such as doing things faster can result in higher quality output if new processes are created that lean out wasted steps.
- Transformational leaders might also emphasize that nothing should be done to compromise the basic ethical and moral values of the organization. They will not succeed if they compromise their ethics, regardless of what goals are achieved.

You might see from the example above that the transactional and transformational leadership orientation entails a different way of thinking and different ways of influencing the followers who work with them. You might also have realized that it is the combination of the two leadership orientations that optimize the full range of performance and development.

Some global distinguishing characteristics of *transformational leadership* are worth stating up front. Transformational leadership involves the process whereby leaders develop followers into leaders. This is a conscious goal; the leader has a development plan in her or his head about each follower. Transformational leadership is fundamentally, morally uplifting. Such leaders stimulate challenge, as opposed to suppressing it when it arises. They are deeply trusted and exhibit the moral perspective to warrant such trust. Their willingness to be vulnerable and to self-sacrifice builds tremendous trust among followers, along with ownership in the form of identification with their mission or cause. Their willingness to self-sacrifice is often associated with similar patterns of self-sacrifice among their followers in a sort of falling dominoes effect. They work to leave behind an organization, community, or even society that is better positioned to succeed than when they first began their work. For these reasons, Burns,[58] Bass,[59] and Sergiovanni[60] referred to transformational leaders as moral agents who focus themselves and their followers on achieving higher-level missions and purposes. The higher levels of identification result in higher levels of commitment, trust, loyalty, and performance.

How can I describe such leaders to you in more practical terms? They are people who come to their tasks not only willing to listen but also determined to know what others are thinking. They take the time to get to know the people they work with, what these people need to know to perform at their best, and how far they can be stretched, challenged, and supported. They are role models of the expectations they have of others.

Leaders oftentimes have to make difficult decisions where they are doing the least harm to the most people. For example, if cost cutting is required, these leaders do not protect their offices from the ax, but try to look at what is best for the overall organization's success. They frequently struggle with what is the right thing to do, and they keep in the forefront a set of standards that makes the execution of their principles predictable. You get to know what they think is right and wrong through their words and their actions. Many want to emulate them because they are respected for taking a stand on important issues, for championing someone's cause, for taking on difficult challenges others have avoided, for being concerned, and for doing something about those concerns. They encourage those around them to use their full intellectual capital and to not fear questioning those things that are most established nor those issues with which they are most closely aligned (see Box 6.1).

Now, as we look at transactional leadership, we see that transactional leaders address the self-interests of those being influenced by them. Transactional leaders offer inducements to move in the direction they desire, which often is a direction that would also satisfy the self-interests of their followers. They exchange promises of reward for cooperation and compliance from their followers to get the task done. The best transactions are constructive, and evidence cited earlier would suggest these are effective in achieving desired levels of performance. Many examples of this type of leadership behavior may be found in almost any organization, even in my initial interactions with you in formulating a compact of expectations and an understanding of how best to develop leadership potential.

It is understandable to wonder how transactional leadership can form the base for transformational given the differences in these leadership orientations. Here is one connection that might help in understanding how these leadership orientations work together. If you honor all your various transactions with people, over time they come to trust you; it is higher levels of trust versus compliance that transformational leadership uses as its base for achieving exemplary performance. But, of course, leadership is not always that simple, meaning that even though you believe you have been absolutely consistent, some followers, peers, or even your supervisors may not concur with your opinion. So, being consistent

> ### BOX 6.1 Levels of Commitment/Loyalty and Transformational Leadership
>
> Pitman (1993) provided evidence to show that the commitment level of white-collar employees in six organizations correlated positively with the transformational leadership ratings of their supervisors. Niehoff, Eng, and Grover (1990) surveyed 862 insurance employees, reporting that commitment to the organization was positively affected by the extent to which top management was inspirational and encouraged innovativeness from employees. Similarly, employee ratings of their shop steward's leadership style predicted members' loyalty, sense of responsibility, and actual participation in union activities (Kelloway & Barling, 1993). In fact, the strongest predictor of levels of loyalty to the union and participation in union activities was the shop steward's transformational leadership. Shamir, Zakay, Breinin, and Popper (1998a, 1998b) reported that, with Israeli Defense Force companies, group morale, cohesiveness, and level of potency were each positively related to trust in the platoon leader, identification with the unit, and willingness to sacrifice for the leader. Den Hartog (2000) reported that 267 Dutch employees who rated their leaders as more transformational were also more emotionally committed to their work. Berson and Avolio (2004) showed that followers at subsequent levels in a large telecommunications company were much more familiar and aligned with the organization's goals when led by leaders evaluated as more transformational.

in the eyes of all your followers who are close and at a distance will be a very difficult challenge that is renewed each time you work with a new group of followers. However, all the evidence points to it being a worthwhile challenge to take on in terms of long-term success.

Further down the range, transactional leadership can also be an active or passive engagement in terms of being a corrective exchange or transaction. Here, the exchange involves a desired change in behavior, learning level, cooperation, or compliance of followers to avoid censorship, reproof, negative feedback, punishment, or disciplinary action. For example, if too many beads are shifted from the left jar to the right in 1 day, then certain privileges are lost by students in Stacey's class. The same logic applies to the number of defects in rejected products, poor customer service, and delivery errors by suppliers.

Both constructive and corrective transactions can be set to be contingent on each follower's performance or, in some cases, the leader's, if follower directed. Some leaders emphasize constructive promises, praises, and rewards that are contingent on achieving expected performance (see Box 6.2). Other leaders manage by exception and pay attention to their followers only when their behavior is off the mark and correction is needed. Even though such constructive transactions are reasonably successful and effective, corrective transactions are less so, particularly in terms of developing learning potential in followers. How well would you learn if you only had someone who always built a list of things for you that you should not do? What about the long list of things you *should* do, try, be encouraged to explore, and even fail at over time? In all, transactional leadership is not enough for people to achieve their full potential, whether they are leaders or followers, individuals or in groups. And as a culture, this style of leadership creates an environment that is often risk-averse and quite low in innovation, because if your contract is being monitored, you are likely not to innovate and take risks.

One example of creating a low-risk culture comes to mind. I was at a senior management retreat for a large medical supplies company. The company was very conservative and embedded in a culture that constantly tried to avoid mistakes. In that business, it was quite important to avoid making mistakes that would place customers at risk. Yet, the company had taken an extreme position on avoiding any mistakes after being caught by the Food and Drug Administration (FDA) for putting out a product that was not properly tested. This decision had led to a huge fine for the company, several indictments, a dramatic loss in market share, and a very tarnished image with customers. The *event*, as it was called internally, also became the turning point in creating a culture that was paranoid about making any mistakes. The key words in the culture became *control* and *comply,* which do not go too well with a third word—*innovate.* During the second day of the retreat, the CEO was challenging the group to give him feedback: "Help me. . . . Don't you have any passion?" A young, Italian manager spoke up finally and said, "I was told by my regional manager that under no circumstances am I to say *anything* interesting at the

---

BOX 6.2   Mission/Purpose and Transformational Leadership

Keller (1992) reported that effective leaders in research and development (R&D) project teams tended to inspire a sense of mission and purpose about the importance of the work being done by the team, they stimulated new ways of thinking and solving difficult problems, and they got members to contribute the extra effort needed to achieve exemplary performance levels. Such transformational leadership was also shown to be more predictive of project quality in research versus development teams.

Keller (2006) did a follow-up longitudinal study with 118 R&D teams from five separate organizations over a 5-year period and replicated and extended these findings supporting his initial ground-breaking research. Specifically, Keller reported transformational leadership predicted 1-year-later technical quality, schedule performance, and cost performance, and 5-year-later profitability and speed to market.

meeting." Here, the company had spent tens of thousands of dollars to bring in its senior managers from around the world, and the employees were being coached to not be innovative, not be creative, and above all else, not say anything interesting. I found *that* interesting and, by the way, not uncommon.[61]

The fact that people come to meetings with their senior managers to not say anything interesting is more the norm than the exception. I find in working with organizations that one of the more valuable roles I play is being the conduit to top management for ideas that lower-level managers will not risk saying. It is incredible to see so much latent potential in organizations that goes untapped because the leadership has not made the organization a safe place to say what you really think.

When I recently asked a group of 90 emerging leaders from America's top technology companies if they would tell their leaders what they really think, on a 1 to 5 scale, they were near 1 in terms of strongly disagreeing with this item. The survey was done in a classroom setting so I could ask them why they were hesitant to speak up, and it primarily came down to two issues. The first issue was that their managers did not care to hear what they thought. The second issue was that they were not going to risk their careers by telling their managers the truth. Unfortunately, we can see from the meltdowns in early 2000 with Enron and WorldCom and later in 2008 with Bear Stearns, Lehman Brothers Holdings, and Washington Mutual that many employees knew full well what was going on but few if any would challenge their organizations going over a cliff.

I recall meeting a young economist at a leadership recognition ceremony in which his sister was receiving an award for outstanding leadership in her community. He was visibly depressed because he felt that he had not stepped up loud enough to challenge the direction that Washington Mutual was headed, which turned out to be dissolution—a hundred-plus-year-old company gone.

When leadership is needed, any leadership is likely to be more successful and effective than avoidance of responsibility to provide leadership. *Laissez-faire leadership* (LF) is the behavior of those individuals in a group who, in the extreme, do not care what happens, avoid taking responsibility, cannot make up their minds, and are satisfied to sit and wait for others to take the necessary initiatives imposed by the tasks at hand. We can call these types of individuals *social loafers*. Our descriptions of Stacey or Sam should suggest that this style is not the one either of them exhibited very often, but they probably exhibited it once in a while, as we all do at various points in time. It is quite human to avoid certain decisions, yet it is ineffective leadership to be seen over time by your peers, supervisors, or followers as primarily avoidant.

Ask yourself now whether you have ever avoided a problem or delayed taking action on a particular decision beyond what others thought was reasonable. I believe we all must admit that we have avoided making a decision; therefore, the answer is always yes. I am sure that someone has certainly seen all of us at some point exhibiting LF. In terms of building the full range of leadership potential, how often you exhibit a certain set of behaviors along the range ultimately determines how effective you are over time as a leader. The frequency with which you exhibit behaviors depends on your perspective or frame of reference of what you consider important. What is important to you will influence where you place more or less emphasis in terms of your choice of actions and decisions. For example, if you understand the importance of identifying the needs of people who report to you and that doing this can have a positive impact on their development as well as your own, then you are more likely to expend energy and time trying to understand each individual's needs.

Think about the last time you were confronted with a choice of sitting back and waiting for someone else in your group to say what was needed to be said for the group to move forward or for you to take initiative. Why were you reluctant to act? What made you finally do what you did? We all are laissez-faire about certain things, and, in fact, it may be used to our advantage. For example, an article appeared in *The Wall Street Journal* about Lou Gerstner 6 months after he was selected to lead IBM out of its worst slump. The article described Gerstner as laissez-faire. This is a label no one today would ascribe to Lou Gerstner's leadership of IBM and how he left it when he retired. With some reflection, one might say he chose not to act before he was prepared to act, despite the fact that employees, stockholders, investors, and competitors may have seen him as laissez-faire. By the way, he apparently spent the first 6 months closeted with IBM's customers, finding out what they liked, did not like, and needed from IBM. Yet, in his employees' eyes, he may have been seen as avoidant. Realize that part of IBM's problem was the company's avoidance of its customers in terms of really listening to their needs, succumbing instead to its own long history of success.

AND THE RESEARCH SAYS . . .

As I said from the outset of this chapter, prior research has supported the idea that, on average, transformational leadership is far more effective than transactional leadership in generating the higher levels of extra effort, commitment, performance, and satisfaction of those led (see Box 6.3 and 6.4). This has been true almost regardless of the level of leadership position, the type of organization, and the culture in which both are embedded.

Constructive transactional leadership is reasonably effective under most circumstances. *Management-by-exception* (MBE), also a transactional style, is more corrective than constructive. But actively correcting a follower for failure to perform as expected is more varied in effects. For example, in an extreme, life-threatening context, looking for exceptions is a positive characteristic of leaders. In brainstorming new ideas in a marketing research firm, it is likely not seen as a positive characteristic. Finally, corrective leadership that is passive (for example, Please don't fix it if it ain't broken.) tends to be generally ineffective across most conditions and situations.

You must be willing to address a follower's sense of self-worth to engage her or him in being committed and fully involved in the challenges at hand. And that is one thing transformational leadership adds to the transactional exchange. People do not comply with what needs to be done; at the higher end of their potential, they are more committed to achieving it because they believe in what they are doing and, therefore, identify with the effort displaying higher levels of ownership. Identification provides the high octane for achieving exemplary performance.

BOX 6.3 Linkages Between a Full Range of Leadership and Performance[62]

Gasper (1992) conducted a meta-analysis of prior literature on transformational leadership. Results indicated that transformational leadership was the more preferred style among followers and was associated, as noted with single sample studies, with perceived leadership effectiveness, follower satisfaction, and greater willingness to put forth extra effort.

Coleman, Patterson, Fuller, Hester, and Stringer (1995) reported the results of a comprehensive meta-analysis. The average relationship (which can vary from −1.0 through +1.0) across studies for the transformational leadership factors and performance ranged from .45 to .60; for transactional, .44; for MBE active, .22; for MBE passive, .13; and for LF, −.28. These meta-analyses included 27 studies. A similar pattern of results also emerged in the relationships with satisfaction and rated effectiveness.

Lowe, Kroeck, and Sivasubramaniam (1996) conducted a parallel meta-analysis confirming that the transformational leadership factors were more highly correlated with work performance and that this pattern held up across two levels of leadership with both hard (number of units) and soft (performance appraisals) measures of performance. The total number of samples, including both published and unpublished works, was .47. Lowe et al. did find some differences attributable to moderator effects in the relationships observed. For example, some differences were found in comparing public and private organizations and when examining the type of performance measure. For example, in terms of performance measures, the following results were noted for relationships between the leadership scales and follower ratings versus organizational measures, respectively: idealized/charisma = .81 versus .35; individualized consideration = .69 versus .28; intellectual stimulation = .68 versus .26; contingent reward = .56 versus .08; MBE = .10 versus −.04 (see Figure 6.1).

Judge and Piccolo (2004) set out to replicate and extend the findings of Lowe et al. (1996) by including a wider variety of leadership measures and by testing the augmentation hypothesis advanced by Bass (1985). The augmentation hypothesis indicated that transformational leadership would augment transactional in predicting performance outcomes as was shown in the research at Federal Express reported by Hater and Bass (1988). Evidence for the augmentation hypothesis showed that transformational leadership accounted for unique variance beyond transactional and laissez-faire leadership in predicting performance. Judge and Piccolo reported that the strongest relationships they found were between ratings of transformational leadership and follower satisfaction with the leader (.71), job satisfaction ($\rho = .58$), and group and organizational performance (.26).

More recent research has begun to focus on the various processes through which transformational leadership effect performance outcomes (Avolio, Zhu, Koh, & Puja, 2004; Bass, Avolio, Jung, & Berson, 2003; Bono & Judge, 2003; Kark, Shamir, & Chen, 2003; Liao & Chuang, 2007; Wang, Law, Hackett, Wang, & Chen, 2005). This research shows that the effects of transformational leadership on performance can be indirect and mediated through constructs such as empowerment (Avolio et al., 2004), trust (Pillai, Schriesheim, & Williams, 1999), and identification with the leader (Walumbwa, Avolio, & Zhu, 2008). This emerging research also shows that the transformational leadership/performance link in some cases was fully mediated (Asgari, Silong, Daud, & Samah, 2008) by levels of job satisfaction, follower satisfaction with the leader, and commitment to the organization.

BOX 6.4   Executive Leadership and Performance[63,64]

Agle (1993) examined 250 CEOs, mostly from major U.S. companies. The executives were rated by their direct reports in terms of their idealized leadership qualities, their achievement levels as CEOs, and the performances of organizations under their tenure. Findings indicated that the more charismatic leaders led more effective organizations as seen by their direct reports as well as their stock performance. Ratings of idealized leadership also correlated with sales increase, market share, earnings, and return on investment (ROI).

Figure 6.1   Evidence for Impact on Performance

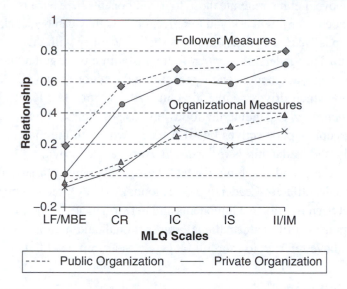

SOURCE: From "Effectiveness Correlates of Transformational and Transactional Leadership: A Meta-Analysis Review," by K. Lowe, K. G. Kroeck, & N. Sivasubramaniam, 1996, *Leadership Quarterly, 7*(3), 385–425.

Transformational leadership involves motivating others to do more than they originally intended and often even more than they thought possible. This can happen when a person goes from doing a task for the money to doing it because she or he identifies and takes pride in what is produced. What is good enough to be paid for is not always good enough to take pride in. This gap is what transformational leadership tends to reduce in individuals, teams, and even organizations.

In sum, true transformational leaders raise the level of identification, moral maturity, and perspective of those they lead. Over time, they develop their followers into leaders. They broaden and enlarge the interests of those they lead. Their shadows are much deeper and longer in terms of their effects on others, and by and large they are very positive shadows over time.[65]

REVISITING THE COMPONENTS OF TRANSFORMATIONAL LEADERSHIP

Transformational leaders do more with colleagues and followers than set up simple exchanges or agreements. They behave in ways to achieve superior results by employing one or more of the four components of transformational leadership briefly mentioned above. Let me reiterate those four components here because, before going on to the next chapter, I will ask you to reflect on how they can be developed in you.

Leadership is *idealized* when followers seek to identify with their leaders and to emulate them. The leadership *inspires* followers with challenge and persuasion by providing meaning and understanding regarding the actions required. At the core is *identification,* which drives people to achieve the vision. The leadership is *intellectually stimulating,* expanding the followers' use of their abilities to question not only other people's perspectives but also their own, even the most deeply rooted ones. Finally, the leadership is *individually considerate,* providing followers with support, mentoring, and coaching. Each of these components is assessed with a survey called the Multifactor Leadership Questionnaire (MLQ; see Figure 6.1 for relationships between full range components and performance).[66] The MLQ comprises all the components of transformational, transactional, and nontransactional leadership that we have referred to as a full range of leadership potential.

Idealized Influence[67,68]

Transformational leaders behave in ways that result in their being role models for followers to emulate (see Box 6.4). They are admired, respected, and trusted. Followers identify with the leader and the cause or mission the leader is advocating and over time come to emulate the leader but in a true idealized sense in that they will question the leader.

Among the things leaders do to earn idealized credit is to consider the needs of others over personal needs, often willingly sacrificing personal gain for the sake of others. Leaders share risks with followers and are consistent rather than arbitrary in their actions. They can be counted on to do the right thing, especially when it is tough to do so. Principles and standards provide the base of consistency for how leaders are perceived, not each behavior. Specifically, leaders can be very difficult and challenging to some and highly empathic and supportive for others all within their range of principled leadership.

Transformational leaders avoid using power for personal gain but will use sources of power at their disposal to move individuals or groups toward accomplishing their mission, vision, and cause. They are the leaders whom people name when they are asked to reflect on their life by describing someone who has had a profound influence on their personal development. An Israeli platoon commander told me that in the Israeli military they referred to this type of leader as someone who leads with you and ahead of you. Often, an idealized leader is perceived as being the central force in moving a group forward and the person who sees what she or he should be doing next: both with them and ahead of them.

Inspirational Motivation

Transformational leaders behave in ways that motivate and inspire those around them by providing meaning and challenge to their followers' work. Team spirit is enhanced. Such leaders display enthusiasm and optimism. They get followers involved in thinking about various attractive future states or scenarios, considering sometimes very different and desirable alternatives. They can inspire others by what they say, by what they do, and at the highest end of the range, by both (see Box 6.5).

BOX 6.5   Transformational Leadership and Sales Performance

Garcia (1995) examined the relationship between transformational leadership and sales performance. The field study was conducted in two large U.S. companies serving a nationwide market. The context in which these salespeople operated could be classified as high-complexity buying centers. Using the MLQ, 101 salespersons were rated by their supervisors. Transformational leadership of the salespeople significantly correlated with the performance rating they received, as well as a sales/quota ratio generated to compare the performance of salespeople across the two organizations. Transformational leadership accounted for 37% of the variance in sales performance effectiveness as rated by the sales managers.

Intellectual Stimulation

Transformational leaders stimulate their followers' efforts to be innovative and creative by questioning assumptions, reframing problems, and approaching old situations with new methods and perspectives. Creativity is encouraged as a high norm for conduct. New ideas and creative problem solutions are solicited from followers who are included in the process of addressing problems and finding solutions. Followers are encouraged to try new approaches, and their ideas are never criticized simply because they differ from the leaders'. Often, the leader focuses on the *what* in problems rather than on the *who*, where blame might be assessed.

Followers, in turn, stimulate the leader to reconsider tried-and-true assumptions, helping the leader and organization avoid going over cliffs. Nothing is too good, too fixed, too political, or too bureaucratic that it cannot be challenged, changed, retired, or abandoned (see Box 6.6). It is quite likely that those things you refuse to question that are essential to your organizations' survival will be successfully questioned by your competitors who will, no doubt, be delighted you left the questioning to them. Maybe this is also what Andy Grove (1996) of Intel meant when he said in his book that one must run a business by being absolutely paranoid. Of course, to be paranoid

> ### BOX 6.6 Champions of Innovation and Transformational Leadership
>
> Howell and Higgins (1990) provided results to corroborate Keller's findings with R&D teams. Specifically, Howell and Higgins reported that the champions of innovation who, in a variety of Canadian organizations, were identified by using a rigorous peer nomination and interview process that also displayed the high end of the full range of leadership exhibited by transformational leadership. Such champions generated innovative ideas and approaches, which were synonymous with being more intellectually stimulating.

is to worry without cause. So, perhaps we should label this healthy, constructive, and adaptive paranoia.

Individualized Consideration

The transformational leader pays special attention to each individual's needs for achievement and growth by acting as coach, mentor, teacher, facilitator, confidant, and counselor. Followers and colleagues are developed to successively higher levels of potential on a continuous basis, paralleling the type of continuous process improvement that is sometimes observed in highly effective total quality/lean systems. Individualized consideration is practiced as follows: New learning opportunities are created, along with a supportive climate for learning to occur. Individual differences in terms of needs and desires are continuously recognized (see Box 6.7). The leader's behavior and affect demonstrate not only acceptance of individual differences but also a desire to attract them to enhance creativity and innovation (for example, some people receive more encouragement, some more autonomy, others firmer standards, and still others necessary attention in the summer, as described with Stacey's students).

A two-way exchange in communication is encouraged, and management by continuous engagement is the norm in practice. Interactions with followers are personalized (for example, the leader remembers previous interactions, is aware of individual concerns, and sees the individual as a whole person rather than as *just* another student, soldier, employee, or customer). The individually considerate leader listens effectively and could be heard saying, "It's not what you tell them; it's what they hear." We must make sure that what was heard was what the speaker intended us to hear. Such leaders may not always get the concerns right, but you have to give them credit for trying.

> ## BOX 6.7 Transformational Leadership and a Culture of Empowerment
>
> Masi (1994) reported a positive relationship with army personnel between transformational leadership and individual empowerment and motivation among followers. Motivation to achieve was also related to transformational leadership. Reports of empowering cultural norms across organizations were modestly, positively related to ratings of transformational leadership. A similar result was found in a study conducted with nurses in Singapore by Avolio et al. (2004) in which the authors found that feelings of empowerment mediated the effects of transformational leadership on levels of organizational commitment.

Such leaders delegate tasks as a means of developing their followers. Delegated tasks are monitored to see whether followers need additional direction or support and to assess their progress; ideally, followers do not feel that they are being checked on at all. Why? How can this be? They trust their leader's intentions. Stated in their terms, "this person is trying to help me by pointing out mistakes, as opposed to pointing a finger at me in some accusatory way." If you asked such leaders, they could most likely tell you fairly specifically where their people are in terms of achieving their full potential and the plan they have in mind to close the gap between the *as is* and the *what could be*.

> *Have you known anyone in your life who displayed the four components of transformational leadership? If so, how did you feel toward the person? How did you perform as a consequence of that person's efforts toward you? How do you perform today as a consequence of their actions?*

COMPONENTS OF TRANSACTIONAL LEADERSHIP

Transactional leadership occurs when the leader rewards or disciplines the follower, depending on the adequacy of the follower's behavior or performance. Transactional leadership depends on laying out contingencies, agreements, reinforcement, and positive contingent rewards or the more negative active or passive forms of management-by-exception (MBE-A and MBE-P).

Contingent Reward

With this approach, a leader assigns or secures agreements on what needs to be done and promises rewards or actually rewards others in exchange for satisfactorily carrying out the assignment. Such constructive transactions have been found to be reasonably effective, although not typically as much as any of the transformational components in motivating others to achieve higher levels of development and performance.

Management-by-Exception

The management-by-exception form of corrective transaction tends to be more ineffective, particularly when used in excess. However, in many situations, this style of leadership may be required. We find, for example, in life-threatening or other high-risk settings, such as nuclear plants, healthcare, and firefighting, that corrective leadership in its active form is seen as being much more positive and effective by followers and leaders (see Box 6.8 and Figures 6.2a and 6.2b). In fact, in most environments where risk is high, the interpretation of corrective transactions is much different than in contexts where risk is low or negligible.

BOX 6.8 Leadership and Platoon Performance

In Figures 6.2a and 6.2b, from a 2-year project codirected by me and Bernie Bass, one can see that the management-by-exception leadership of both platoon leaders and platoon sergeants positively predicted the platoon's readiness. Platoon readiness was evaluated on the basis of its performance with a field exercise at the Joint Readiness Training Center (JRTC). JRTC hosts a 2-week simulated exercise in which platoons are taken through near-combat missions to evaluate their performance. The transformational and transactional leadership of both the lieutenants and the sergeants positively predicted platoon performance over a 3-month period with correlations in the .3 to .6 range. (This project was funded by the Army Research Institute, 1996–1997, Contract #DASW01–96K–008.)

The corrective transaction may be active or passive. When active, the leader arranges to actively monitor deviations from standards, mistakes, and errors in the follower's assignments and to take corrective action as necessary. Such leadership involves a constant vigilance for possible mistakes. When passive, the leader waits for deviations, mistakes, and errors to occur and then takes corrective action. Now, here comes another one of those reflective questions.

Do you think you spend too much or too little time in your leadership role focusing on mistakes? How do you think this affects people's willingness to be creative and innovative, which by definition is a deviation from standards?

Figure 6.2a Platoon Leader Effectiveness in JRTC Predicted by 360° MLQ Ratings of 18 Platoon Leaders in Garrison

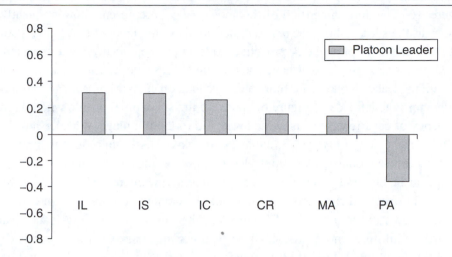

Figure 6.2b Platoon Sergeant Effectiveness in JRTC Predicted by 360° MLQ Ratings of 18 Platoon Leaders in Garrison

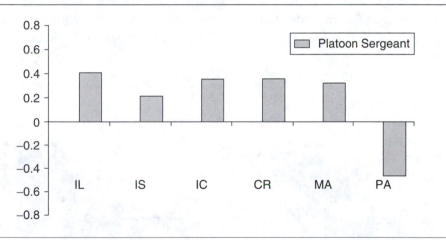

NOTES: IL = Idealized Influence; IS = Intellectual Stimulation; IC = Individual Consideration; CR = Contingent Reward; MA = Management-by-Exception (Active); PA = Passive Corrective; JRTC = Joint Readiness Training Center; MLQ = Multifactor Leadership Questionairre

Nontransactional/Laissez-Faire Leadership

Nontransactional/laissez-faire leadership is the near-avoidance or absence of leadership and is, by definition, the most inactive, as well as the most ineffective, according to almost all prior research on this style of leadership. In the very extreme, nothing is transacted between a leader and a follower with this style.

Fundamental to the full range leadership model presented here is that every leader displays each style to some degree. An optimal profile is shown in the right side of Figure 6.3. The third dimension of this model (*depth*) represents how frequently a leader displays leadership. The *active* dimension is self-evident in that I have shared with you examples of active or proactive leadership. The *effectiveness* dimension is based on research results that have shown active transactional and proactive transformational leadership to be far more effective than other styles of leadership or nonleadership. The left side of Figure 6.3 portrays the suboptimal profile where higher frequency of occurrence occurs at the lower end of the full range of leadership.

In the right side of Figure 6.3, the leader displays laissez-faire leadership infrequently, transactional leadership styles of passive and active management-by-exception at higher frequencies, and contingent reward more often. The most frequently observed are the transformational leadership components. In contrast, and as shown in the left side of Figure 6.3, the poorly performing leader leans toward exhibiting more laissez-faire 'leadership, passive management-by-exception, and much less, if any, transformational leadership. By the way, you could replace *leader* with *team* and, on the basis of results with teams in industry, education, and the military, this statement would be accurate.

In a study of team leadership, Sivasubramaniam, Murry, Avolio, and Jung[69] reported that the collective transformational leadership of self-directed teams

Figure 6.3 Contrasting Leadership Profiles

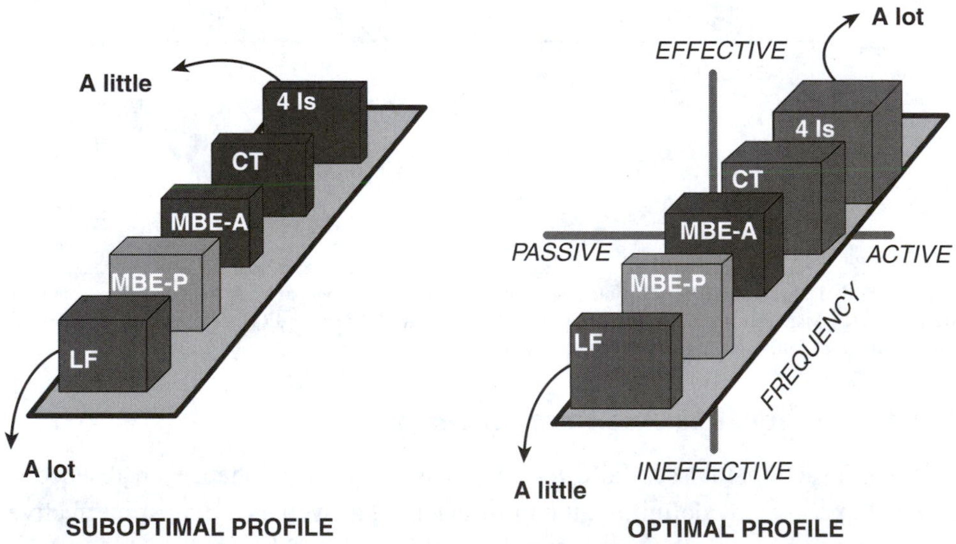

SUBOPTIMAL PROFILE

OPTIMAL PROFILE

NOTE:. CT = Constructive Transaction; MBE-A = Management-by-Exception (Active); MBE-P = Management-by-Exception (Passive); LF = Laissez-Fair Leadership.

positively predicted its performance over a 3-month period. Team laissez-faire and management-by-exception leadership negatively predicted performance (see Box 6.9).

Among the components of transformational leadership, *idealized influence* and *inspirational leadership* are most effective and satisfying; *intellectual stimulation* and *individualized consideration* are a bit less so. All four Is of transformational leadership are more effective than constructive transactional leadership. However, constructive transactions remain reasonably effective and satisfying for most situations except where a leader has no control over the ways a follower may be rewarded for satisfactory performance. Actively taking corrective action—that is, managing by exception and arranging to monitor the performance of followers—is generally less effective and satisfying. Waiting for problems to arise or remaining oblivious until a mishap occurs is seen as poor, ineffective leadership and is typically highly dissatisfying for followers. Most ineffective and dissatisfying is laissez-faire leadership, wherein the individual avoids leadership and abdicates responsibilities.

BOX 6.9 Team Transformational Leadership and Performance

Sivasubramaniam, Murry, Avolio, and Jung (2002) contrasted the higher order factor of transformational leadership and corrective transactional leadership in teams to predict how potent the teams perceived themselves to be over time, as well as to predict performance over a 3-month interval. Student teams participating in this study rated themselves at Month 1 and again at 3 months on how they perceived the collective leadership of their respective teams. Leadership ratings taken early on were highly predictive of subsequent leadership ratings for both transformational leadership and corrective management-by-exception. Transformational leadership directly predicted the performance of these groups and also predicted performance indirectly through levels of group potency. A similar pattern emerged for avoidant leadership.

Many research studies have been conducted in business/industry, government, the military, educational institutions, and nonprofit organizations showing that transformational leadership, as measured by the MLQ derived from the full range model, was more effective and satisfying than transactional leadership, although the best of leaders frequently do some of the latter and more of the former. These studies are described in more detail in Box 6.11.

BOX 6.10 Top Level Leadership and Performance

There is relatively little research linking top level leadership styles to performance. What is currently available provides for mixed results. For example, Waldman, Ramirez, House, and Puranam (2001) found that CEO charisma was not related to subsequent organizational performance as measured by net profit margin and shareholder return or return on assets, respectively. On the other hand, Agle, Nagarajan, Sonnenfeld, and Srinivasan (2006) and Waldman, Javidan, and Varella (2004) reported that CEO charisma was associated with subsequent organizational performance.

BOX 6.11 An Integrative Summary of Full Range Leadership and Performance Outcomes

- Transformational leadership among Methodist ministers was associated with greater Sunday church attendance and membership growth (Onnen, 1987).
- Transformational leadership was higher among presidents of MBA teams completing complex simulations with greater financial success (Avolio, Waldman, & Einstein, 1988).
- Transformational leadership was higher among strategic business unit managers whose departments achieved greater future financial success (J. A. Howell & Avolio, 1993).
- Managers who were seen as transformational by their followers earned better performance evaluations from committees composed of their superiors (Hater & Bass, 1988).
- Naval officers who were rated as more transformational by their followers earned early promotion recommendations and better fitness reports from their superiors (Yammarino & Bass, 1990).
- German bank unit performance over longer versus shorter periods was higher in banks led by leaders who were rated by their followers as more transformational (Geyer & Steyrer, 1998).
- University faculty satisfaction was correlated positively with ratings of transformational leadership (F. W. Brown & Moshavi, 2002).
- Self-ratings of transformational leadership positively predicted the performance of West Point cadets over 6 months (Hannah, Avolio, Walumbwa, & Peterson, 2010).
- Ratings of platoon leader transformational leadership positively predicted unit performance in simulated combat conditions (Bass et al., 2003).
- Howell and Boies (2004) concluded that champions of innovation seen as more transformational were supportive of new and innovative ideas and were better able to connect ideas to organizational performance outcomes.

> ### BOX 6.12   Transformational Leadership and Project Unit Performance
>
> Thite (1997) examined the extent to which transformational leadership was better suited for leading technical project teams as compared with transactional leadership. Respondents were from 36 organizations involving 225 teams and 70 project leaders. Results indicated that the most versus the least successful project teams, using company criteria for determining performance, had project leaders who were rated as more transformational and active transactional. All the transformational scales and the contingent reward transactional scale were positively correlated with team outcomes.

As noted above, transformational leadership adds or augments transactional leadership in its effects on follower motivation, satisfaction, and performance (see Box 6.12).[70] In terms of their interplay, constructive and corrective transactions may have only a marginal impact on followers unless accompanied by one or more components of transformational leadership. For getting the most out of transactions, the follower needs to feel valued by the leader, the follower needs to find meaning in what she or he is doing, and the follower needs a sense of ownership in what is being done.

LINKAGES TO DIRECTIVE VERSUS PARTICIPATIVE LEADERSHIP

Transformational leadership can be directive or participative as well as democratic or authoritarian. Sometimes, transformational leadership is misunderstood as elitist and antidemocratic. Since the 1930s, democratic and participative leadership has been pronounced as the modern way to build the intelligent, learning organization. Indeed, most managers have learned that, before making a decision, it pays to consult with those who will implement the decision, although fewer pursue a democratic vote or strive for consensus in a participative discussion with all those involved and affected by their decisions.

There are many good reasons for encouraging shared decision making, empowering followers, and self-managing, not least of which is that it is your job as a leader to develop followers into leaders. The quality of followers you leave behind is part of your legacy. Yet, many circumstances call for a leader to be decisive and directive. Novices may wish direction and advice on what to do and how to do it. Even when no leader is appointed, someone must begin to take initiative, and that person may soon come to be seen as a leader. In extreme contexts where danger is high, people expect directive leadership, but they also expect you to listen so that you have the optimal level of situational awareness.

Many have confused transformational leadership with democratic or participative leadership. The idealized leader, by providing radical solutions to address her problems, can direct followers who are counting on her to help them get out of a crisis. Perhaps they are at a stage of learned helplessness, not knowing which way to turn, and only a directive transformational leader will make things happen in a positive direction. Again, the inspirational leader can be highly directive in her appeals. The intellectually stimulating leader may directly challenge her followers. The individually considerate leader could rise above the demands for equality from her followers to treat them differently according to their different needs for growth, challenge, and development (see Box 6.13). At the same time, the transformational leader can share in building visions and ideas that could result in a more democratic and collective enterprise. She can encourage follower participation in the change processes involved. In the same way, transactional leadership can be either directive or participative.

BOX 6.13   Peer Ratings of Cadet Transformational Leadership

When peers of military cadet leaders were asked what characterized the most important traits of a good leader, they described traits associated with inspiration, intellectual stimulation, and individualized consideration, such as having self-confidence, having persuasiveness, showing concern for the well-being of others, having the ability to articulate one's ideas and thoughts, providing role models to be emulated by others, holding high expectations for himself and others, keeping others well informed, and maintaining high motivation in himself (Atwater et al., 1994). As noted earlier, these same leaders were also evaluated (by using an interview procedure for assessing moral development developed by Lahey et al., 1991) as being more highly morally developed then their peers at the same institution.

HOW OTHERS DESCRIBE THE HIGH END OF THE FULL RANGE OF LEADERSHIP

When we have asked in numerous workshops and interviews what constitutes transformational leadership, many respondents have offered the following descriptions. So, in their words, or perhaps in your own, we can see the following attributes and behaviors associated with the four Is of transformational leadership.

Idealized influence leadership was attributed to leaders who set examples for showing determination, displaying extraordinary talents, taking risks, creating in followers a sense of empowerment, showing dedication to the cause, creating a sense of a joint mission, dealing with crises, using radical solutions, and engendering faith in others.

Inspirational leadership included providing meaning and challenge, painting an optimistic future, molding expectations that created self-fulfilling prophesies, thinking ahead, and taking the first step, often with risk to oneself—the *Ahead of Them* part described earlier in the chapter where we discussed exemplary platoon commanders in the Israeli Defense Forces.

Intellectual stimulation was judged present when the leaders questioned assumptions, encouraged followers to employ intuition, entertained ideas that may have seemed silly at first, created imaginative visions, asked followers to rework the same problems they thought they had solved, saw unusual patterns, and used humor to stimulate new thinking.[71]

Individualized consideration was apparent for leaders who answered followers with minimum delay, showed they were concerned for the followers' well-being, often assigned tasks on the basis of individual needs and abilities, encouraged two-way exchanges of ideas, were available when needed, constantly encouraged self-development, and effectively mentored, counseled, and coached peers and followers.

Another type of leader Bass has labeled the *pseudo-transformational leader*. These are leaders who act like transformational leaders from an impression management perspective, but they are not really transformational leaders. Why? They have no intention of sacrificing their self-interests for the good of others. In fact, they typically do just the opposite, taking advantage of other people's interests for their own good, if not their survival. This description led me to focus on what constituted authentic transformational leadership and authentic leadership in general, which I will take up later in this book under New Developments.

Table 6.1 lists examples of good and bad leaders, along with some distinguishing attributes that look like they are transformational and those that are labeled pseudo-transformational.

Where do these leaders come from in terms of their life streams, and how can we know when they are for real and when they are just full of impression management behavior, hell-bent on deceiving us for self-aggrandizement? Again, that is where authentic leadership will come into play in terms of addressing this question.

Table 6.1 Examples of Pseudo-Transformational Versus Transformational Leaders

Pseudo-Transformational	Transformational
Idi Amin	Andrew Carnegie
Jim Bakker	Charles DeGaulle
Nicolae Ceausescu	Dwight Eisenhower
François Duvalier	Mahatma Gandhi
Jimmy Hoffa	Dag Hammarskjöld
Adolf Hitler	Nelson Mandela
J. Edgar Hoover	Edward R. Murrow
Joseph Goebbels	Abdel Nasser
Howard Hughes	Erwin Rommel
Benito Mussolini	Marshal Tito
Ferdinand Marcos	Bishop Desmond Tutu
Pol Pot[a]	Lech Walesa

Some Distinguishing Attributes	
Self-aggrandizes	Envisions a more desirable future
Dominates	Seeks consensus and is empathic
Exploits others	Respects differences and develops independent followers
Manipulates	Unites though internalization of mission and values
Unites through fear/compliance	Is self-sacrificing and trustworthy

SOURCE: From "Charismatic Leaders and Destructiveness: An Historiometric Study," by J. O'Connor, M. D. Mumford, T. C. Clifton, T. L. Gessner, & M. S. Connelly, 1995, *Leadership Quarterly, 6*(4) 529–555. Reprinted with permission.

NOTE: [a]Not originally included in the O'Connor, Mumford, Clifton, Gessner, and Connelly (1995) article.

In this chapter, I have discussed the basic components of the full range model of leadership and have demonstrated the hierarchical ordering of these components in the full range suboptimal and optimal model profiles. I have shown where the full range model links up to more traditional styles of democratic and participative leadership. Finally, I have made an important distinction between transformational leaders who look like and behave like transformational leaders but who are not because of the perspective they maintain, which is that they come first in their desires to dominate others and most often take advantage of the goodwill of the people who follow them.

SOME THINGS WORTH REPEATING AND REFLECTING ON

- Transactions often form the basis for effective transformational leadership.
- The full range model has received a broad range of empirical support demonstrating the hierarchical ordering of effects of transformational, transactional, and laissez-faire leadership on performance.

- Further work on impression management and moral development will no doubt help differentiate the pseudo-transformational leaders from the authentic ones.
- For your own reflection, consider where your leadership strengths and weaknesses fall with respect to the optimal and suboptimal profiles presented earlier. What did your profile look like this past week?

By using the term *full range,* we intended to stimulate you and our colleagues to think about what was missing in our model that now needed to be included. So, what can you recommend that will make it the full range model of leadership?

A SHORT EXERCISE

I would like for you to think about the significant leaders you have had in your life stream. Now, please describe one specific behavior that represents each of the components of the full range leadership model.

- Can you come up with at least one behavior for each leadership style?
- Now, can you fill in one behavior that represents your style for each component?
- How much emphasis do you think you place on your behaviors at the higher end?
- Ask a trusted peer if your perceptions of your full range are accurate, and if not, why not.

CHAPTER 7

BORN

A happy man [person] is too satisfied with the present to dwell too much on the future.

Albert Einstein

Since I completed the first edition of this book, I have become even more convinced that there is an archetype in many people's minds that leaders must be born. I find that many will accept the fact that there is now data to show that leaders are largely made not born, but in frequent conversations after presenting this data, it still seems reassuring to most people to think that leaders are really much more born than made. Indeed, I have found fewer stereotypes as strong as this conviction.[72,73]

Over these past 10 years, we have now come to label those who believe leadership is born as the *entity group* and the ones who see it made as being *incrementalist*. The entity folks see humans as being fixed with certain endowments such as traits, whereas the incrementalist, as their name might imply, view that change is always possible. When I first wrote about the born versus made issue, I honestly felt that we should not restrict the potential of human growth by assuming that it is largely heritable. I believed then that human beings are simply more elastic than that.

However, I now realize there is an even more important issue to be addressed with respect to focusing on accelerating leadership development. The more you believe in the entity perspective, the less likely there is anything we do that will move you to develop; whereas the incrementalist comes to the developmental stage with a more open view of what might change. The view itself is part of the readiness that individuals have to develop to their full potential. And going back 10 years and now forward, I take a very strong position on this topic. Leaders are made, and so are followers for that matter.

So regarding the debate on whether leaders are made or born, the answer is yes, and it is an important yes because if you say no, it diminishes your developmental readiness to learn and grow. The question we need to ask is, "What type of learning experiences, beyond an individual's genetic endowments, are required to be an effective, if not an exemplary, leader?"

What is emerging in leadership development literature is a more sophisticated view of this question. It is not only that an event shapes leadership development but rather that different events, at different points in time, and for different individuals will have a varying impact on one's leadership development. For example, there are some events we can say are weighted more heavily in terms of their developmental load. An event that requires a significant transition in one's life or career can have a more substantial impact on the person's development versus a simple change in the way that person works in the same position. These developmental events can be organized into a taxonomy of sorts and then used as a framework for deciding how best to use them for accelerating the development of a particular leader. For instance, Dragoni, Tesluk, Russell, and Oh (2009) reported that the developmental quality of leader assignments had a positive relationship to the competencies observed in individuals who had experienced those assignments.

Recall our discussion of the life stream. Perhaps genetics is what you enter the stream with, but the real question is what you come out with downstream in the life course (see Box 7.1).

BOX 7.1   Interview With Colin Powell

In an interview, General Colin Powell, former chairman of the U.S. Joint Chiefs of Staff and secretary of state, said, "I think leaders can be shaped. You have to have the fundamental instincts for working with people. But the instinct can be improved upon through training and education, so that you understand what works for you. In my career I've come across people who were terrible leaders because they had no gut instinct for leadership and no amount of training helped them. I've also come across brilliant natural leaders who became even better when they developed their skills." ("Colin Powell's thoughts on leadership," 1998, pp. 56–57)

So, to what extent do you think leaders are born versus made?

I am asking you to consider this question at the outset of our discussion here because it affects the way you perceive what can and cannot be developed, which we now know is based, in part, on the implicit model of leadership in your head. By implicit, I mean the automatic model that guides your thinking before you even think about it. So, as part of your model of what makes up a leader, how strong a theory do you have about what is made and what is born? Below are some questions that relate to whether you are an entity or incremental type thinker to help you along in terms of what constitutes your model. The more you answer true for the first 4 items, the more you lean toward born versus made.[74]

Implicit Theories of Leadership Developability

True or False About You

1. The kind of leader someone is, is something basic about them, and it cannot be changed very much.

2. Leaders can do things differently, but the important parts of who they are as leaders cannot really be changed.

3. Everyone is a certain kind of leader, and there is not much that they can do to really change that.

4. Leaders cannot really change their deepest attributes.

SOURCE: Adapted from "Stereotype formation and endorsement: The role of implicit theories," by S. R. Levy, S. J. Stroessner, & C. S. Dweck, 1998, *Journal of Personality and Social Psychology, 74*(6), 1421–1436.

If you believe that leadership is something you are born with, then your expectation about yourself and others is that leadership is relatively fixed at birth in the form of natural leaders. So, if I were asked to develop leadership in myself or to develop it in others, my expectation would be that I can do very little to develop someone's leadership much further than it already has been developed. Such expectations alone can affect how successful you will be as a leader. Why? Because the beliefs you have will become a self-fulfilling prophecy. Yet, a positive lesson for leadership here is worth stating: Be careful what you expect and believe; it may very likely come true. Recall Dov Eden's work on both the Pygmalion and Golem effects.[75,76]

An individual who believes that leadership can be continuously developed actively seeks out development opportunities to enhance his own or someone else's leadership potential. In searching for such opportunities, he signals to others that this competency can be developed with the right mix of developmental challenges. We also now know that not all challenges are equal in terms of their contribution to leader development.

One might say that certain predispositions set boundaries within which leadership potential can be developed. One of those predispositions relates to what you believe can be learned and what you believe is hardwired and tied to heritability.

At the risk of me sounding sarcastic, why would anyone write a book on leadership development if he or she thought leadership potential was preordained versus predisposed? I firmly believe that leadership development is, to some extent (30%), predetermined by the nature of one's personality, intelligence, and emotional makeup. Evidence accumulated over the past decade has indicated that personality and intelligence are, to some degree but not all, genetically transferred from one generation to the next.[77] Yet, most evidence on personality predispositions indicates that about 50% of the similarity in personalities with identical twins is attributable to heritability, while 50% is not.

One could say with some degree of confidence that we have at least 50% to work with in terms of developing the person and the context in which that individual develops and could agree that the rest is up to the individual's predispositions. Notice that I said *individual* and *situation* because we believe the individual and the situation must be considered to assess leadership, to develop it, and to enhance one's ability to achieve one's potential. We must keep in mind an important distinction between leadership as a process and the leader as a person embedded within that process. We must also realize that most behavioral geneticists today think that heritability and the situation are so intertwined that to see them as separate makes little sense. For example, there are some people predisposed to getting a particular type of cancer but do not because they change their lifestyle and it reduces or eliminates the potential for cancer occurring.

A basic premise that I have attempted to thread throughout this book is that we must consider both the individual and the situation in order to develop a deeper appreciation of the full range of leadership development potential. Leadership is almost always affected by prior events occurring in the situation and the time period in which leaders and followers are operating. For example, how Mayor Giuliani led after the 9-11 attacks on the United States positioned him to be a highly regarded and courageous leader. Yet, the day prior to the attack on New York City, he was reviled by many for racial profiling and being the bully mayor. Amazing how the situation transformed this leader. . . . Is he born or made?

Prior to the meltdown in the technology sector toward the change of the millennium, many saw Warren Buffet's leadership of Berkshire Hathaway as ineffectual and out of date. Yet, when the technology sector crashed because he did not invest in something he did not understand, suddenly he became a leader of wisdom and vision. By the way, he was seen again as a visionary for not getting his company involved in the derivatives and hedge funds fiasco in 2008. In these situations, one can see how impactful the situation is to our views of leadership and perhaps even the leader's development. Was Warren Buffet born to be a leader? I doubt it. When asked how he learned to be such an ethical leader, he responded that he watched the respect and dignity his father accorded customers in the little grocery store in Omaha, Nebraska. Born or made?

We may witness a leader's behavior during crisis, and under those conditions we may think the behavior is not only appropriate but also highly desired, and we may even label the leader as inspiring. Under normal day-to-day circumstances, the leader's behavior would seem completely unacceptable and inappropriate, but in crisis, we are thankful someone took the first step and perhaps, most important, a step toward resolving the crisis, which is why Giuliani was so revered during the day of the attack and the days following. Giuliani later recalled in an interview on the CNN show *Larry King Live,* when asked why he led the way he did, on that day, he said something along the lines that he kept hearing his father say, when everyone goes crazy, move in close and don't back away. This is exactly what he did, moving his team to the epicenter of the attack so he could report out exactly what was going on. Born or made?

Another example of such a situation comes to mind from a story I read concerning an Israeli colonel. Colonel Eli Geva had grave reservations about the role of the Israeli military in the Lebanon War. Part of his reservations stemmed from the fact that the Israeli military was not adequately trained to be an occupying force and that it was being asked to occupy Beirut, Lebanon. When told to move his troops into Beirut, Colonel Geva indicated to his superior that he could not comply with the order. In not complying with this order, Colonel Geva knew full well that his career in the military would be over. Unlike in most other military organizations, the Israeli officer is often trained to improvise and to question, yet in this situation, Colonel Geva's commander was adamant about his response to this directive. Colonel Geva had no other choice but to either comply with the order or relieve himself of his command. He made the latter choice, which ended his career in the military. This type of decision for a young rising star would never have occurred in another situation, the Yom Kippur War. Ironically, officers in the Israeli army today learn about Colonel Geva's case and are asked to analyze the situation and to understand why he made the difficult choice he did and its implications for developing military leaders who should question authority when such questioning is warranted. Over time, the context may very well become the figure of our attention.[78]

In many contexts, we now find managers saying that a manager is much more a coach and facilitator than a director and commander. Mort Meyerson, former CEO of Electronic Data Systems (EDS), said after taking over his new appointment at Perot Systems following several years of retirement that almost everything he learned as a CEO at EDS about leading had to be abandoned or retired for this new work situation. Such conclusions are now more commonplace among senior executives who find themselves embedded in a workforce that is technically more sophisticated and competent and that requires less oversight and day-to-day direction. Now, the leader must coach, facilitate, and gain control through commitment (see Box 7.2).

Coaching and developing leaders was not quite the style of Mr. Agnelli, the CEO and chairman of the Fiat Corporation. Mr. Agnelli was oftentimes viewed as king of the Fiat's empire in Italy, an empire that had amassed nearly 250 companies. At a conference in Turin, Italy, he was speaking to a group of top Fiat managers, and in the middle of his speech, he paused to say something like, "I know some wonder when I am going to step down, well I will step down when the physical solution tells me to." Unfortunately, for many leaders like Mr. Agnelli, they believe their reign will last forever, and when they do have to deal with the physical solution, they have not adequately prepared their second in command to assume the position of leadership. This was the case for Mr. Agnelli, because after he passed away, there was no clear successor, and for several years the Fiat Corporation floundered and nearly collapsed.

BOX 7.2 Crisis and Charismatic Leadership

Rivera (1994) examined in a laboratory setting where there were two types of charismatic leadership—crisis-induced and noncrisis visionary leadership. Followers' performance under both types of charismatic leadership was superior to performance under transactional leadership. An assessment of performance over time indicated that crisis-induced, charismatic leadership was not sustained at the same levels over time as visionary and transactional leadership with a second task performed by followers.

Pillai (1993) examined how followers and leaders coming from healthcare organizations responded to crisis situations. Specifically, this author was interested in examining a basic question often raised in the charismatic leadership literature: Is a crisis required for the emergence of charismatic leadership? The author reported that the perception of a crisis did not relate to emergence of charismatic leadership in the investigation. Pillai (1996) reported that, in a survey of 101 healthcare organization units, the leaders being seen as more charismatic correlated negatively with stress on the job and whether their followers thought they had been in crises over the past 3 months.

BOX 7.3 Environmental Stability and Leadership Performance

J. C. Brown (1994) set out to identify the leadership competencies associated with superior performance in times of turbulence versus stability. Superior and average performers were pooled from some *Fortune* 500 firms that had engaged in transformative processes within the past 5 years.

Conducting behavioral event interviews resulted in the identification of four clusters of competencies that differentiated the top and average performers. The competencies represented four components of leadership similar to the components of transformational leadership discussed in the full range model. They were (a) visionary leadership, (b) a strong conceptual and systems thinker, (c) involving and empowering others, and (d) personal qualities (for example, venturesome, high energy, open, and responsive).

Hicks (1990) conducted a small-sample study of 11 leaders in a missionary organization and found that unstable conditions were not necessarily required for transformational leaders to be effective. In addition, a stable environment was not a prerequisite for leaders to lead who were more transactional.

So, thus far the results are not consistent on how crises affect the emergence of transformational leadership. In some cases, and perhaps it depends on the nature of the crisis, transformational/charismatic leadership will *not* emerge. Bass and Bass (2008, p. 595) conclude: "Charismatic effects can emerge not only in crises, but as a consequence of the charismatic's vision and its articulation, which create a sense of need for action by the followers."

Returning to the born versus made issue, in a study conducted with identical twins, the authors reported that self-ratings of leadership had a 50% overlap with identical twins as compared with fraternal twins. Specifically, by using the MLQ (self-ratings) discussed earlier,[79] a strong relationship was found in how twins rated themselves with respect to leadership styles. If a member of a twin pair thought he was inspirational with followers, it was likely that his twin thought the same was also true for himself. Because most personality instruments use self-ratings, these results parallel those findings obtained by using a similar methodology to assess personality.

Now, I referred above to 30%, not 50%, in terms of leadership being heritable. In more recent research, where we have examined how many leadership positions an individual has held over his or her career, we found the heritability of leadership was now only 30%. Using what we considered to be a more objective indicator of leadership—positions held—we found only 30% heritable. What this might suggest is that the self-ratings, as is often the case, may have been biased.

You might be thinking, where is the evidence for the impact of experience on leadership development? This is an excellent question in the light of the main focus of this book. First, let's be clear on what we mean by *experience* and its connection to leadership and the development of an individual's perspective-taking capacity. Then we can discuss the relationship of experience to leadership development.

Certain life experiences, including family upbringing, significant engagements with role models, education and training, dramatic life events and crises, and work experiences, are accumulated and take the shape of what a colleague of mine called a life biography or life script. Let's take a moment to look at this life script from the perspective of people entering a leadership training program.

Instructors often come to realize that all people enter training at some point in their stream of life events. (By the way, you can also apply this logic to being a leader or manager responsible for training others on the job.) Not all people have followed the same life course, have had the same life difficulties or opportunities, or are equally developmentally ready, but they all end up there that first day of training with some anticipation of learning something about leadership. Not all people believe that much can be done about this, however, and some are simply not developmentally ready for the experience. Some are there on their own accord, and some are forced to be present.

BOX 7.4 Born to Lead?

Johnson, Vernon, Molson, Harris, and Jang (1998) conducted the first-ever study linking genetic predispositions to leadership ratings. Their results indicated that leadership was, in part, heritable when comparing results for 247 monozygotic twins. Each twin rated his or her own leadership style by using the MLQ. A great deal of shared variance in higher-level leadership, such as transformational, was seen as being linked to the twins' common genes (average genetic correlations of .5).

Subsequent leadership research suggests that approximately 30% of the variance in leadership style and emergence in leadership roles respectively can be accounted for by genetic factors, while the rest is due to environment and the interaction of the environment with heritability (Arvey, Rotundo, Johnson, Zhang, & McGue, 2006; Arvey, Zhang, Avolio, & Kruger, 2007; Ilies, Gerhardt, & Le, 2004). These findings support Plomin and Daniels's (1987, p. 1) conclusion that "behavioral-genetic research seldom finds evidence that more than half of the variance in complex behavioral traits is due to genetic differences among individuals . . . most behavioral variability among individuals is environmental in origin." This conclusion is in line with Mumford, Stokes, and Owens (1990, p. 48), who suggested that "hereditary and environmental influences often work in tandem."

What is important to consider here, as well as in your own situation where you are in a leadership role, is that you need to understand as much as you can about each member's developmental readiness to help that individual achieve full leadership potential. This is, in part, at the heart of what I referred to as individualized consideration in action. I also said earlier if you are not ready to sacrifice 5 minutes each day, then perhaps you are not developmentally ready to learn more about building your own leadership potential. Some people are ready, some people can be prepared to be ready or motivated to action, some people require direction, and some people should be left alone for a while until such time that it makes sense to intervene in their life courses or streams.

The developmental readiness of people relates to the unique perspectives they have built about how best to influence others and themselves.[80] Perspectives here could be a model or theory of the self. Each form of influence is related to the experiences people have accumulated or their life biographies or both. Some people who have an emerging biography may think the world is mostly driven by self-interests and to influence others one must align each person's self-interest around what needs to be accomplished. This can be labeled the *pure transactional approach,* or what Karl Kuhnert referred to as the *operators.* Give them the rewards they desire, and they will work to maximize their self-interests.[81]

On the other hand, there are people who believe that although self-interest is important to promoting motivation and achievement, it is not the only driver influencing others to either develop or perform. Their perspective or model of how things work is different, and this is likely a result of differences in their life scripts versus the transactional types. It is quite possible they have seen others sacrifice their own interests, even lives, for the good of a group, organization, or community, if not for its very survival.

Recall Stacey. She sacrificed her potential to win the most prestigious award in teaching for the good of a group of students she had not yet met. Recall the stream of fifth graders coming to her classroom to say good-bye. Do you think this was based on self-interest? When Stacey takes her own time to meet with students over the summer, those students come to understand that she is doing it because she believes in them and that her satisfaction is derived from their achievements. Many of them come back to say good-bye out of respect for the sacrifices Stacey continually makes for her students. In the classroom, when she emphasizes the need for mutual dependence to help each student achieve his or her full potential, she is developing a perspective (more deeply, a model of life) in students that they must give back to others for everyone to succeed fully. She is also teaching them the importance of internal controls. Perhaps most important to transformational leadership development is that one should measure how well leaders are doing, not simply by their own accomplishments but also by the accomplishments and achievements of others. Again, we are back to the legacy of leaders.

Interestingly enough, Andy Grove, the former CEO of Intel, and Bill Gates of Microsoft stated the key to their respective financial and developmental success is, in large part, the fact that their companies had a higher mutual dependence on each other in terms of investment, learning, and development than probably any other two companies. I will have more to say about this as we look at what some have referred to as *shared leadership* in teams. It suffices to say that this book began by highlighting the importance of our mutual dependence in helping each other achieve one's full potential, or vital force, and we will see much more of this when we discuss teams and shared leadership. The notion of mutual dependence is probably best captured in a quote by John Gardner:

> *The achievements of Greece in the 15th century B.C. were not the performances of isolated people, but of individuals acting in an age of shared excellence.*

Consider the following questions: How can you strategically shape your life biography to maximize your full leadership potential? Is it possible to do so? How much range do you think you have to make a difference right now?

Consider that some of your chapters are obviously already fixed, especially the ones already written. However, even with those chapters, you can go back and derive different meaning from what affected you at an earlier point in your life stream. This occurred for me when a former CEO of a large financial services company was reading to me something he had memorized that was written back in 1840 about discipline. He kept reading—and I never saw the message here in the way I see it today—and the message was how you must value followers for them to value leadership.

Every day, portions of a new chapter can be created by you, ones over which you have some degree of control in terms of your own leader development. So, the choices you make each day will determine your life biography at later points in your life. What is your business plan for personal leadership development?

I recall when Carrie came to my leadership class at the University of Nebraska I asked her to talk about her life stream. Twenty years earlier, she had sat in the same seats of those students in front of her. She started by saying when she was a business student she decided to create Carrie Inc. She would have a vision, mission, values, and board of directors to guide her life journey in business. As she shaped her business plan, she made some very difficult choices to realize her dream. For example, she decided that she would not have children as she wanted to invest all of her energies into her career. When she said that, many of the folks in the class, especially the women, sat there in silence soaking in the type of hard business choice she had made about her business, Carrie Inc.

In a general sense, exploring any new experiences in and of itself is an important facet of developing one's leadership perspective. For example, engaging in how other disciplines diagnose problems, collect data, and evaluate solutions can be helpful in terms of challenging your own assumptions about what is right versus wrong, which might shape your life stream and course.

Perhaps Albert Einstein captured it best by saying, "The true value of a human being is determined primarily by how he [or she] has attached liberation from the self. . . . Everything that is really great and inspiring is created by the individual who can labor in freedom" ("Albert Einstein," n.d.). Often, the liberation allows us to consider widely different ideas and perspectives, which can lead to break-through innovations.

Several research projects point to some areas you should consider as you begin to take hold of what your life biography should be like in developing your full leadership potential as well as the potential of others. I present a profile here based on what has been found that characterizes high-potential leaders. I present information you can use in choosing alternative life courses, as opposed to picking a different set of parents, which could also have affected your potential to lead given the results reviewed above for identical twins. And I will present one more study recently done on twins that I think you will find interesting.

Prior research now shows that leaders who have been evaluated by their followers as more transformational were shown to exhibit a broader range of learning interests. This broader range stimulated a willingness in others to come to these leaders with ideas that were on the boundaries of acceptability or sometimes even beyond those boundaries. They demonstrated a passion for learning new and different things, which often was diffused into the climate and culture of their work unit. They followed an accepted principle that says answers to one's problems can be found by consulting other fields that have not addressed the particular problem directly but nevertheless have generated some interesting and potential solutions. This occurs in science all the time when a drug or herb discovered for one purpose appears to have the potential for curing a disease for which it was not initially developed.[82]

Another facet of human development that comes through strongly in prior research is that of gaining experience in situations where one has to influence others without the authority of a position—a more common occurrence these days in organizations around the globe. These situations can be both formal and informal with respect to influencing others.[83] So, those individuals in high school who took on a broader range of responsibilities for which they had to influence others but perhaps had no formal position power were people who engaged the full range of leadership more effectively later in life. These same people also have been shown to develop a more mature thought or implicit model of leadership that helps guide them in effectively developing others. They are freer from inner problems leaving them more able to focus on dealing with the problems of others.[84,85]

Individuals who have been extremely challenged, sometimes way beyond what they thought possible, but received support in their failures and constructive advice from parents were often the ones who grew up to be the best developers of people. They learned early on what could be derived from both failures and successes. As they passed through life, they continually sought to work with a mentor who would not simply make life easy by championing all of their cherished causes but rather encourage them to dig down deeply to provide their best efforts. And when their best efforts resulted in a failure, they were encouraged to reflect on aspects of the process that could be improved for another try at the goal. They debriefed failures along with successes.[86]

Because we are reflecting, another finding from this work is that those leaders who were most effective went through life crises pursuing one of two learning options. The first option was to not examine deeply what happened and to feel good about the fact that the crisis and stresses were over. The second option was to derive as much meaning from what could be learned by going through the crisis, perhaps via some postmortem analysis of events. These two approaches represent very different perspectives in terms of learning styles, and they affect how willing the leader is seen by others to want to learn from mistakes, even those one might consider the worst possible mistakes that should have been avoided. Stated another way, even in the worst situations, such leaders turned or transformed the threats of a crisis into a learning opportunity.[87]

A more poignant example of leading under duress is the three learning objectives that Victor Frankl set for himself while in a German concentration camp. Imagine trying to use such an experience as an opportunity to learn, and you can appreciate more fully the title of his book on the subject, *Man's Search for Meaning,* or what we have called one's perspective on life and leadership.[88]

I have worked with two companies (one mentioned earlier) that went through major ethical violations that almost bankrupted each company. I found in both cases that many people there did not want to talk about *the event.* In both cases, strict compliance standards were put in place that ensured such deviations in business practices would never occur again. As a consequence, both companies suffered from a control-dominated culture that had lost its ability to innovate. When I asked people what they had learned from these events, by and large, they simply said, "Not to do *that* again!" Unfortunately, in not doing *that* again, most other deviations that would lead to innovation were also not being done. By and large, little, if any, debriefing of the event was done to separate out recoverable and unrecoverable mistakes in their businesses.

Let me point out something that might be very obvious at this point in our discussion. The life experiences that you accumulate both strategically and beyond your control (you always have the control to revisit and reexamine) shape your perspective on how to influence others. The way you go about developing yourself as a role model can also have a significant impact on the way others choose to develop around you or as a *direct* or *indirect* consequence of your efforts. If you are in a prominent leadership role, then the choices you make regarding your own development can become a set of choices for others to consider to the extent that they model your style and behavior over time. Respected leaders, by the way, are mirrored in their behavior and choices. This can be good or bad if the leader is pseudo.

Let me briefly review one last twin study. We set out to examine whether individuals had a history of rule breaking or rule conforming. Again, we compared identical and fraternal twins and found that 30% of their leadership across their careers (positions held) was due to heritability. We also found that rule breakers (not law breakers) were more likely to ascend into higher positions of leadership than conformers. These are folks who challenged the rules growing up, however, did not hurt anyone or break the law. More importantly, if their parents used authoritative parenting, this contributed positively to them becoming leaders. Notice this was authoritative not authoritarian, which meant they set clear rules and standards and reinforced them rather than simply beating up on their kids without standards.

Looking back, with respect to whether leaders are born versus made, I have attempted to approach this issue from several angles. First, in terms of your own development, I have argued that you have some choices over the experiences you accumulate and that those experiences, within some limits, can affect the leader you are, the leader you will become, and the way you are ultimately perceived by others. They can also affect your perspective of the roles you think are appropriate for followers and, of course, the roles they choose to adopt.

Second, what you select to expose yourself to in terms of life experiences signals to others the type of experiences they can engage in if they choose to model your behavior. Also, what they choose to expose you to is part of how your life biography will unfold. For example, if you had a group of followers who absolutely feared to challenge your ideas when they came across new developments in other fields, you are, in effect, shaping the types of experiences that people bring to you and, in turn, your own life biography's development.

Returning to the issue of self-interest, with perhaps a sort of ironic twist, when you stifle the development potential of those who follow you, you are in effect stifling your own development by the types of ideas and experiences people are willing to present to you. So, it is in your own self-interest to engage other people's ideas and challenges. We return to this issue later, for those autocratic types that just threw the book down and said, "Are you yanking my chain?"

In this chapter, my intent was to convey to you that although limits are set by our genetic predispositions, a tremendous range also exists in which we can work to develop your leadership potential to the highest points along the full range of leadership. Realizing that these boundaries exist is an important basis for you to be an individually considerate leader with others. Using the excuse that leaders are born and not made to avoid developing followers, however, will limit your own full potential as a leader and your followers' leadership potential as well.

I want you to reflect on a set of questions, or perhaps one in particular, if you choose. These questions look at your earlier life biography and how it has shaped your perspective over time in terms of leading others up to this very moment. Use 5 minutes of your reflection time to consider these questions, and then consider how you are going to create the next chapter in your life biography. Keep in mind that what gets included in your life biography is not completely in your control but that, on a good day, we would say at least 50% is. Actually, even when events occur due to serendipity, you can be mindful of how those events can shape your development, and therefore regain control of your development.

Coach Bear Bryant shared a story involving the enigmatic dynamics of a love-hate relationship between a coach and a player. Bryant's former player, Bob Gain, was a discipline problem. Bryant remembered being harder on him than on any other player he had ever coached. Years later, Gain was serving in Korea, and on the night before his platoon's first battle, he wrote a letter to his "old damn coach." Bryant was amazed. In the letter, Gain admitted his disdain for Bryant but ended with, "I love you tonight for what I used to hate you for." Is this perhaps a case example of authoritative development?

- *What type of learning style would best characterize your parents' interactions with you?*
- *What is the worst life crisis you have had to deal with, and what positive things did you learn from it through self-reflection?*
- *What is your most important assumption, and what would your reaction be if someone questioned it?*
- *During the next 3 months, what would you like to include in your next life biography chapter? Why?*

BOX 7.5   Leadership Challenges Viewed by the HR Leadership Community

Based on a 2006 survey of top human resource (HR) leaders, the number one challenge for HR directors is identifying and developing the leadership talent needed for growth and expansion of their respective organizations (Fegley, 2006). In a second national study, 44% of organizational leaders surveyed concluded that enhancing the effectiveness of leadership training was their number one or number two priority (American Society for Training and Development, 2007).

One of the ways to improve on the effectiveness of leadership training is to make both participants and their managers accountable for making it stick. As noted earlier, with Kegan and Lahey's (2009) work, organizations and individuals have very strong immunities to change.

I suggest the immunity is higher if the managers do not know the return on development investment. Avolio, Avey, and Quisenberry (in press) advocate a strategy for estimating the return on developmental investment using the quantitative effects generated by prior meta-analyses. Specifically, if you know the strength of the training impact and you know the costs, you can then estimate the return on development investment (RODI).

For example, Collins and Horton (2004) conducted a meta-analysis of 83 training studies gleaned from the management and leadership literature from 1982 to 2001. Their findings replicated earlier findings indicating that managerial training produced positive outcomes with effect sizes ranging from $d = 0.35$ to $d = 1.37$. With these effect sizes and similar types of results reported by Avolio, Reichard, et al. (2009), we can begin to estimate how much money we should invest in training given the effects and what we can expect in return. Ironically, only 10 to 20% of organizations ever actually evaluate the impact of leader development programs on performance (Avolio, Sosik, Jung, & Berson, 2003). Avolio, Avey, and Quisenberry (in press) estimated using the findings from Avolio, Reichard, et al. and the formula below with estimates of costs provided by large U.S. corporations that the RODI was generally 200% for a well-validated program.

$$RODI = NTdSD_y - C$$

N = number of participants in developmental intervention

T = expected time duration of change in leadership behaviors (converted to fraction in years)

d = effect size of intervention, also considered as the average difference in outcomes between trained participants and untrained counterparts

SD_y = standard deviation of dollar-valued job performance among untrained employees. When dollarized performance metrics are not available, the performance metric may be a function of 40% of annual salary. In this case, 40% of one's annual salary is a conservative estimate of that individual's dollar value to the firm in terms of performance.

C = total cost of training the expected number of participants

SOME THINGS WORTH REPEATING AND REFLECTING ON

- One's leadership development is affected by the life experiences accumulated.
- Specific life experiences appear to be linked to the development of positive forms of leadership.
- What you model as a leader can determine what you receive in return from your followers, which can either enhance or inhibit your development as a leader.

A SHORT EXERCISE

Take a piece of paper, and lay out your lifeline in 5-year increments. In each of the 5-year periods along your lifeline, identify any events or moments that positively impacted your leadership development. Try to discern what you learned from those trigger events that shaped your development. You may want to add to this exercise by asking people who knew you at that time in your life about those events and how they might have perceived the impact of those events on your development as a leader. You may find very different views than yours about those events, which is why we say leadership and its development are in the eye of the beholder.

CHAPTER 8

COCREATED LEADERSHIP

The fundamental movement over the next 25 years will be in the dispersing of power in organizations.

Bill O'Brian, CEO of Hanover Insurance

It is quite common for people to think of leadership as being associated with a particular individual. Yet, leadership in many organizations today is not just vested in a single individual but in a larger collective, such as teams or team systems. For example, it is difficult to think about Google without thinking about its two founders, Larry Page and Sergey Brin, as well as the now-CEO Eric Schmidt. Unilever, several years back, had two CEOs who served as the coleaders of the vast organization that now spans more than 90 countries.[89]

In this chapter, I would like to turn our attention to examining leadership as it is distributed within and between levels. Leadership has probably always been a cocreated process involving a leader and at least one follower. However, it has taken years to recognize the importance of everyone but the leader in the leadership process.

AT THE INDIVIDUAL LEVEL

Much of our discussion up to this point has focused on individual-level leadership such as Sam and Stacey. This leads to a very basic question: If there is just a leader with no followers to lead, can one observe leadership? Some of my colleagues might argue yes, there is self-leadership, but beyond that I would argue that a key ingredient is missing—the *other* person in the leadership process, the person being influenced. This can be a follower, a peer, a customer, a supervisor, or some combination of these people. Most discussions of leadership deal with, at minimum, an interaction between two individuals. Here, our observations center on the treatment of an individual by the leader. Is the leader inspiring? Is the leader demonstrating individualized consideration? Like the cells in the human body, this is clearly a very important building block for the leadership system of the organization, and that is exactly how I want you to think about the beginning of building a leadership system. It starts one cell at a time, and here the cell is the leader and someone else, and then another, and another, and the context, and then the future state that is emerging, and . . . well, let's stop here for the moment. And like cells in the human body, we can say that each of these cells has a cultural footprint that affects the type of interactions we will observe within and between cells. The footprint can be the values of each individual, the founding leaders, as in the case of Google, as well as the values of the organization.[90,91]

Taking a step backward to move forward, in any traditional organizational setting, we must first understand the leader's perspective on how she believes others should be treated; this forms a broad or, in some autocratic cases, narrow basis for interactions with others. If the leader sees the world as a series of transactions based on mutual self-interest, then the basis for the leader and follower or peer-to-peer interaction is to satisfy the self-interests of those who work with her; if the self-interests are satisfied, then desired targets should be met. With this perspective, the leader changes the incentives to channel motivation and performance. By the way, the follower can also serve in these transactions by recognizing what the leader accomplishes and channeling motivation and performance by leading up.

Let's now assume that some hypothetical organization is composed of five people, including the leader. Thus, in each interaction the leader has with each of her four followers, she clearly states the goals and expectations for a transparent transactional relationship. The compact of understanding is then composed of a series of "if you do this, then in return you get that" statements.

At an optimum level, all of the parties understand what they need to do to be rewarded for their efforts (individual or collective) and their contributions to the organization. One transactional relationship leads into another, forming a set of norms in the organization that help guide what is expected of each of the members and what they will get in return for meeting those expectations. The culture itself becomes more transactional over time, as do the values. An optimal exchange occurs when set expectations are clear, performance meets expectations, and recognition and rewards are provided equitably. It seems perfect in form and substance, so why not stop there?

In this rather simple organization, what has begun at an individual level of interaction between the leader and follower can eventually become part of a larger leadership system characterizing the entire organization. In the case of the Google organization, it has now gone from two founders to thousands of employees. The leadership system by expressed design is promoting a set of expectations that everyone knows about and that guides the interactions of members in that organization, whether they are with the leader or with other members interacting with each other. What we see occurring in organizations such as the hypothetical one above is quite interesting. What started as an interaction between a leader and her followers grew into a leadership system and culture. And if the system is developed carefully and strategically, the leader will have more than the 5 minutes we have required to be a reflective leader (see Box 8.1). This occurs where the system can substitute for the specific interactions between leader and follower that, at earlier points in the relationship, required greater levels of monitoring and vigilance.

A good example of that is the organization in the United States called Costco, which was founded by Jim Senegal. Jim Senegal has a simple transactional formula to guide Costco transactions: Provide the best product value to members of Costco at the least expensive rate. Every interaction that his 147,000 employees have with members in their stores is a product of that formula. Senegal believes you retain customers and encourage them to return to your store to buy new products if you just keep to that simple formula in every interaction.

A most recent example exemplifies his focus on this simple, core organizing principle that guides employee transactions with customers. In late 2009, Costco announced that it would drop all Coke products from all of its stores. This was a huge step given that many Costco members are devoted Coke product customers. Jim Senegal released a statement to the news media simply saying that Costco could not pass on to its customers the best price given the amount Coke had decided to charge its customers, and rather than increase the Costco price, he preferred to stay true to this core value.[92]

There are many other examples of this transactional focus at Costco. One is called the salmon story. This story began in the fish department where it decided that each year, it would increase the quality of the salmon fish purchased from suppliers while reducing the cost to the customer. For 10 years running, it have done just that, and now other departments try to get their salmon stories heard throughout the company.

Perhaps you are wondering what actually is going on here. We moved from leadership of the individual to leadership that is more systemic and can substitute for some lower-level interactions required at the beginning of a relationship. The same may be true of our relationship. If you extend what you have learned from reading this book to the next level of analysis, which is the people you work with and those whom you are interested in developing to their full potential, then you can substitute for what you have learned in this book. And I anxiously await your substitution, as that is one of the ways we are able to positively distribute leadership throughout organizations as characterized by Jim Senegal.

Perhaps another example might help in terms of what I mean by distributing leadership. A local entrepreneur started an organization to build the next generation of laser tools for industrial application. He said at the groundbreaking ceremony for this new company that he wanted to build an organization based on the principle that employees would always be comfortable challenging each other's ideas and especially his own ideas. He suggested that to survive in this new business required that employees ask difficult questions before their competitors did. Too many organizations train their employees to leave their brains at the door. The leadership system requires that this be so, as it inadvertently rewards people for shutting down versus speaking up. If the entrepreneur has his way, it will not be so in this new organization.

BOX 8.1   How Transformational Leadership Relates to Reputation, Cooperation, Friendliness, and Warmth

In a study conducted with government councils with first line supervisors and their work groups, Weierter (1994) found that transformational leadership positively related to perceptions of work group reputation, cooperation, friendliness, and warmth. These factors were later described as potentially substituting for transactional leadership behavior. In other words, they had become part of the leadership system that ended up guiding subsequent employee behavior.

Some years ago, I attended a recognition day ceremony at a large sunglasses factory in northeastern United States. At that meeting, an operations worker was describing how he had made a suggestion to the chemist in his area and how his suggestion had led to a change in the chemical processes used to bond gold to sunglasses frames. In the first several months, his unit had saved the company more than $700,000 by increasing the level of bonding to the metal, thus reducing the amount of gold going down the drain. He was asked when he had discovered the alternative way of processing the gold. His reply was, "Several years back." I asked him why it took several years to get his idea implemented. To paraphrase what he said, "It took me several years to learn that I should not leave my brain at the door when I come to work and speak up. The previous plant manager did not care to hear our ideas. Phil [the current plant manager] cares, and I bring my brain to work every day now. Once I made the recommendation to our chemist, it was implemented within a few days."

Let's step back and take a look at what the entrepreneur was trying to establish in his new organization and what Phil was doing in the sunglasses plant. It is quite common in organizations for people not to tell their leaders what they really think or, worse yet, what they have known for some time. If you are going to embrace the higher end of the full range of leadership, you will quickly realize the shortcomings of this approach. Leaders who control their organizations with an iron hand think they are less vulnerable. History would suggest otherwise (see Box 8.2). Humankind has never created any better control system than what comes with internal control based on commitment. No walls, contracts, punishment systems, regulations, or laws have ever been able to control people's behavior, especially how they think, any better than when those individuals have internalized the control. In other words, they believe, and therefore they do whatever needs to be done willingly, even in the extreme where they sacrifice their own lives for a cause. That is one incredible control mechanism.[93,94,95]

When I was touring the Great Wall in China, someone told me something that relates to the human condition described above. The guide said the Great Wall would never be breached from the outside. It was too tall and strong. Rather, it would most likely be breached from the inside, because someone who simply no longer believed in the leadership of China would open the door and let the barbarians in, so to speak.

BOX 8.2 Transformational Leadership and Participation

Cheverton and Thompson (1996) examined the relationship among follower ratings of leadership, organizational context, and psychological participation. The sample of leaders included middle- to senior-level managers in business and nonbusiness settings. The authors indicated that nonbusiness leaders displayed transformational leadership more often and that higher levels of psychological participation were noted among followers of transformational leaders. Transformational leadership created a climate for greater levels of participation. In a comprehensive meta-analysis of the literature, T. J. Weber, Carsten, Harms, and Avolio (2009) reported, in addition to increased levels of participation, that ratings of transformational leadership were positively correlated with organizational citizenship behaviors.

The entrepreneur described above fully understood that, by building at the foundation of his organization the norm that ideas were welcome, over time the system of leadership that would evolve should be more receptive to, if not demand, divergent, challenging ideas. No brain hooks should appear at the door where employees can leave their thoughts on the way into work. Employees of that organization would be led and would lead up.

Something else is going on in the example of a start-up organization that is perhaps not so apparent. Not only is the leader attempting to establish a framework for future interactions he desires in the organization, but also he is recognizing that the people he selects may come from organizations that did not appreciate challenging the ideas of one's superiors. And the habits of the past are easily imported into the present unless a conscious, disciplined effort is made to address those habits, and such habits are quite common in organizations and in many cultures throughout the world.

For example, in a workshop I conducted in Mexico where we were discussing dependent followership, one participant said that it is common for Mexicans to say, in Spanish, "How may I serve you?" as opposed to "Excuse me, how may I assist you?" This simple expression indicates the subordinate role that followers typically play in these cultures. Similarly, on a trip to Korea this past year, I learned firsthand how difficult it is for people from a *shame culture* (a culture where individuals go out of their way to save face, oftentimes at the expense of telling leaders what they really think) to question authority. It is so ingrained not to question managers that one has to change the societal leadership system to effect change at the organizational level, a challenge many Korean Chaebols (Korean conglomerates like Samsung) confronted as they attempted to globalize their organizations and workforces.[96]

As an individual leader, you are often forced to assume what has been developed or not developed in those you are attempting to influence. The habits of the mind can be so ingrained that they can create significant reservations among employees to make any changes without feeling totally incapable of success. So, even though the local entrepreneur is starting a new organization, this in no way guarantees that old habits may not come through the door. In fact, without a clear statement of the CEO's preference, reiterated in many different ways, it is likely that new employees will not come in naturally questioning the ideas of others, particularly those they consider their bosses. They have typically been trained very differently in schools and in work organizations to respect or defer to authority, which is fine as long as the people in authority know what they are doing and, more importantly, are doing the right thing (see Box 8.3). Why challenge is seen as being anathema to having respect for leaders remains a central problem in the *least* innovative organizations. Unfortunately, this is not always the case, and to protect the democracy of a country and any organization requires that people question the unquestionable, the undiscussable, and the unmentionable.

To build a leadership system requires that we understand two very basic points. First, we can determine what the system will be by stating up front what our ideals are and then behaving in a way that is absolutely congruent with those ideals. It is fair to say, we are now building a life script for the organization.

Second, people come into an organization with preconceived notions or models in their heads, not blank slates. So, consistency is crucial to overcome the habits imported from past experiences inculcated from other groups and organizations. That is why I said earlier that consistency, or better yet, predictability, around trust building will be one of your greatest challenges and accomplishments, if eventually achieved. It is also why companies like Nordstrom, Disney, Amazon, and Southwest Airlines are a pain in the butt to get into. These organizations expend a great deal of energy on selecting and socializing employees to the desired cultures. One of my MBA students told me that he had 15 interviews before he was offered his first job at Amazon.

For some people at the groundbreaking ceremony described earlier, what appeared as a simple statement was quite profound in terms of its implications for building a leadership system. This crucial point of initiation can be a very effective start in building a system that will take on its own life. How so? First, people will remember and hold you to what happens early, as it is based on a primacy effect. We recall things better that are at the outset of a relationship. Many couples can recall their first date, but the second or third may blur, for example. If the leader is consistent with his espoused ideals, those who work at the organization will come to realize it is just the way people need to be treated, as Jim Senegal has done at Costco.

Relationships with customers and suppliers first will take on the characteristics of the relationships that are observed internal to the organization, but eventually they will migrate to external relationships with suppliers and customers if they are properly nurtured and reinforced. And at some point, the founder could actually step back and see that the leadership system, once created, is in line with his espoused beliefs and desires. Yet, consistency and continuous reinforcement are necessary for it to evolve to a systemic cultural level. Many forces are against this entrepreneur's espoused beliefs, not least of which are the managers who frequently do not have the confidence to be vulnerable and be questioned by followers. Also, some people at that groundbreaking ceremony may be cynical about such words and think it is just management-by-magazine, or based on what is popular versus rigorous or right. Specifically, these are the right buzz words to say. Now really show me. But the benefits (and here I mean financial) can be profound for the leader who can move on to other activities as the system takes over reinforcing ideas, values, and principles that were initiated by the leader (see Box 8.3).

BOX 8.3   Transformational Leadership in India

Pereira (1986) set out to generalize the model of transformational and transactional leadership within the Indian context. The company in which data were collected is Larsen and Toubro Limited in India, and at the time of the study, it was the fifth-largest private-sector firm in terms of assets. Self- and other ratings were collected from 58 managers. Pereira confirmed the hierarchical ordering of constructs in the full range model, reporting that transformational leadership accounted for a significantly greater share of the variance in ratings of satisfaction with the leader, job effectiveness, communication of followers' needs to senior leaders, and organizational effectiveness.

In a recent study of 50 Indian firms, the pattern of relationships shown in Figure 8.1 was observed between the type of culture in those organizations and financial performance.

Figure 8.1   Organizational Culture and Performance

Indicators:	Inducement (Transactional)	Investment (Paternalistic)	Involvement (Transformational)
• Roles	Narrow	Broad	Flexible
• Supervision	Direct	Developmental	Facilitative
• Competitive	Price	Product Differentiation	Innovation
Outcomes:			
• ROI %	7.03	9.64	11.02
• ROA %	16.37	15.98	20.89

SOURCE: Sivasubramaniam, Murry, Avolio, & Jung, 2002.

NOTE: Productivity compared to closest competitors.

Let's take a moment here to capture what is going on in the organization's leadership development cycle as it has implications for understanding leadership at a systemic level, particularly systems that are quite commonly in use today, such as project teams.

CORE ATTRIBUTES

The basis for the system began with an idea or a perspective of what the leader desired and articulated in relation to a value, principle, goal, or some combination.

The leader is responsible for clearly articulating what is desired and developing a script that people come to understand and believe in over time: This is the way we do business. Leaders define what the scripts should be and which ones specify the roles, expectations, and interactions we observe over time. Jim Senegal has a script for his employees that started with the best product for the lowest price.

Consistency is generally crucial to embedding what a person wants to establish in the leadership system and is proportionately more crucial to the extent the beliefs the person is trying to change are heavily ingrained in the way people already think.

The leader initiates what later she or he will also become part of, or embedded in, so choose carefully the leadership system you are trying to build. The leadership system can become a main support system for your agenda or a terrible obstacle or immunity to change when change is needed. This was exemplified in IBM, which had built this incredible organization that eventually became completely immune to change when all the signals on the outside said CHANGE. This may now be happening to companies like Microsoft, which started out as renegades but now are large corporate bureaucracies struggling to be the source of their own change. As you assume a role of leadership, ask yourself, What script do you want to write? What line do you intend to share each and every day in your verbal and nonverbal interactions? The leadership play will unfold without any direction, as we are wired as human beings to be authors and to make meaning of our lives.

Paradoxically, by not choosing to develop scripts and a leadership system, you are, in effect, creating a system, albeit loosely coupled. People import habits from the past; thus, if you do not decide what the leadership system should be, it will be something it has been because people, like nature, abhor a vacuum. People will create a system to frame their interactions; this is deeply rooted in human nature because we cannot allow intentions to just happen. So, if you are laissez-faire in your design of a leadership system, it will be created for you without your input based on someone else's intentions; some might even call this a self-organizing system. If good people are involved, it may end up being a good system; if not, then it is all left up to chance.

A reasonable question for you to ask is, "Okay, so what is the bottom line here?" The bottom line is that you can select and develop, over time, the leadership system you choose to be embedded in at some future point. And you can create what eventually exists as a basis for each interaction. It takes discipline and determination to create a system that goes against the habits of the past, and you can rest assured that people will look for any slight deviation from what you espouse, retreating to methods they are familiar with and have used in other organizations.

*The difference is knowing what you want and knowing what the end is supposed
to look like. If a coach does not know what the end is supposed to look like, he
won't know it when he sees it.*

Coach Vince Lombardi

The Team Leadership System

We now have a foundation for discussing team leadership and organizational system development. The development of a team leadership system is introduced here, and we get into more detail about what constitutes shared leadership later on in the next chapter.[97,98,99]

How do you start building a team leadership system? The first thing to realize is that each member comes to the team with a conception of how a team works—a mental model of sorts or perspective that forms the basis for interactions regardless of whether one states them explicitly or not, which will have an impact on behavior.[100] As a team leader, it is important to ensure that each member has the perspective that, over time, the goal of the leader or leaders on the team should be to bring these implicit models into some sort of alignment. Some authors call this process creating a *shared mental model* for guiding team development and performance.[101] One point is clear: Any system out of alignment, human or otherwise, is not able to optimize its performance. Such systems are also inherently unreliable. So, at its foundation, the leader and team need to appreciate and understand the diversity of perspectives brought to the group and, through that understanding, find a way to align each member around certain principles that can guide the team system's development over time. In a self-directed team context, we should substitute the word *leaders* for *leader* in the previous sentence.

Place yourself in the role of team leader. One of the first steps is for you to understand the perspective of each member and, of course, for each member to understand yours and that of their fellow team members. As with the entrepreneur above, he made it clear what his starting point was in terms of the nature of interactions he desired in the new organization and that it was important for him to understand the habits and perspectives brought into the group. The goal is to integrate the diversity of the group around a common purpose; the integration comes through the goal created and the principles for how members treat each other in the group.

Several points that parallel those mentioned above are worth reiterating. First, think of a team composed of individuals as having the potential to develop into a full range leadership system. Second, one basic responsibility of a leader is to help define a system in which she or he will eventually operate over time. Third, a system composed of human beings is, in large part, based on the integration of each member's mental model into a cohesive or collective model that comes to guide the group or team's behavior as a leader's behavior does at the outset of a team's development. In the team's literature, such models are called *transactive memory*. The transactive memory of a team means each member has a way of thinking that quickly guides actions to be in alignment with each other.

The shared leadership in highly effective teams represents a collective understanding of how members want to relate to each other, and the purpose, or the goal, of the relationships is often idealized in the way we described this term at the individual level. It also determines, to a large extent, the methods and styles of relationships with other individuals and groups, both within and outside the organization.

As organizations move toward a team leadership system, they typically need to rebuild the system of leadership that has existed in their organizations in the past or in what you expect to embed this team system over time. I say *rebuild* here because we are assuming that one system existed prior to moving to teams, a system that was more hierarchically based and tied to superior–subordinate relationships. This is an awesome challenge for many organizations today because the habits are so ingrained in terms of the old system of leadership that it takes tremendous consistency to convince people we are truly trying to move to a team leadership system-based organization where influence is more horizontal than vertical.[102]

Many organizations that have tried to make the transition to teams often lament that it is not working very well. I am not surprised. People are very aware of discrepant signals in organizations and inconsistencies, particularly when one is trying to initiate a radical shift in ways of thinking and operating. It is one basis for widespread cynicism in organizations. Thus, when you say you want to go to a team system and the principles are in place but the behavior is not, what type of conclusions do you expect others to draw over time? Of course, we typically find that what people say is not what they are doing, so the system is being created but it is not the one desired. One would label that inauthentic, and I will have more to say about authentic leadership in a subsequent chapter.

Reflect on a situation where a gap existed between what was espoused and what you observed in practice. How did the gap affect your perspective, your motivation, and ultimately your performance?

To start building a team system, you should have in mind the system features you want to end up with over time. In other words, envision the type of processes you would want to occur if all your ideals were achieved. What would the interactions look like between you and the other members and among the other members of the team? If you have clearly envisioned the process and have acted consistently with the principles that support that process, you have a good chance of achieving your desired ideals over time. Are you wondering, "What does he mean by *chance*? It seems as if we did everything he said." This is all true, but selection also plays a role in what people do. In the human system, the quality of the resources is based on how you select people into the system. In the example that began this chapter, we saw that the leader had an enviable situation in that he had the chance to pick a new workforce from scratch. Consequently, he should begin to put the basic principles into action to form an organizational system while selecting new people into the organization, which is an advantage many organizational leaders do not have, let alone many project leaders, who have to build the team with what they are given or have versus some ideal selection process. Yet, if you have the ideal, then consider the nature of the resources that will best fit your system and select the best for the group.

If you are currently working, consider how difficult it would be for a team in your organization to self-organize with respect to picking the challenges and resources needed to accomplish those challenges. What institutional habits and systems would prevent this initiative from being successful? How might you change the team's context so that it is receptive to self-organizing teams? How can you create what Facebook, Linux, and Twitter have created in the virtual world? These are very viable communities that continue to self-organize around specific foundational principles that loosely guide the direction that has been set.

BOX 8.4   Virtual Leadership

A growing issue for developing leadership is how to lead virtually, which involves leading people from different departments, organizations, countries, and sometimes even competitor companies (Avolio, Kahai, & Dodge, 2000). In virtual teams, "challenges are more likely to occur when distributed work occurs in different time zones, when local communication and human infrastructures fail, when team members' hardware and software platforms are different, or when local work demands require the immediate attention of collocated managers and workers, thereby creating pressure to pursue local priorities over the objectives of distant collaborators" (Weisband, 2008, p. 6).

Kahai and Avolio (2008) investigated the effects of leadership style and anonymity on the discussion of an ethical issue within a simulated virtual team context. Kahai and Avolio reported that group member participation in discussing how to address the ethical issue was higher when leaders were transactional versus transformational.

Xiao, Seagull, Mackenzie, Klein, and Ziegert (2008) conducted a field experiment focusing on surgical teams in a real-life trauma center. These authors reported that when the team leader was in the adjacent room, they had more impact on communications with the senior member in the room. However, when the senior leader was colocated, the amount of communication among the team leader, the senior member, and the junior members was more balanced.

Balthazard, Waldman, and Atwater (2008) examined leadership and group member interaction styles, comparing virtual and face-to-face teams. They reported that group members in face-to-face teams were generally more cohesive, more accepting of a group's decisions, and more synergetic than were virtual teams. Face-to-face teams scored higher on constructive interactions, while virtual teams scored significantly higher on defensive interaction styles.

Currently, we know very little about how to address the following questions:[103]

- How does the technology impact how leadership style influences follower motivation and performance?
- How will trust best form in teams when mediated through technology?
- How will the leadership and cultural location of teams and technology connecting members impact the quality and quantity of their performance?
- How will the nature of the task and its complexity impact how leadership affects virtual team performance working across time, distance, and culture?

Teams Embedded in Organizational Cultures

Today, the culture of an organization has never been more relevant to building an optimal leadership system. Why today? The more organizations have decoupled and deleveled their structures and built networks, the less structure there is available to provide guidance to what are and are not appropriate standards and norms for behavior. In attempting to replace managerial structures, the specific need is to establish the type of culture the leadership of an organization wants in place to guide the development of relationships throughout the organization's phases of development, and in many cases, this means across time, distance, and complex cultures.

Another way of looking at what has been described here is that organizations are not of the same form as they were even 10 or 20 years ago. Leadership is migrating to the lowest levels, and more and more people have direct influence in shaping an organization's destiny as well as interfacing directly with clients and customers. Today, almost everyone faces the client. With these changes comes a need to reengineer relationships in the organization to take into consideration that, increasingly, the formal structures are blurred and the informal structures have more influence on bottom-line performance.

Back in the late 1970s, a CEO by the name of Bill O'Brian took over the lead at Hanover Insurance. Bill envisioned the changes on the horizon in the insurance business and decided that big corporate headquarters with a large staff would soon be outdated and that the largest concentration of staff should be where it can be most useful—with a company's customers. So, he began a campaign to localize decisions at the point of contact with the external customer. In his initial attempt, he failed, in part because of the ingrained beliefs of who was in charge. For months, people kept sending the same requests to headquarters for decisions to be made that they were repeatedly told were their prerogative. Bill had to transfer the corporate staff to the field to get the decisions to be local.

He also began a weekly letter to more than 10,000 employees, describing examples that fit with a localization philosophy. He found through the use of strategic redundancy and consistency of action that he could shift the perspective from a top-down decision-making structure to one based more on lateral integration and distribution of shared power. It took much more time than he thought initially to attack and change past habits that had been imported into the present situation he and Hanover were confronting (see Box 8.5).

We see the same types of localization efforts going on in organizations throughout the world. For example, many healthcare systems are trying to transform the patient and physician relationship. The idea is to make healthcare delivery more patient centered, and to do so one must reduce the hierarchy in the old patient-physician relationship. This is extremely challenging for many healthcare providers as the model has been active physician and passive patient receiving care versus collaborating and cocreating care.

Ironically, the famed Mayo Clinic in Rochester, Minnesota, was doing patient-centered, collaborative physician care nearly 100 years ago. Why? There were the three founders of the Mayo Clinic, a father and his two sons, who said from the start that the organizing principle that would characterize the Mayo Clinic was collaborative physician, patient-centric care. A century later, the clinic is seen as the model for patient-centered, collaborative healthcare practices, and its organizing principle has been used to transform other healthcare organizations such as the Cleveland Clinic in Ohio.

In some organizations in which teams have really taken hold, like at Xerox, the need to examine how peers lead each other in ever-changing team compositions, as well as how they participate in multiple teams at the same point in time, has become a prominent issue for people in the field of leadership development.[104] Part of the change that is underway is technology driven. More people are connected to

each other, and information is accessible in ways it never has been before in organizations. As information becomes more transparent and accessible, the ability for
many, many others to make decisions that have resided at higher levels has now
migrated down organizational hierarchies. Evidencing this change is the reference
that many Marines now make to what they call the *strategic corporal*. What they
mean is that strategic decisions traditionally made at much higher officer levels are
now being made daily by corporals ("Three Block War," n.d.).

In traditional organizational structures, the manager was the central unit of information, dissemination, and retention; this is no longer true in most organizations
today. This condition is forcing organizational leaders to rethink the structures and
processes in the company, the roles of managers, and the roles of those who still
report to those managers. Organizational leaders who have recognized these changes
and dramatic shifts in structures and technology, as well as in worker needs, have
been reconsidering how their business structures should be designed. This can be
witnessed in almost every sector of the world economy in terms of the tidal wave of
reengineering, the dialogue on the knowledge criterion, and the relearning of organization and all the things being reinvented. Yes, we are into the age of *re*. It is a
worldwide housecleaning project to prepare for life in this new century. Yet, to date,
we are still exploring how we should lead in these new age organizations, and
frankly, for some, they operate as though it was still the Roaring Twenties.

BOX 8.5   Transformational Leadership and Computer Mediation

Kahai, S., Sosik, J., and Avolio, B. (1997) conducted a laboratory experiment to examine the
impact of different leadership styles delivered via computer mediation in order to simulate virtual
teams. Confederate leaders were employed to deliver the leadership styles across groups/condi-
tions. Participants were undergraduate students involved in an idea-generation task. Results indicated that leadership can have an impact on group processes and outcomes when delivered
through computer mediation. Both directive and participative leadership had a positive and significant impact on the number of ideas generated within the experimental sessions, the satisfaction with participation, and the levels of participation. Directive leadership increased
participation in the task versus decreasing it. Anonymity built into the system used for computer
mediation moderated the effects of leadership on group processes and performance.

The use of anonymity in computer-mediated interactions can also be a powerful tool for integrating the diverse opinions of group members in that it is a mechanism to encourage participants to focus on what is said versus who said it. With early instructions between leader and
follower, this may be a useful strategy for developing more open and effective communication.

(Continued)

(Continued)

Kahai, Avolio, and Sosik (1998) examined 58 four-member groups consisting of either graduate or undergraduate students taking part in three tasks. In the first, they made a private decision about an issue and then discussed that issue via computer mediation, followed by a second opportunity to decide on the issue privately. The authors reported that different forms of anonymity increased participation/discussion in these groups. Anonymity also increased satisfaction with the process. Large differences were also found in the pattern of results if the groups started with initial differences of opinions. Being more anonymous was a positive predictor of group interactions with larger differences in initial opinions. These results have significant implications for the development of teams and for dealing with conflict or difficult issues in team processes over time. Using computer mediation can help in addressing the polarization that often goes along with groups composed of diverse membership. Similar findings have linked anonymity and transformational leadership to enhancing the creativity of teams.

An essential ingredient to business success seems to be the development of a culture that is highly adaptive and prone to re-creation. By adaptive, I mean a willingness that pervades the culture to get rid of or abandon something that does not serve the needs of the business in order to move onto something that is more effective.

At Levi Strauss, people have to reapply for their own jobs periodically to ensure they are still relevant to the organization.[105] John Kotter indicated that "only cultures that can help organizations anticipate and adapt to change will be associated with superior performance over long periods of time" (p. 44).[106] Bass and Avolio have designated the adaptive culture as one that is more transformational.[107]

Firms must avoid being seduced by their own success, or what Danny Miller called the *Icarus paradox*.[108] I have called it the *failure of success*. When we become too comfortable with our successful products or programs, we fail to kill them to move on to better products and programs. Indeed, the roots of failure for most organizations are their formula for success.

> *Unless you learn to manage the aftereffects of winning, the forces that led your team to the top will turn around and destroy you.*
>
> Pat Riley, former head coach of the New York Knicks

At an organizational level, we are witnessing a dramatic transformation that has been stimulated by events, some of which were discussed above. Taken together and referring to Figure 8.2, a future scenario has been emerging that has caused

Figure 8.2 Organizational Development at Any Level Requires Change

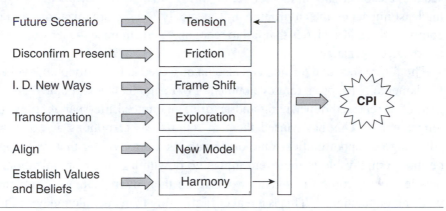

NOTE: CPI = Continuous Process Improvement.

enough tension in organizations for the leadership to rethink its total leadership system.[109] Where some degree of tension does not exist, there is no motivation for systems to evolve and change. The leaders in organizational systems must be able to hold tension until the new ideas pop.

Whether at an individual, team, or organizational level, as the future scenario becomes more evident and the extent to which this new future state is dramatically different from the present or past, some accommodation must be made. (Accommodation is a soft way of saying adaptation or transformation.) Tension, like adaptive conflict, is a good thing if it leads to a productive dialogue and a constructive change in the way one operates, a group functions, or an organization transacts its business. Transformational leaders focus the tension into positive energy to create the desired future scenario.

For many leading organizations around the world, changes in technology, the globalization of markets, and the changing nature of the workforce have contributed to reconsidering the nature of what constitutes the total leadership system and culture. Some leaders have seen a cliff on the horizon, it has caused tension to make changes, and they have explored ways to make the needed changes in their organizations. Others just do not see the cliff coming where significant and even fundamental change is required, and because they do not see it, they eventually fall into the abyss. The ones who see the cliff and see it in time will make the necessary adjustments, accommodations, and, ultimately, transformations. Those who do not—well, let's hope for a readily available parachute.

We are seeing today, in 2010, that many newspapers are going out of business because they failed to notice the tension being created by the rise of the Internet and its availability to provide news anytime and anywhere but not necessarily accurately. The same would be true of the U.S. automotive industry that failed to see the tension arising in the market requiring smaller, fuel-efficient cars that had the least impact on the environment. Repeatedly, we see organizations and indeed communities and societies that fail to recognize and embrace the tension and adapt in advance to change.

The future state and tension can also be observed at the individual level and are fundamentally the basis for development. For example, many people realize today that, after repeated downsizing and layoffs, guaranteed life-span employment no longer exists. This has caused them to rethink career options and also to take advantage of opportunities some organizations are providing that will help them be more employable in the event things go downhill at their organization. Other people have become free agents working on their own—about 30% of the U.S. working population.[110] This is a real cliff affecting many people today and into the foreseeable future. It is also a cliff for organizations that now must develop the full potential of their workforces—unfortunately, often for someone else.

At the center of transforming from a control culture to a challenging one is the ongoing battle between balancing *control* and *flexibility*. You can imagine which side usually wins out, can't you? An amusing reference to what takes place in an organization's structure where control rules is represented by Gordon MacKenzie's (1998) *Orbiting the Giant Hairball*. Too often, organizations rely on past policies, decisions, and processes for determining future direction; this creates a tie-up that inhibits people from breaking out of their old orbits. Gordon described his former job at Hallmark Cards as operating in the role of "loyally subversive."

Sometimes the future arrives unexpectedly. We witnessed this in the economic crash of the Pacific Rim countries during 1997 and until January 1998 when a cliff appeared suddenly on their horizon. In 1997, I was visiting Korea and addressed some executives on the need to identify and adapt to domestic changes in world markets that were already on their horizon. As is true in all Asian cultures, the members of my audience politely listened to my call to develop more transformational leaders and followers at all levels of their organizations.

Many Korean Chaebols appeared flush with resources. They also appeared to have a high degree of complacency with success. About 6 months later, I attended a national conference in the United States at which the top three Chaebols were present; each of the presenters basked in the glory of their successes, reporting the billions of dollars generated by each of their groups that year. Interestingly enough, in 1997, even while I was in Korea, a call came for the huge Chaebols to restructure, to empower their workforces, and to help smaller and nimbler firms get off the ground. Unfortunately, they had to fly a bit higher until the wax on their wings melted before they were willing to challenge how they had designed their leadership systems.

Shortly after I returned from Korea, the value of the Korean won dropped nearly 50%, making Korea a paradise for foreign shoppers but a disaster for the Korean population. At the time, they were heading over the cliff. In nearly every Korean newspaper article and conversation, one saw or heard over and over again the three letters *IMF*. They stand for International Monetary Fund, which stepped in to bail Korea out of near-financial ruin. It is amazing what a year can bring to a seemingly prosperous nation.

I started my presentations in Korea during my second trip by asking whether IMF stood for what the chairman of the Chaebols said when asked about the crisis in Korea: "It's my fault!" Unfortunately, the leadership of these venerable organizations had ceded control to the hands of the IMF and the new government at that time. The then–Korean president Kim Dae-Jung urged the leaders of Korea's largest organizations to take drastic corporate restructuring measures—unfortunately, the message was on the wrong side of the cliff. The situation became so severe that the chairman of Samsung agreed on January 22, 1998, to sell off 128 billion wons' worth of real estate from his group and pledged 90% of his salary to support employee welfare funds following layoffs. When you do not see the cliff coming, it tends to restrict your options the closer it gets to you.

Roll forward another 10 years, and now you have organizations throughout the financial sector of the United States folding left and right. What is amazing is that the leaders of these organizations, and I am mean thousands of them, did not see the cliff coming, or if they did, they ignored its impending consequences. It would be hard for anyone to imagine that the U.S. government would own a large share of General Motors or Citigroup. I am sure it would be hard for employees at Lehman Brothers to imagine that over night, this venerable Wall Street firm would be gone. The same would be true for Washington Mutual (WaMu) in the northwestern United States after nearly a century in operation. One might ask, "What were these leaders thinking?" The answer might be, "Not much."

BOX 8.6   Vision and Firm Growth[111]

Baum, Locke, and Kirkpatrick (1998) examined the relationship among vision attributes, vision content, vision communication, and venture growth over a 2-year period. This was the first study to examine the effects of vision on the overall performance of an organization. Vision attributes (clarity, challenge, future orientation, and ability to inspire, for example), vision content (growth image), and vision communication each positively predicted the venture growth of the firm. Vision content and vision attributes were also indirectly related to growth performance through vision communication.

Referring back to Korea, many executives said to me while I was visiting before the full effects of the crash, "Once we address the financial crisis, we will work on the leadership problem." Why business leaders insist on separating leadership from the "business of business" still amazes me each time I hear such comments. It is like the Israeli bank human resources director who told me recently that her CEO was delaying any type of leadership development effort until their new business strategy was fully deployed. Leadership development should coincide if not drive strategy deployment, and it is much more effective to do it at the front end than to recover it at the back end.

As organizations (or countries) enter periods of fundamental change and transformation, some will likely question whether it is for real or not, as that is natural for all of us to do. This is a reasonable thing to ask amid change and confusion. If we step back and reflect on what has happened during the past 25 years or more, we see patterns that suggest the dramatic transformation is very real and perhaps only in its infancy. What I mean here is that we still have many organizations operating in 2010 and designed for 1910 in terms of their leadership systems.

Looking back 50 years, the turbulent 1960s and 1970s saw a great deal of discussion about the role of participative management in the design of leadership systems.[112] One at least had to consider being more participative in a period when both leadership and authority were being questioned throughout the world, particularly in the United States because of the Vietnam War debacle. The credibility of the entire leadership system was in question, and many of these questions were creating tension in how organizations conceived and designed their leadership systems. With more of former president Nixon's tapes now being released, one can only appreciate in retrospect how important the process of questioning authority truly was at that point in U.S. history. Here was a president who nearly single-handedly brought down the longest standing democracy through his own and his followers' corrupt actions. Indeed, I would suggest we have never recovered trust in the U.S. presidency since these tragic trigger events.

Interestingly, the push toward building total quality and lean systems has made it essential that management and leadership question their roles as directors and controllers. Deming and others assured that these questions would be asked, and thus the tension was created for change quite a while ago.[113] Service quality entered the picture in a huge way in hospitality industries, in manufacturing, and eventually in education and healthcare demanding that employees at the point of contact with customers need to be able to make decisions more rapidly. It was a business necessity, not something nice to have to continue operations. And then with the information technology explosion, many of the pieces that were difficult to pull together started to fall into place, albeit not so easily in some organizations that resisted changing their leadership systems. This is as true of the command and control organizations that have resisted opening up their systems to become more transparent as it has been of societies such as North Korea or even China. What these societies have discovered is that there is no way to control the flow of information into the country and that what people are learning about the outside world is now beginning to transform the worlds inside these nations. Indeed, this is a global phenomenon powering dramatic changes in counties from the Balkans to changes in women's rights in the Middle East. You might say that these organizations and societies have a very high level of tolerance for tension.[114]

As we have now entered the new millennium, the speed of reaction time is not only a competitive advantage but also an expectation in terms of doing business. The timelines in almost every organization for delivery services have been compressed, and everything must be shorter. This ranges from getting patients out of hospitals in days versus weeks to delivering pictures framed over night versus months.

Bass, in referring to the challenges facing the U.S. Army, stated, "It is expected to be an Army which will deploy extremely quickly, be logistically self-sufficient, be intelligence-rich and facile with instant information about its own and enemy forces and conditions" (p. 47).[115] How could one think that, with all these elements changing, the leadership system and cultures in organizations did not need to change and transform radically? Well, those leaders who saw the cliff emerging started to explore and put into place systems that would prepare their organizations for the realities of the new global marketplace. This may have led the founders of Google to create the 20% work rule. What this means is that engineers can work 20% of their time on work of their own choosing. This rule provides for the flexibility to adapt at the local engineer level. By the way, during this 20% time, one engineer invented the now-ubiquitous Google Maps program.

> *When a man [or woman] ceases to wonder, he [or she] will cease to ascend on the scale of being.*
>
> Alfred North Whitehead

Many companies have gone through the early phases of exploration and transformation and are leading the change in the way organizations are defined today. I will use one example, referred to above and perhaps not immediately considered by most people: the U.S. armed services. As in other organizations, technology has had a profound impact on the way the armed services conduct their business. Also, with the ending of the Cold War and a single comment made by then–Soviet president Gorbachev, many things changed in the way the services did and currently do business.

When President Gorbachev first met General Colin Powell, he supposedly leaned across the table and said to General Powell that he needed to find himself another enemy. Powell said in a speech I attended following the fall of the Berlin Wall that he was taken aback with the president's comment. The former Soviet Union had been a great enemy for the United States to prepare for during the past 28 years of Powell's career. In some ways, Powell thought we were losing "the good old days," when the lines were clear, as symbolically represented by the Berlin Wall. Powell indicated that, during the first two thirds of his career, he learned to near-perfection how to contain the communist threat. And now, 2 years from retirement, everything in his business had changed. The containment strategy was no longer relevant, and he realized that the world was moving into a much more unpredictable period. The former Soviet Union and its allies needed to be included, not contained, to maintain security. This has led to a radical reinventing of our military strategic operations and thinking.

A cliff had quickly emerged, and the question became, Do we have the right armed forces strategy and operations for the next millennium? What type of hairball had we created since World War II in the military? And like any other organization, this new future state and the tension it created led to a vast search for new ways of conducting business in the armed services.

To be successful now, the U.S. armed services would have to be more responsive to rapidly changing conditions, reduced in size, trained more specifically, and able to use the most advanced information technology, while winning over communities rather than simply defeating them. Sounds a bit like General Electric, IBM, Xerox, 3M, HP, Intel, Toyota, and ABB, doesn't it? Things changed for the U.S. Army and, in fact, all militaries in the way they have had to do business, requiring a serious "re"consideration of their leadership system. This serious reconsideration is an ongoing exercise today around the globe as the U.S. Army deploys to places like Afghanistan that offer a very different landscape literally and figuratively for what the military needs to do to be successful. War, like business, has changed, and the tension was in the air 30 years ago, if noticed. Frankly, I am an advocate for making war obsolete altogether.

Like many CEOs, General Powell had to learn how to question his old assumptions and systems. He humorously suggested in his remarks that he only wished Gorbachev had waited until after he had retired to change the world. Because it happened on his watch, however, Powell did what needed to be done to begin the transformation process in the U.S. military.

During the phases of exploration described above, as organizational systems begin to move toward transforming the way people relate to each other, there is a need to bring some consistency and alignment to the new ways of working

together. Generally, in most organizations, alignment occurs at its most fundamental level around or in line with the culture that emerges and, of course, is
based, in part, on the national culture in which an organization is embedded. For
example, as information becomes more readily accessible to everyone and as
everyone's involvement becomes more crucial to success, there is a need to support, if not initiate, collaboration. Thus, in many organizational systems, we see
the emergence of collaboration and cocreation as central features or values that
leaders are trying to develop in the organization's culture. Valuing the individual
and her or his ideas along with having greater respect for differences of opinion,
or loyal subversiveness, also becomes an important core value in the transformed
culture. Collaboration is required just as in any other form of interaction or directive that accomplishes what must be achieved by the organization.

It is now common to hear organizational leaders say they have moved from
being the manager of a control system to a coach and facilitator who is now
viewed as the keeper of the value system in the organization. Mort Meyerson, the
former CEO of Electronic Data Systems (EDS) and then-CEO of Perot Systems
mentioned earlier, remarked that, at EDS, everything in his job was about some
form of control. When he was asked by Ross Perot to come out of retirement to
lead Perot Systems, he discovered that most of the control processes he had
learned and practiced at EDS had to be abandoned in his new work environment.
Apparently, he did mean abandoned.

In a more open system, leaders have the advantage of reaching out and reinforcing open communication as a fundamental value in the organization but not
without risk. For example, one senior executive got so excited about valuing
open communication in his organization that, at the annual meeting of his division, he committed to responding personally to all e-mail messages he received
from his division's members. By the next morning, he had received 900 messages. A colleague indicated that there must have been a lot of people waiting to
talk to him. The executive had to reconfigure the compact he made on the fly to
make it possible to reach the goal he wanted to achieve in shaping the culture in
his organization. You can be open and accessible without being deluged and
abused. One could also interpret the rush of 900 messages as advance warning
of a cliff on the horizon.

Let's take a moment to reflect on what has been said in this chapter. The con-
fluence of emerging forces will continue to affect the nature of how organizations
develop themselves. In fact, you can ask yourself a few very simple questions:
What is organization? What does it mean to you now, what did it mean, and what
will it mean in the future, considering the types of changes mentioned above?
Perhaps your answer may be like that of Lee Ward Hock, the founder of Visa,

when he suggested that the less obvious a company's organizational structure is, the better that is for business. For many organizations, this statement has a greater ring of truth to it than in even the recent past—like yesterday.

Amid tension and change, many will continue to ask, "Is all of this for real, or is it simply some program or 'flavor of the month'?" Some ask this question because they are afraid they might miss out on something that is happening. Some ask because they are afraid of the impending changes and would like to hear that the answer is really *no*. They may say inside, "But I really like telling people what to do." Others ask because they are perhaps already living the role of the chief learning officer, and such questions bring into focus the next cliff on the horizon before it is upon them.

To answer such a question and to lead, you must step out of the current time context in which you are embedded, examine the next potential context, and envision into what your organization is emerging. Another way to put it is to use *what-if* scenarios to see what will happen if certain things really do change in the environment we intend to operate in over time. In 1955, most, if not all, managers in companies like IBM, EDS, GE, AT&T, and Honeywell were men. This hit me straight on when I walked into a local restaurant that had a picture of all the IBM employees standing outside the main and foundation plant in Endicott, New York. Two things struck me about the picture: One, virtually no women were in it, except what appeared to be a few employees' wives with their children. Two, every face in the crowd of several thousand was White.

Now, let's ask questions that one of those managers may have asked himself while that picture was being taken on that day: If women became managers, what implications would that mean for human resources polices? If everyone could talk to the CEO simultaneously, how might that affect the organization's culture? If each consumer had different preferences that we could meet almost immediately, and they each came from different cultures, how would that affect how we market and produce goods and services in our organizations? These seem like obvious questions today, but they would not have been within that time period and context. Yet, they should have been asked by the leadership of the organization. Now, we are taking a picture of you and your organization's employees. Do you have any thoughts about what will emerge in the future?

When Ameritech was undergoing a dramatic transformation from a regulated telephone company to an innovative telecommunications organization, one consultant asked the senior managers to write a *Fortune* article on what Ameritech would become 3 years hence. Why don't you consider this an exercise for your unit or organization?

Speaking of seeing the future in the present, some years ago I was sitting in a meeting at a large European conglomerate with a top executive who had traveled extensively around the world. Looking around the all-male room in 1992, he said, "Let's start to aggressively hire women for our high potential management positions." He then exclaimed, "So far, the best ones are still in the market!" One can see the future in the present if one takes the time to look, to reflect, and to get feedback.

It appears that the dramatic changes going on within organizations and the contexts in which they operate are very real and are driven by many complex, dynamic forces. You need simply to witness the transformations occurring in the leading companies around the world, and you can see that the future is already emerging and requiring a very significant change in the configuration of the leadership systems and cultures in which they are embedded.

The relevant questions now seem to be, What systems must we retire (and this includes ways of thinking)? What systems must we transform? And how will this affect the people we select and develop for the new leadership positions in our emerging organizations? Many organizational leaders and, I am sure, their seconds in command, if they are being heard, are asking themselves these same questions; to be fair, many still are not. My challenge is to get you to ask these questions, reflect on your answers, and decide which directions you will explore—sooner or later.

Now, I would like to comment on the future. The emergence of alliances, open source development, social networks, and user innovations as well as increased reaction time to market, advances in network technology, the emergence of a Generation X and soon Y workforce, and the need to be fully aligned with your customers all point to the fact that collective, or collaborative, leadership is an area we must seriously explore and develop for organizations into this next millennium. One only needs to imagine in her or his organization a situation where 80% of the units formed are self-organizing. This is incredible even to conceive of in current organizations where the organizational structure is very obviously bureaucratic and noticeable. You might say that such an organization does not yet exist, but it is possible.

One direction for sure that must now be explored is the topic of our next chapter: shared leadership in teams. People will want to share more in the leadership system, to be full owners and stakeholders. They are already being asked to be more involved with customers because it is doable with advanced information technology and because it is actually the right thing to do. They do know more about customer needs. For all of these reasons, we must now consider how the new leadership system will look in our future organizations.

Okay, the camera is ready to snap a picture, which, by the way, is digital, and you can check out the picture on your PC or phone and discard it if it is blurred and try again. Let's see, was it Kodak that recently laid off 10,000 employees? Do you have any thoughts about some cliffs on the horizon for your leadership?

SOME THINGS WORTH REPEATING AND REFLECTING ON

- A migration of leadership responsibilities is occurring in organizations that is fundamentally changing the leadership systems of those organizations.
- Creating loyally subversive followers is an essential ingredient for fundamental and transformative change in organizational systems.
- The future is in the present for those who take the time to uncover it for themselves and realize that tension can facilitate change.
- If we fail to predict the future, we have to live in it nonetheless.

Let me leave you with one question to reflect on: *How have you reinforced your loyally subversive followers lately for questioning the current state in your organization or work unit?*

A SHORT EXERCISE

Please take the Continuous Process Improvement (CPI) in Figure 8.2, and think about how it applies to the development of your leading a team that was very resistant, if not immune, to change.

- If you were to go through the phases depicted in this CPI figure, how could you apply those phases to addressing the initial resistance or immunities to change?
- What type of friction would you expect to occur?
- How could you overcome that friction through changes in leadership style or using the 4 Is?

CHAPTER 9

SHARED LEADERSHIP

According to African humanistic thinking and a term they use called vital
forces, *a person is not a person unless connected with others.*

The focus of this African life philosophy is that individuals derive their sense of
meaning and self through their relationships with others. This makes sense if we
look at some of the examples that I mentioned regarding the identification associated with being a firefighter, for example. We know that one's self-identity is in
large part defined by the collectives we belong to, such as the communities we live
in or choose to be a part of (for example, when I was in Nebraska, being a
Nebraskan Husker). They even referred to the Husker fan as being part of a larger
collective called Husker Nation.[116]

The type of deep connection represented in the concept of vital forces is that it
becomes a way of sharing values and perspectives that, over time, become automatic filters for how one perceives one's self and others. For example, in Husker
Nation, a fan is someone who shows total respect for the competition. The potential downside of creating such groups is that it also creates in-groups and out-
groups, which can be quite dangerous as we have seen throughout history in
movements associated with the Nazis, Fascists, apartheid, religious cults, and so
forth. Consequently, we want to have a healthy connection on the inside in terms
of our identities, but we do not want to go so far as to put one group down to lift
another up. More importantly, we also want enough people in the in-group willing to take leadership and challenge the group's direction.

People come to teams or organizations with their own identities—sometimes
several, as I noted in terms of the selves we develop in our life course—and it is
those identities we are trying to align when we say that all followers or team members now identify with a leader's vision and each other's efforts. Indeed, each person's contribution can be unique and, at the same time, enhanced through his or
her relationships with others, especially where the group exhibits a high degree of

trust and transparency. This appears to be the essence of the vital force of a group or team. It is not a trade-off between individualistic or collectivistic thinking; rather, their integration creates the vital force in highly developed teams as well as in larger organizational systems. In fact, the absence of the vital force is noticed in the maladaptive conflict frequently observed as teams come to grips with how to work together and what is their common purpose.

Coming from the most individualistic nation on earth, I have always struggled with the notion of how we can blend the uniqueness of each individual with the specific need to collaborate and coordinate, which characterizes highly developed teams. Clearly, we are seeing more and more organizations talk about the importance of social networks and collaboration but still lead using a hierarchy of roles, which I, in fact, would endorse. In my opinion, you will never take the hierarchy out of human interactions, but rather you can accommodate it and adapt it to highly sophisticated levels of collaboration. This is a strategy commonly done with organizations that have to respond to crises where they have a very strict hierarchy of command called an incident command system, with lots of flexibility thrown in at all levels of the organization to respond to demands on the ground. Thinking of these first-responder-type organizations, among others, I have come to consider vital forces a stimulus concept with regards to how this could be accomplished without losing the benefits of the individual, the group, or the team.[117]

Have you observed how companies typically treat the team concept? Generally, they want people to identify with something, which is often a trivial representation of what really constitutes a team. Call it a team, label everyone an equal contributor, do some hokey ceremonies, and put a large sign over the door saying something like Welcome to Team Torino. These same companies also usually provide a day or two of training to jump-start the team with many activities that have little if anything to do with leadership. And interestingly enough, this type of team training is usually done with people from different teams, not the team they are trying to develop and in my view focuses too much on abstract, *soft* processes that most managers hate to discuss and are even more disposed not to do once back at work.

My general impression is that such approaches often generate more cynicism than team development. What happens when you tell a group of people they are a team, and they do not trust each other? There is something much more profound to be discovered in the vital forces in teams and organizations. It starts with an individual who is a full contributor and who is willing to sacrifice for the team's goals, mission, and vision because he or she identifies with the collective but will not and should not give up who he or she is as an individual. Such individuals are all together on the inside as one unit in that they fully identify with its mission. Being together on the inside is at the core of what I mean by building the vital forces in organizations. Its closest cousin in the leadership literature is being identified with a cause, belief, mission, or vision. This, too, represents being together on the inside in terms of your thoughts, your emotions, and your behavior.

I have had many discussions with colleagues regarding a very popular way of thinking in Africa referred to as *Ubuntu* philosophy. In terms of discussing shared leadership, I can say that if I translated Ubuntu directly, it would mean *unity through diversity*. These three words have dominated my thinking about teams and shared leadership since I first came across them. They are at the essence of what President Nelson Mandela set as a national goal for South Africa when he assumed the presidency. He said quite often that there is one South Africa, or one nation. Yet, like the former Yugoslavia, it has a highly diverse population with groups that have very little in common in terms of an indigenous culture. President Mandela battled the historical tendency in most conflicts to create a blood-over-brains solution to enforce change and reverse that logic to being brains-over-blood by using "unity through diversity" as a mantra for change. This is truly a remarkable vision, given that apartheid was fundamentally based on separation versus integration and that although the laws have changed, it will take time for the implicit models in people's minds to change to even come close to the new laws.

By the way, the new CEO of Ford Motor Company, Alan Mulally, has pursued the same vision, calling Ford employees to focus on Ford, and for there to be just one Ford. He has been determined to stop the internal fighting that was killing this venerable company. So far, it seems to be working: Having a unity through diversity strategy, Ford has posted two profitable quarters back-to-back, coming off the heels of the worst recession in U.S. history.

South Africa has had to move from a control-dominated society under apartheid to a society where the controls are within people operating within a democratic collaborative system. In choosing this direction, many have had to change their fundamental perspectives about different groups to appreciate their diversity and how all members together each can accomplish more successes individually. Of course, the way for South Africans has been strewn with many difficulties. As controls for compliance have been removed, the crime rate has soared in South African society. Over 15 years later, commitment and trust are still not in place to replace the controls that guarded behavior, and now the guards must be in the way people think, or stated another way, they need to be internalized in everyone. As a nation, South Africans remain in a period of extreme vulnerability.

Most South Africans I met only knew the system they grew up with, and many, I believe, did not know what they did not know about the outside world. In the United States, I grew up believing fundamentally in individual liberties and heard this all the time from teachers, lawyers, parents, and presidents. We protect this liberty as a nation, often in the very extreme sense, even though we do not always apply it to all of our diverse groups in the United States.

For example, we frequently did not apply this to African Americans, Hispanics, or Native Americans. However, I think we are doing better, but it has taken us 250 years, with much work remaining, to accomplish.

In South Africa, apartheid was what people were taught to believe in, and it was endorsed not only by the government but also by the church. I must say here that I am not excusing any past mistakes in this country, and they are huge ones. I am merely trying to explain the context in which the people of this nation were embedded or grew up over time. Framing this context for you is crucial to put into perspective the challenge of creating unity through diversity.

I must add that, in a much less extreme sense, the challenge is not much different for a team that must work with discrepant models in people's heads about how best to work together to become a high-performing system, as I suggested through Ford's example. The same is true for the different teams that work in the U.S. healthcare system that are frequently at odds with each other at the expense of patient safety. We see this behavior in the frequent conflicts between union and management. For example, the Detroit mayor, David Bing, has continually reached out to the city's unions to say that the city cannot continue to pay 68% of employee wages to benefits and not go into bankruptcy. The city is near failure, and the unions and management are not in agreement, which could result in Detroit being the first major U.S. city to claim bankruptcy.

> *If you treat a man as he is, he will remain as he is. But if you treat him as if he were what he ought to be, and could be, he will become what he ought to be, and could be.*
>
> Johann Wolfgang von Goethe

I can extend the splits to many more examples that prevent groups and organizations from being successful. The challenge we have ranges from firms that have tried to merge unsuccessfully, such as Time Warner and AOL, to liberal and conservative politicians, those that endorse climate change legislation and those that oppose it. Even where they may hold common interest, if not survival, leaders face the challenge to create a high level of unity through the requisite diversity noted in Ubuntu philosophy. Indeed, it may be one of the enduring challenges of leadership in every community, organization, and society.

People become embedded in their past in terms of how they define themselves. This type of embeddedness came out very poignantly for me in a workshop I conducted for a large South African bank. Midway through the retreat, I kept trying to get a young, Black woman to contribute to our discussion. She would contribute with me at the breaks but not in the larger group. She was the only Black person in the room and the only female. At the end of the second day,

I approached her and said that I thought she had enormous potential and that it was a positive challenge for me and this organization to unleash her full potential. I wanted her to confront the opinions of these other managers to benefit them as well as her. She looked at me with sad eyes and said that, for her whole life, she was taught never to confront a White man. Now, everything was different; she fully understood the need, but her automatic response was to question whether it was appropriate each time she attempted to question her White, male colleagues. She knew intellectually that she must do it. Yet, these implicit models are very difficult thinking systems to retire. In South Africa, people have to retire their implicit systems in parallel with creating entirely new ones, making this nation one of the most interesting cases for studying transformational leadership in the past and into the current century. The same is true for the airlines, Delta and Northwest, who just began merging. I say *just began* because the legal and financial transactions that are completed oftentimes are just the beginning for merging the implicit models that have guided each of these venerable, large, and complex airline systems. In fact, the more you create a strong and unified corporate culture, the harder it should be to merge with another culture, unless they are identical, which never happens.

The collective experiences and thinking from the work described above led me to the creation of a figure designed to represent the development of groups to teams and then to highly developed teams. At the far left of Figure 9.1 is a group of people who happen to find themselves together for some reason; this is usually a prerequisite for being a team in that all members share some common purpose but not necessarily a common organization or even common geography. The starting point is to have a common purpose.

Notice the different patterns that are used to represent each individual as being different perhaps in perspective, talent, performance potential, and desire. As one moves from left to right in Figure 9.1, the group structures itself by members laying out expectations for each other. Again, the patterns are different, and in the structuring process, we do not lose individuality in the group, although some compromises have to be made on the basis of whatever expectations are set for the group. In working with teams, this is the point that parallels the building of what we have called a compact of understanding, or some call it a team charter.

I have had the opportunity to interview many teams, teams that had become quite successful in developing to their full potential. One question I have asked at the end of interviews has always been answered in the same way by all of these respective teams. Members of the most highly developed teams said that if they could go back and do it all over again, they would have set clearer expectations early on for themselves. I heard things like, "Thinking we were all adults, we short-circuited this process, and it led to very bad, destructive conflicts."

Figure 9.1 Team Leadership Development

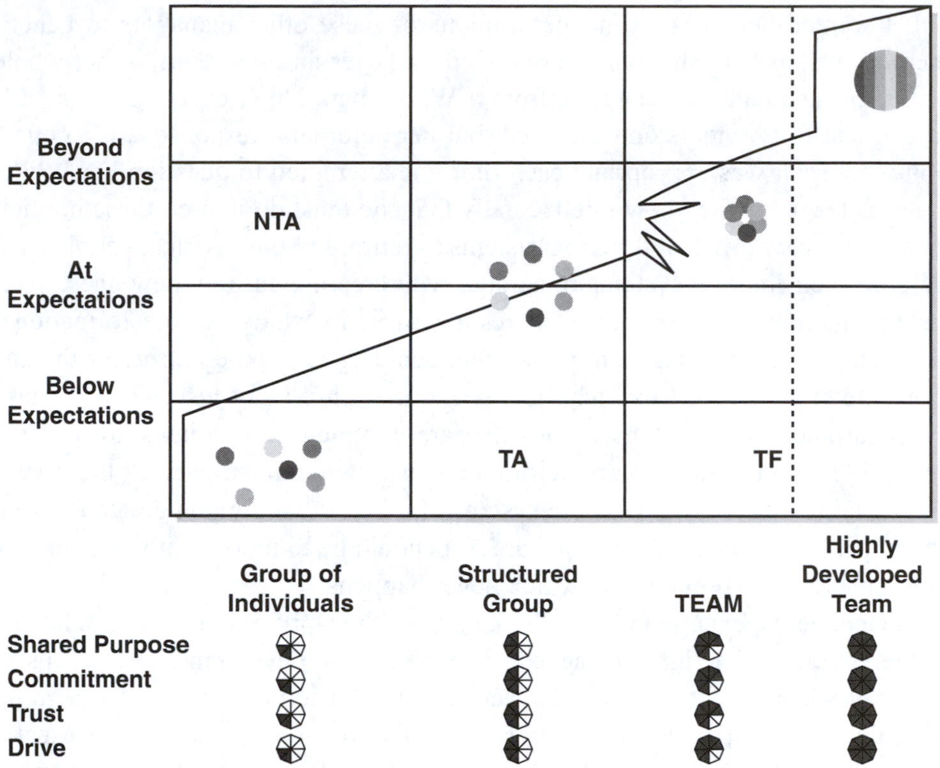

SOURCE: Avolio (1999).

NOTE: NTA = Non-Transactional; TA = Transactional; TF = Transformational

I now believe that "normal" storming stage in a group's development is actually a consequence of poorly articulated expectations. It may also be a result of what Richard Hackman described as insufficient direction being given to the group from the outset.[118] In my opinion, if we can get the compact of understanding correct up front, we can move from early formation to adaptive conflict, which becomes the basis for building a highly developed team leadership system where leadership is fully shared among members (see Box 9.1). And by saying *shared*, I mean where members disproportionately influence each other to do something at any one point in time. Stated differently, it is rare that each member is influencing another equally at any one point in time.

Jehn has also come up with a useful framework for classifying the effects of different forms of conflict.[119] For example, Jehn identified both *relational conflict* and *process conflict* as being detrimental to performance and satisfaction. *Task conflict,* which focuses on the content in a group's work and goals, was identified as being situational in its impact and showed positive effects under certain conditions. Moderate to high levels of task conflict were positively related to group performance. Group development and performance can be largely affected either positively or negatively by the type of conflict. Quickly resolving relationship and process conflicts was seen as being essential to effective group performance.

Included in Figure 9.1 is a squiggly line that appears before a structured group (structured around expectations of each other) becomes a team. In any development process, there is a need for tension to create exploration, change, and ultimately transformation. This is as true in individual development as it is in group or organizational development. Groups must test their system to know how well they are working together. Indeed, an essential stepping-stone for teams is to build in rigorous tests to qualify their system as ready to deploy.

Analogous to the challenge associated with transitions in teams is the recent 787 Dreamliner airplane that Boeing just built with a lot of new technology and processes, including being the first plane largely built from composites. In late 2009, the plane took off on its maiden voyage and now will undergo months of stress tests to make sure it will perform under a broad range of conditions. What other teams that you have worked with or on have done that kind of stress testing before "flying"? I can tell you that from my experience, the answer is very few in most organizations including healthcare, government, or in the private sector. However, most sports teams, special forces teams, disaster intervention teams, firefighters, and other teams that address life-and-death situations do so as part of their routine in building a high-performance team. The components of Boeing's system can be seen in their relationships, tasks, process, and common goals. Their process can be applied to every team's development.

BOX 9.1   The Nature of Different Styles of Conflict

Lehnen, Ayman, and Korabik (1995) examined the types of conflict styles used by male and female leaders. The sample included managers and vice principals in Canada, rated by their followers. Results indicated that self-rated transformational leadership was more strongly associated with using an integrative conflict management style. The relationship between transformational leadership and satisfaction was shown to be mediated by the conflict management style used by the leader. Leaders who described themselves as more transformational used integrative conflict management styles and had followers with greater levels of satisfaction. This relationship was stronger for the female versus male managers in the sample. Male transformational leaders described themselves as using more of a compromising style of conflict management.

The occurrence of events testing a group's system was labeled by Gersick as *punctuated equilibrium*.[120] What Gersick meant was that there are certain points in a group's development where fundamental, or what might be called nonlinear change, occurs. Some will have more dramatic tests than others, but in the end a test must occur where the basic expectations and principles of the group are examined by the group and transformed, if needed, to address new challenges and opportunities. If members come away from challenges saying, "We all did what we expected of each other," or "We even exceeded each other's expectations," then a higher level of trust and cohesion will result. This is reflected in a closing of the circle in Figure 9.1. Members have learned that placing confidence in their team members is fully justified. They have also learned how each member performed under stress or extreme duress, so they are much closer to understanding fully each other's strengths and weaknesses. It is a clear transition point in time when many teams recognize that they need some outside input and coaching in order to achieve a full-blown transformation in perspective.

The process depicted in Figure 9.1 as represented in Ubuntu philosophy suggests that members have gone from the *I* to the *me* to the *we* or *us*. *I* is in reference to one's self only. *Me* is in reference to others. And *we* represents myself within a larger collective, or a highly developed team unit. Generally at the *we* stage of development, I am much more willing to sacrifice my own self-interests for the good of the team as needed.

The transition or transformation that occurs in going from *I* to *me* to *we* is a crucial point in time where reflection on what is happening to one's self and the group is essential for further transformational leadership development. Reflective learning provides each member the opportunity to examine where he or she is with respect to the group's development, as well as where other members are in their respective development trajectories. Indeed, it is perhaps a more difficult type of reflective learning than occurs in individual leader–follower interactions in that each member is reflecting on an entity he or she is more a central part of than in more traditional leader–follower interactions. It is also analogous to asking someone to step out of his or her culture and not to think so individualistically, then asking, "Okay, now what do you see?" It is difficult to step out of what we are fundamentally embedded in overtime and what gets hard wired in each of us. It is analogous to saying that even though you only know French just try to understand German. The process of decoding is quite a challenge. Using the debriefing process described below, what we consider *tuning* can be helpful to unpacking what is going on in the team.

After Action Review Process Steps and Template

1. What did we intend?

2. What happened?

3. What worked well? Why?

4. What did not work well? Why?

5. What will we do differently?

6. What did we learn?

What Did We Intend?			

What Happened?			

What Worked Well?	Why?	What Didn't Work Well?	Why?

What Will We Do Differently?			

What Did We Learn?			

Let's return to the transition or transformation point depicted in Figure 9.1. If the group successfully addresses its challenges and members have come away generally satisfied with each other, we can start to describe them as a team. Indeed, by working together, each member does accomplish more, and the team accomplishes more over time.

As a leadership system, we expect to see the four Is of transformational leadership. Members care about each other's development (individualized consideration). They are willing and even eager to challenge each other's perspectives without thinking that someone is being attacked (intellectual stimulation). Often, they have inspired each other to get through the difficult times together (inspirational motivation). Ultimately, they have a higher identification and confidence in the team's ideals, central purpose, and vision in some cases (idealized influence).

In comparing the team to the group, the group operates collectively on a more transactional level. Members can be highly corrective or even avoidant where no structure for expectations of members exists. So, what we often see at the lowest end of development is members avoiding taking responsibility or some taking it and others not. We see people correcting each other, and this often leads to arguments over who said what and, in the extreme, to out-of-control *storming*. Relationships within the group are in conflict, and the process feels out of control. We see attempts to set agreements and contracts as the basis for developing trust and commitment. Self-interest usually is more dominant than collective at the beginning, although some members may feel conflicted because they would like to work as a team but are having problems with members who seem to be in things for themselves. This clearly indicates a lack of trust.

At the far right of Figure 9.1 is a highly developed team. We chose *highly developed* because we were interested in the membership's perspective and thought that performance would follow perspective and development. In terms of perspective, we thought that members of highly developed teams, just like highly developed leaders, were willing to sacrifice that which they most desired for the good of the team, if they needed to do so for their team. However, optimally no one has to sacrifice, but rather everyone finds a way to align self-interest with collective interest. Their perspective is more highly developed because self-interest no longer rules the day. This does not mean that self-interests are ignored, just that when it is important to do so, members will delay without reservation their self-interest to move closer to the idealized goal of the team. Why? Because, at the highly developed stage, they have complete identification with the team and its goals, yet as represented in the figure, they each retain their own individual identities. The retention of each member's identity linked together in a common purpose forms the basis of a team unit's vital force. We show in Figure 9.2 what we started with to build the team. Individual identities are pulled together through leadership and a common purpose into an extraordinary force. By the way, "to join forces" is a dictionary definition of the verb *team* ("Team," 2008).

Figure 9.2   To Join Forces

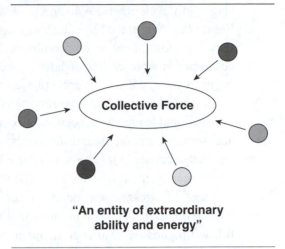

"An entity of extraordinary ability and energy"

SOURCE: Avolio (1999).

The retention of individual identities paradoxically provides the basis for shared leadership and often constructive and adaptive conflict. Members have to share each of their unique contributions. If more than one person can do the same thing, we might say we have one too many people in the room. By bringing together the diversity resident in a team, we typically provide the synergistic value associated with teams that are described as high performing by numerous authors, including Kazenbach and Smith in *The Wisdom of Teams*.[121]

The symbol chosen to represent the highly developed team is that of a circle that retains the shadings, but shows them in harmony, or blending together. One manager remarked, on first seeing Figure 9.1 and hearing of the different phases of development, that he agreed up to the last phase. He thought the symbol we chose should have been a square, not a circle. I asked him why. He said that, in a team, everyone makes equal contributions. He was from the United States and has what I have come to witness many times—a very typical, U.S.A.-centric view about teams. A team means we are all going to move toward making more similar contributions. I disagreed with his point and said that, with the circle, at any one point in time, contributions to the team are likely never equal. Sharing usually means someone has more than someone else to give, and in highly developed teams, the same is true. The allowance of unequal contribution makes great teams truly great.

The circle symbolically represents that, in highly developed teams, some members lead when it is their opportunity to lead and some members follow in an exemplary fashion; this can change again and again over time. So, whoever is central or more in control at one point in time will move to the periphery as others who have the knowledge, expertise, or persistence need to move to the center of a challenge, threat, or opportunity. Only by combining the unequal contributions of members in the team, or their distinct competencies, can we have shared leadership and highly developed teams. Of course, over a long time and with the right selection strategy, we can say that the team, theoretically, will approximate a box versus a circle. However, as people always say to me, "In the real world, things just don't happen that way. So, let's stick with the circle for now."

We have also looked at attributes of the group and team that coincide with stages of development. A listing or description of these attributes is presented in Figure 9.3. We placed the attributes into the phases of team development where they are most likely to be prominent. This should not suggest to you that they could not emerge earlier or later in the process of development. Most evidence suggests they typically overlap phases of team development.

Seltzer, Numerof, and Bass reported that when other factors were held constant, transactional leaders who focused on corrections and mistakes increased the stress and burnout among their followers[122] (see also Box 9.2). Seltzer and his colleagues concluded that stress was more highly correlated with the excessive use of active management-by-exception and the absence of transformational leadership. In times of stress, team members not only need to know what they are doing wrong, but they also need to know that they have the support of other members, a full willingness to challenge members' ideas, the drive to attain their goals, and the ideals to do so in a fair and principled manner. Team leaders and members must balance the drive for new ideas and performance with consideration for the varying needs of each individual. Burgess, Salas, Cannon-Bowers, and Hall have recommended that the type of leadership required for teams working under stress is very much in line with the full range model of leadership.[123] Strategies they recommended include checking team member performance, providing feedback, monitoring performance, gate keeping, and troubleshooting to locate and correct errors, which would all fall within the transactional range of leadership. Transformational strategies recommended for handling stress included developing individual member competence to handle uncertain events or ambiguity, to build a thorough understanding of the mission, to establish an alignment of members' goals with those of the team, and, probably more important, to provide an established trust between members for support when it is most needed.

BOX 9.2 Stress, Burnout, Turnover, and Transformational Leadership

Densten and Sarros (1995) examined the relationship among leadership, stress, and burnout in police service organizations in Australia. Earlier research by Selzer, Numerof, and Bass (1989) demonstrated an inverse relationship among burnout, effectiveness, and satisfaction. The study involved a sample of 480 police personnel evaluating middle- to senior-level ranks. Higher levels of idealized leadership and transactional contingent reward were related to less emotional exhaustion and, to a lesser degree, personal accomplishment burnout. Leadership accounted for 14% of the variance in emotional burnout.

Figure 9.3   Summary of Team Development Phases

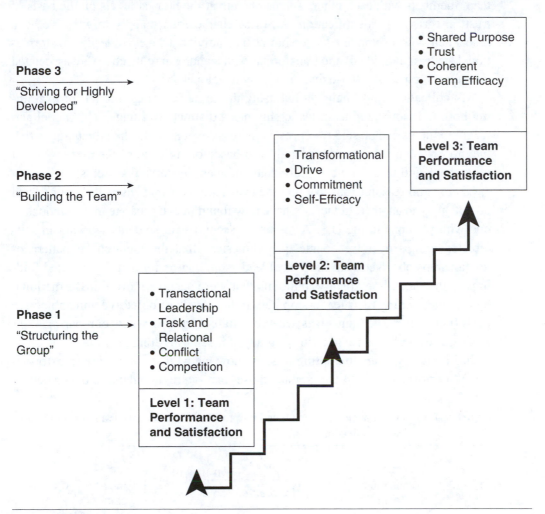

Viewing Leadership at Two Levels

I have now introduced a parallel version of the full range model at two levels. The first version was at the individual leader and follower level, and I spent time up front describing the model and perspectives associated with each level along the full range. In this chapter and the previous one, we began discussing the same model of leadership as part of building a team leadership system. Yet, the only thing that has changed is what we applied leadership to as opposed to changing the concepts along the full range of leadership. Members of teams are inspiring, and so, too, can be an individual leader. Leaders can show individualized consideration, and so, too, can team members with each other. Teams operate at the highest levels on the basis of trust, integrity, and identification. All these characteristics apply to what we have associated with exemplary leadership at the individual level. Indeed, transformational leaders (individual) and transformational leadership (collective) are associated with teams, especially those that are highly developed.[124]

My colleagues and I believe that using the same full range model for examining both individual and team leadership has a distinct advantage. The model and its components can be said to represent a cross-level model. The advantage is that the more we move to networked and team-based organizations, the more we must move back and forth between individual and team leadership systems.

There is no reason to suspect that the leadership concepts discussed at one level do not apply to another. In fact, we have now found in two separate investigations—one with platoons in the U.S. Army and a second with students working in self-directed groups over the course of a semester—that the hierarchical pattern of relationships observed with individual leadership and performance paralleled findings with teams. Specifically, platoons that were seen as more transformational by members rating their leadership had higher levels of objective and subjective performance.[125] The same was true for student groups when comparing their measures of performance in terms of grades for semester-long projects.[126]

In Figure 9.4, I am attempting to show how teams that were more transformational performed over time versus those that were avoidant and corrective.

Figure 9.4   Performance Patterns Over Time for Avoidant Versus Transformational Team Leadership

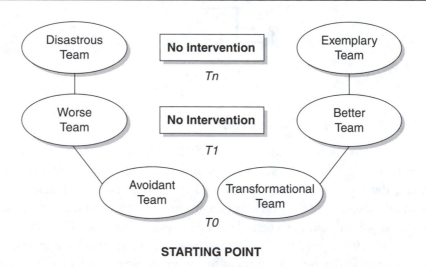

SOURCE: Avolio (1999).

Interestingly, the good teams became even better at an accelerated rate, whereas the bad teams became disastrous. Figure 9.5 presents the actual values or path coefficients, which demonstrate that the leadership in a team is formed relatively early on (Month 1), and it predicts both the subsequent leadership in the team and the team's level of potency and performance.

Going back to the concept of vital forces, I believe that one main element in team development that has often caused teams to fail when it has not been properly developed is the total leadership system. Through proper transactions and the use of transformational leadership to augment transactional, each individual's contribution to development and performance is maximized. It is the mechanism or process that facilitates the ideal of creating unity through diversity. Consequently, the sharing of leadership becomes feasible when commitment has been built into the team, along with members' identification with each other, the mission, and the vision (see Box 9.3). A Zulu expression, *Umphakati*, perhaps captures this best: Within the best teams, "we are all together on the inside." This would represent a very pure definition of identification and would provide a firm basis for members being willing to share in their leadership and followership responsibilities as well as to sacrifice as needed for the good of the team. Stated another way, if we all identify with what is important, who cares who is leading as long as it is the best person or people for the task at that particular moment in time. Such levels of trust and identification are not easy to build, but once built, they can have dramatic, positive effects on a team's effort, performance, and perhaps most important, sustainability (see Box 9.4).

Figure 9.5   A Time-Based Model of Team Leadership, Potency, and Performance

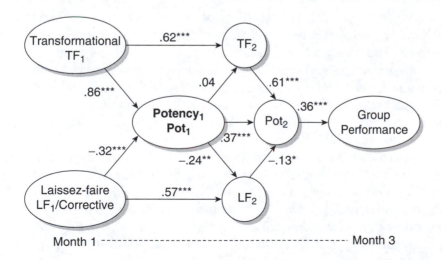

SOURCE: Sivasubramaniam, Murry, Avolio, and Jung (2002).

Note: $*p < .05$; $**p < .01$; $***p < .001$

BOX 9.3   The Role of Leadership in Building Teams

Pearce and Conger's (2003) definition of shared leadership states: "a dynamic, interactive influence process among individuals in groups for which the objective is to lead one another to the achievement of group or organizational goals or both. This influence process often involves peer, or lateral, influence and at other times involves upward or downward hierarchical influence" (p. 1). Pearce (2004) adds to this earlier definition of shared leadership, suggesting that it is a "simultaneous, ongoing, mutual influence process within a team that is characterized by 'serial emergence' of official as well as unofficial leaders" (p. 48). Shared leadership can also be "viewed as a property of the whole system, as opposed to solely the property of individuals, effectiveness in leadership becomes more a product of those connections or relationships among the parts than the result of any one part of that system (such as the leader)" (O'Connor & Quinn, 2004, p. 423).

One common factor often identified with failure to implement a team system successfully has been lack of emphasis on the role leadership plays in building effective teams, which has typically been examined at the individual not at the team or shared level (Sinclair, 1992; Stewart & Manz, 1994). Yet, only a few models of team effectiveness (Gladstein, 1984; Kozlowski, Gully, Salas, & Canon-Bowers, 1996) have explicitly considered leadership to be one determinant of team effectiveness. This, too, will change as more authors realize the central role leadership plays in team development.

BOX 9.4   Connecting Between Team Transformational Leadership and Performance

Bass, Avolio, Jung, and Berson (2003) examined the leadership in U.S. Army platoons, focusing on both individual and team leadership. In the initial pilot study, 18 platoons participated. Three months prior to attending a 2-week training camp, the platoon officers and the platoon itself were rated in terms of the full range of leadership. Leadership ratings of the platoon commander, the sergeant, and the platoon itself predicted performance in Joint Readiness Training Corp. (JRTC). Specifically, transformational leadership and active transactional leadership predicted more effective performance in JRTC. Passive leadership and laissez-faire leadership were negatively related to performance.

Avolio, Jung, Murry, and Sivasubramaniam (1996) provided initial results by using a newly designed instrument of team leadership behavior called the Team Multifactor Leadership Questionnaire (TMLQ). Initial results with this sample and the platoon samples from the U.S. military produced six interpretable factors. These six factors primarily replicate the full range model discussed with individual leadership, including the following scales: Inspiring, Intellectual Stimulating, Individualized Consideration, Transactional Contingent Reward, Active Management-by-Exception, and Passive Management-by-Exception/Laissez-Faire Leadership.

Sivasubramaniam, Murry, Avolio, and Jung (2002) contrasted the higher-order factor of transformational leadership and corrective transactional leadership in teams to predict how potent the teams perceived themselves to be over time, as well as to predict performance over a 3-month interval. Student teams participating in this study rated themselves at Month 1 and Month 3, respectively, on how they perceived the collective leadership of their respective teams. Leadership ratings taken early on were highly predictive of subsequent leadership ratings for both transformational leadership and corrective/passive management-by-exception. Transformational leadership directly predicted the performance of these groups while also predicting performance indirectly through levels of group potency. A similar pattern emerged for active management-by-exception leadership.

SOME THINGS WORTH REPEATING AND REFLECTING ON

- The early foundation for building an effective team leadership system is clarifying expectations, roles, and goals.
- Teams must go through adaptive conflict and tension to develop themselves to higher levels of potential and performance.
- Task conflict can contribute positively to group performance and satisfaction, whereas relational and process conflict contribute negatively and should be eliminated as soon as possible.
- Shared leadership rarely, if ever, means equal contribution.
- A direct parallel exists between leadership at the individual level and leadership in teams, which allows us to take the same concepts that work at the individual level of leadership and apply them directly to teams.

Let me leave you with some core questions to reflect on:

Have you ever been on a team where all of you were truly together on the inside? Do you know of a team that has fully achieved unity through diversity? What would you have done for that team versus what others did that did not achieve that level of unity?

A SHORT EXERCISE

I would like you to use the After Action Review (AAR) questions referred to in this chapter in your next meeting. Allow yourself 5 minutes at the end of your meeting to go though the steps and to discuss how you could have improved what you did as a group. What was your group's reaction to using this process?

CHAPTER 10

TRANSFORMATIONAL LEADERSHIP SYSTEMS

An Eastern monarch once charged his wise men to invent him a sentence to be ever in view, and which should be true and appropriate in all times and situations. They presented him the words: "And this, too, shall pass away." How much it expresses! How chastening in the hour of pride! How consoling in the depths of affliction.

Abraham Lincoln

Are you familiar with the NIMBY acronym? It means, *not in my back yard.* I use it here because often people will say to me in workshops, "You know, what you are teaching us sounds great. In fact, you should teach my boss these concepts. But in our organization, its chances of success are nil." *Not in our organization.* I often wonder how such strong views are shaped. Is it part of the identity of the individuals that keeps them from seeing their possible selves in the making? Perhaps, it is in the collective identity of the organization that has developed such a strong view of leadership that to break it down, revise it, or transform it, is nearly impossible to do. And yet, I marvel at those individuals who simply do not accept how others define them, but rather they author their own story and identity, and that becomes the guidance for their leadership model. Of course, without all of the other players in our life script, what gets written as our life novel is in large part shaped by the individuals and situations we interact with over time. The life novel is never single-authored by any means.

Madeline Cartwright was a principal at Blaine Elementary School in Philadelphia, Pennsylvania. Blaine Elementary School was in one of the worst sections of inner-city Philadelphia. At that time, 60% to 70% of the parents of students attending Blaine were drug addicts. The school was a horrible building, filthy and dirty, with few redeeming qualities. When Madeline took over, she was appalled at the conditions in the school. It came to a head one day when she asked a group of students to simply talk about what happened to them on the way to school that morning. It was an innocent enough question, but what she heard was so disheartening that her resolve to make a difference was firmly rooted. One student talked of the gunfire on the streets that he had avoided. Another talked about her fears in having to go by one of the many crack houses on her street. A third mentioned the sound of the cracking glass beneath her sneakers from the shot-out store and car windows. Another mentioned her father being taken by an ambulance to the hospital for a drug overdose and wondered aloud whether he would be there when she returned home; often, they brought him back the same day. Her description was so matter-of-fact that this obviously was a common occurrence in her home.

Exhausted by the morning's events, Madeline and another teacher left the building to go to lunch at a local McDonald's restaurant. Halfway through their lunch, Madeline remarked on how clean the restaurant was compared to the school, indicating that the McDonald's, compared to her school building, was like paradise. She did not know how teachers could expect children in her school to feel good about themselves when the hallways were so filthy, the bathrooms stunk of urine, and the windows were taped from being broken time after time? Again, Madeline's resolve to make a difference in the school was growing each day.

When she returned to the school that afternoon, she asked the head of the maintenance department to take another shot at getting the bathrooms and school in shape and asked what he needed to achieve her request. He responded politely that the maintenance staff were doing the very best they could and that they could not do much better, given their resources. Madeline did not accept this response.

On a Friday afternoon, she went down to the maintenance department to ask the custodians to leave her some supplies for a few cleanup jobs she wanted to do over the weekend. Although reluctant, the head of maintenance complied with her request. She was the principal of the school, after all, giving him a specific order. Belonging to a "hairball" organization has some advantage, and having those traditional views of leadership can be an advantage for exercising power for a good cause.

Over the weekend, Madeline went into the worst part of the school—its bathrooms— and hyper-cleaned them. When the maintenance staff returned on Monday, she indicated that, from now on, those bathrooms were expected to be *that clean.*

Interestingly, when several of the parents heard this story, they were amazed that some bureaucrat would get down on her hands and knees to scrub bathrooms for their children (see Box 10.1). Not too long afterward, some of those same parents began to volunteer to help in the school. Her actions created some positive tension, and things began to change in the school.

With these beginning actions, Madeline was changing how others in the school viewed the identity of the principal, from a maintainer of the status quo to an agent who would assume personal responsibility for change. It was a change that Madeline talked about in her own identity as a leader and a change that members of her school community were also seeing emerge before their eyes.

In the spirit of making the children feel good about themselves, Madeline instituted a rule for the children that was directly against district policy—most districts' policies, I am sure. She sent a letter to parents indicating that if their children came to school in dirty clothes, she would ask them to change and would wash their clothes on the spot. Fortunately for Madeline, her husband was quite handy and was able to buy and fix up a washer that was placed in the school's gymnasium. And if students came to school in dirty clothes, the clothes were washed. When Madeline took a position, she reinforced it 100%, with no deviations. The last thing these kids needed was more deviations in their lives.

To increase attendance in school, which on a bad day was around 30%, Madeline took charge of calling each parent to see why the child was absent from school. If there was no answer at home, she got in her car and went straight to the family's home. If the child was home and not sick, she took the child in her car to school. Attendance quickly soared to 80% and to 90% on a good day without Madeline having to use her car very often to recover students.

The superintendent, who was extremely supportive of Madeline's efforts, was getting heat from other administrators and politicians for the radical steps Madeline was taking, in part because she was redefining for herself and the school what principal leadership meant. He knew that Madeline would do what needed to be done for the sake of the children, even if it meant violating district policies. He identified with her efforts but also had to work within the system he was heading, and at times he had to reign in her efforts. It was never easy. In the end, he became the champion in Madeline's leadership story, which helped Madeline in the transformation of her school system (see Box 10.2).[127]

BOX 10.1 Transformational Leadership and Innovation

Following the work cited in Box 4.4, R. E. Keller (1992) studied 66 project groups containing professional employees from three Research and Development (R&D) organizations. Keller assessed intellectual stimulation of the project leaders as evaluated by followers. The level of intellectual stimulation predicted the quality of projects completed. Keller also reported that transformational leadership had a greater impact on project quality for R&D project teams engaged in research versus teams engaged in product development. Transformational leadership was more impactful when the products were being conceptualized, as opposed to what might appear to be a more transactional process of getting products developed and shipped out the door. By the way, R. T. Keller (2006) replicated and extended this work in a 5-year longitudinal investigation, again finding further support for these positive linkages.

(Continued)

(Continued)

Similarly, Howell and Shea (1998) studied the impact of champions of innovation on 40 radical product innovations in 13 organizations. More effective champions were described as engaging in more ambassadorial and scout activities, whereas less effective ones operated as guards. The former characteristics contributed to teams that had a greater sense of potency and new product innovation success. Teams that were "guarded" created less penetrable boundaries that resulted in less optimal environmental scanning and isolation. In terms of the context, the authors also reported that support for innovation in the organizational culture was an important factor in enhancing a champion's success.

Continuing in the spirit of making the students feel good, Madeline knew that most of these children continually heard from their parents and others in their neighborhoods what they *couldn't* do and what they *couldn't* accomplish, which would become part of their identities: You cannot succeed given your starting point. Madeline instituted a policy that any time a child in the school came across the word *can't,* she or he should cross it out. At a school assembly where this new rule was announced, she picked up an old book, took a red pen, and crossed out the word *can't* each time it appeared on a page. She told her students that *can't* was no longer part of the English language in this school.

> *In most organizations, most really new things get accomplished by subterfuge and cunning.*
>
> Ted Levitt, editor of *Harvard Business Review*

BOX 10.2 School Administrators, Transformational Leadership, and Performance

Leithwood, Jantzi, Silins, and Dart (1990) concluded that transformational leadership practices were more strongly related to school restructuring outcomes than were transactional leadership practices. Management-by-exception had a strong negative correlation with school conditions and processes. Developing a shared vision and consensus about group goals and providing intellectual stimulation contributed most positively to the conditions and processes associated with school restructuring and performance.

Leithwood and Jantzi (1990) examined the leadership practices of administrators in each of 12 schools. These schools had been identified as having highly collaborative environments. The driver developing this collaborative culture was the top school administrator, who displayed transformational leadership. Specifically, "principals have access to strategies which are transformational in effect and, hence, assist in the development of collaborative school cultures" (p. 276).

Leithwood and Steinbach (1991) examined the everyday problem-solving strategies promoted by school principals. Nine elementary school principals were designated as expert problem solvers versus typical principals of less effective schools. Expert and typical type principals varied substantially in how they approached dealing with problems. Comparisons of expert versus typical principals are provided in Box 10.3.

There is much more to tell about Madeline's efforts back at the school, but I think it suffices to say that no one thought she could accomplish what she accomplished by simply choosing to lead up, down, and horizontally. Her secret to being successful was that she saw possibilities first in her role and identity as a leader and then in her process of dealing with obstacles, while modeling the way for others. The modeling part took courage, as she met with a lot of resistance from school leaders that did not see themselves as transforming agents. Her perspective was different from that of the average transactional bureaucrat, who feels compelled to work always within the system's boundaries, no matter how flawed it might be (see Box 10.3). She saw many of the threats in her school's community as an opportunity to inspire others to challenge what they thought they *can't do*. She also exhibited something essential to leading under duress: She had the moral courage to follow what she believed and the physical capability to do something about her beliefs. Many leaders know what is right, but a lot of leaders do not have the moral courage to act on what they know. It is knowing what is right and having the courage to act that make the difference, in combination. She was only one person, but what an amazing vital force she created once she got the staff, parents, and teachers working along with her and fully identifying with her efforts. This meant that they were coming to know what was right, and she was building their efficacy or confidence to take the actions to make a difference.

Transformational leaders often believe that they face a challenging problem rather than what others might describe as an impossible crisis with no alternatives. Viewing it as a challenge versus a crisis leads them to open channels for input, as opposed to closing sources of information like the guards who curtail innovation described above. They become more open to incorporating ideas and suggestions from their followers, peers, or supervisors into final decisions even when the opinions differ from their own. Transformational leaders express their desire to hear more arguments before coming to a conclusion. They are not the types of leaders who seek consensus when the building is on fire. They are dealers in hope, and their hope constitutes both the will and the search to find many different ways to success. And, like Madeline Cartwright, when they have to take a stand out ahead of others, and often alone, they do.

BOX 10.3   Different Principal Leadership Styles

Expert	Typical
Interpretation	
Seeks out and takes into consideration other views	Assumes that others share interpretation
Looks at problems in relation to the larger whole or mission	Views problems in isolation
Goals	
Works to get staff agreement	Is more concerned with achieving own goals
Has less of a personal stake in her or his solution	Is strongly committed to preconceived notions
Principals/Values	
Places highest value on respect for others	Allows impact of decisions to fall on clients
Constraints	
Anticipates obstacles	Does not anticipate obstacles
Adapts flexibly to unanticipated obstacles	Responds ineffectively to obstacles
Views obstacles as opportunities	Views obstacles as obstacles
Solutions	
Outlines clearly the process for problem solving and the expectations of others	Is unstructured
Checks collaborators' interpretations of problems	Assumes that others have same interpretation
Remains open to new and challenging views	Sticks to her or his own views
Ensures that follow-up is planned	Plans rarely
Affect	
Uses humor to diffuse tension and to clarify perspectives	

What can we do to develop the type of leadership we observe in the principal in Box 10.3? When I work with organizations, I use Figure 10.1 (see p. 142) to reinforce several important points about developing a full range of leadership potential. Let me highlight these points for your consideration.

- Leadership development is a time-based process and cannot be accomplished at one point in time. Indeed, one may have to wait for events to occur to nurture leadership development, which I would call *natural learning*. You can create meaningful events, but you must also be prepared to take advantage of those that arise in your life stream as well. This is where serendipity and taking advantage of opportune challenges and events when they arise in your life stream play significant roles in your leadership development.

- The context must be considered when planning the leadership development intervention to anticipate obstacles and enablers that impact the transfer of those things learned in the workshop back to the job.

- Boosters are needed to reinforce what has been learned and to provide support during crucial transition periods. These boosters can help to keep learners more accountable as well as to further address the immunities that keep systems and people from changing. In the follow-up boosters, change typically occurs after people have had a chance to reflect on what they were taught in foundation workshops and especially where they are receiving reinforcements for trying new ways of leading.

- The more training interventions are seamless with respect to transferring what was learned back to the job, the more impact training effects will have over time. Stated another way, if we use unrealistic cases or artificial modeling exercises, we should not expect a positive transfer of leadership training. We should always incorporate issues of relevance to our target audience, something we now refer to as authentic leadership development. This simply means making it real and valid.

- Training should be conceived of not as a discrete program but rather as an organizational intervention supported by other interventions over time in a continuous stream of attempts to shape the leader's view or identity and then how that identity gets translated into actions. Training must have a clear, central purpose that will affect how people perform in their roles.

The training cycle begins with an appreciation or awareness of each trainer's ideal/implicit model of leadership. From there, it works through building an understanding of the full range model, applying that model in terms of feedback on the trainee's leadership style, then developing a plan for intervention and mechanisms to follow up on the plan. The intent over time, after a series of applications and substantial practice, is to encourage the trainee to adopt new ways of leading and following in order to achieve a higher level of development and performance. The cycle is continuous and iterative in the sense that it repeats itself at each new level of awareness and application. It also can be sloppier in reality than I have described above as events can dramatically shape how quickly or slowly leadership development occurs.

Earlier, I introduced the idea of the life stream in terms of explaining individual development. In the context of the model presented in Figure 10.1, we are converging several life streams into an event called a *leadership training workshop*. How then can we optimize the development of each participant when the readiness and needs may be so different?

One way to approach the problem of individualizing training programs is to assume it is important from the outset and to find mechanisms before, during, and after the intervention to address each individual's readiness and potential. This often requires a significant change in developer's thinking about training (see Box 10.4).

One strategy I use to address these differences is to create peer learning partners who are often connected after the workshop to facilitate and support the transfer of learning back to the work context. It may be individuals from the same

Figure 10.1   Leadership Development Cycle

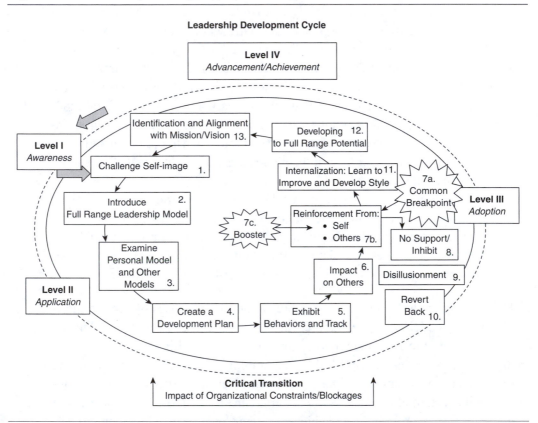

SOURCE: Adapted from Quinn's empowerment cycle (Quinn, Anderson, & Finklestein, 1996).

NOTE: Most leadership development efforts involve I and II. Developmental impact depends on critical transition/booster. Change in internal perspective must eventually align with external opportunities, constraints, and perspectives.

or different organizations. The learning partnerships can be set up on the basis of the individuals' mutual goals, proximity to each other, willingness to work together, need to work together, developmental readiness, or some combination. The main point here is that I use peers to facilitate the process of development beyond the formal training program. Another goal is to enlist peers in sharing the responsibility for maximizing each other's development by supporting it where it counts—back at work.

In addition to using peers in face-to-face interactions following a formal training intervention, I am exploring the use of various forms of information technology to see how I can enhance training effects on learning and performance.[128] For example, I can send an individual, via cell phone, some developmental tips based on feedback he received on my leadership surveys and the goals he set prior to or during the workshop. I can also send a question for him to reflect on that addresses a learning point from the workshop. With many applications now moving to the smart cell phone, I can use this facility for many creative follow-ups, including sending short message videos to stimulate thinking about one's perspectives on leadership, challenges, positivity, and so forth. Indeed, we all may very well find that the smart cell phone, or whatever it emerges into, could be the major breakthrough for developing leadership, because unlike the trainer, it is always with the learner and can be used as a means to boost training effects.

In addition to the follow-up noted above, it is essential to consider the context we are dropping leaders back into following any leadership intervention. For instance, if we are training people to be more individually considerate, what mechanisms exist to support this style of leadership in their home context? Are people rewarded for taking the time to develop other people or to take on the role of a learning partner? Where is the recognition for such behavior, and who might be its champion at more senior levels?

The *booster* concept in the leadership development cycle is rooted in several principles. First, what individuals learn about leadership development may take some time to take root in identity, thought, intentions, and then actions or behaviors. Recall, we all have our implicit theories of what constitutes our leadership style and our identities, and they do not readily change after one or two interventions. The booster is a mechanism for getting people to revisit and reflect on what they have learned after they have had some specific experiences to tie to the model and workshop intervention.[129]

If we start out by assuming that the first training workshop provides participants with a frame of reference against which to catalog and interpret subsequent experiences, the first booster can be used to reflect on how the person has changed his or her scripts to interpret events related to leadership development.

Recall, I indicated that one can create, to some degree, one's own life biography or "novel."[130] What I should say is that this process is cocreated, as followers, peers, and supervisors also become part of how you shape the views you have of your leadership. This is all part of that larger change process being undertaken, of which you are ultimately in the role of being the lead author.

Second, booster sessions can also provide an opportunity to hear how others are applying the model in practice. This can be done in a learning group that periodically meets with or without a facilitator or by bringing back the entire group for a follow-up workshop.[131] It can also be accomplished via a website discussion group or blog. The booster is an opportunity to revisit one's plan for personal development, to revise it, and to estimate progress toward achieving its goals and objectives. This pattern of thinking and behaving is very much engrained in the idea of doing reflection and after-action reviews for debriefing.

Third, the booster is a symbolic representation that leadership development is CPI. CPI represents *continuous personal, people, and process improvement*. The booster helps to continuously revise what one has been doing to improve on her or his plan. It can be a corrective intervention or simply something used to reinforce continuing with the plan that, at present, seems to be hitting all its targets.

The booster session or follow-up sends a signal to everyone that the organization is serious about the change process and that they are going to work on it until the change that is desired is achieved. This takes a lot of discipline, which many organizations typically do not show.

I believe that leadership training should be seamless with respect to the context in which it is intended to be embedded. I mean here that it should be tied to something real that someone wants to transform. I call many of the workshop activities in which I have trainees participate *real play* versus the traditional term, *role-play*. What issues must the leadership system address in the organization? Why not make these issues target points for change in the leadership intervention? Of course, some people are more or less ready to deal with real issues, so the ones you pick can be "low-hanging fruit" to start off, and then you can move incrementally to more significant challenges. By using this strategy, I can build the collective efficacy and potency of the group I am working with to take on even more significant challenges. By building collective efficacy in a group, I can effect a transformation, both in context as well as in performance.

An example of this strategy occurred in some work I was doing with Abdul Latif Jameel in Jeddah, Saudi Arabia. We started an in-house MBA program with a large Toyota distributor that is headquartered in Saudi Arabia but has locations throughout the Middle East. As part of their course work, teams of students had to work on a real strategic issue that the company was going to address or was addressing. The teams would become internal consultancies, developing proposals for change that were presented to the board of directors. The board of directors essentially graded their proposals by either funding or not funding them.

One of the first teams of MBA students made a proposal to the board, which the board enthusiastically funded. The project was to develop a system that addressed some of the key problems distributors were having getting parts to their Lexus customers around the country. The team then went ahead and implemented the proposal providing evidence that the cost savings from this one initiative was sufficient enough to cover all of their tuitions for the MBA program. Upon hearing these results, the board reaffirmed its commitment to the program by agreeing to put through 75 managers.

In the above example, you come to realize that, at some point in the process, you recognize that you have moved from being just a trainer to being an organizational change agent in the trainees' eyes as well as in your mind. I hope these are always completely intertwined. If you have recognized this already, then you can see my philosophy of taking leadership development and building it into a strategic intervention. Remember the basic principle: leadership must be viewed as an integrative process and system. It is difficult to conceive of training leadership in any way that does not include the context in which leaders, peers, and followers must operate over time and, more importantly, change, with demonstrable impact on key performance indicators.[132,133]

During the past several years, I have been involved in situations where an organization totally reengineered its systems and processes only to find out afterward that it had totally destroyed trust and loyalty, making the old leadership system even more dysfunctional. In one instance, I attended a meeting with a group of reengineering experts at which the presenter kept saying proudly to the senior executives in the room that, in their work, they don't use the "f" word. He did not mean the one you might be thinking of, or at least the one I initially thought of, to be perfectly honest. He meant *facilitator*. Reengineering was a technical process that was not going to be muddied by those soft interventions that used facilitators and talked about group processes such as leadership. This group of senior managers, who were engineers themselves, met his comments with smiles and nods of approval.

I have come to realize that I must talk in system-level terms and use appropriate technical jargon to help senior executives understand that any training intervention undertaken will affect multiple systems with each frequently tied to or, more likely, embedded in the other. This is at the basis of what people in leadership today might call a *complex dynamic*. According to complexity theory, if you change even one small aspect of an organizational system, it could impact everything else. For example, look at the changes that occurred because one U.S. Supreme Court case ruled in favor of abortion rights called *Roe v. Wade*. What about the emergence of President Mandela in Africa and the consequences for leadership in other African nations?

How about the impact one Australian Aboriginal runner had on a host nation for the Olympics in terms of an Australian's view of diversity? One moment, event, or individual can have a profound impact on many things that change the course we pursue.

In another example, an organization was investing millions of dollars in a new Enterprise Resource Program (ERP) information system. The culture of the organization was very resistant to change, and after 6 months of false starts, the senior management asked the consultants implementing ERP to rewrite the code to fit their organization's culture and processes. Although the consultants were against doing this, they finally agreed with their client. What did they agree to do? They agreed to take an information processing system designed for modern business functions and retrofit it to an organizational culture, structure, and system designed for the 1950s. Their new design took them back over 50 years.

We have learned in healthcare contexts that the safest and highest-quality care for patients is definitely a systemic issue. However, we also know that each individual must take ownership for the patients' healthcare for the system to function properly. It does not matter what technical or operational system you put in place; if the staff at all levels and within all units does not take ownership for the patients' healthcare, we know that some patients will die due to mistakes. One cannot help but take notice that some physicians and nurses say that one of the leading causes of deaths in the United States is entering a hospital.

Let me summarize the main thrust of this chapter. Our focus has been on examining the context and how it is intertwined with the implementation of a leadership development intervention. I have argued that it is difficult, if not impossible, to achieve the goals of any leadership intervention without considering the context in which it is embedded. Yet, one cannot be overwhelmed by the context either, and sometimes a leader such as Madeline Cartwright must first attack the context to ignite a significant transformation in the way people think and behave. Change the context first, create positive tension, and then worry about changing people's perspectives later. In this chapter, I have attempted in a very direct way to reverse the figures (usually leaders and followers or teams) with the background or context in which they operate. I gave examples to show that, by attending to the context, we have a chance at also changing the individuals who operate within that context. We cannot be separated from the contexts in which we interact. At the very least, if you change the context, you gain people's attention, which is a prerequisite for successful development.[134]

Let me raise the importance of the context to the success of leadership interventions using the following example. I worked with a Wall Street firm that decided to go to teams. A visionary leader kicked off the process, supported by an energized Organizational Development (OD) staff that put every ounce of effort into moving the support and technical operations to a team-based environment. People in the New York City offices put up enormous resistance to the proposed change. The resistance was so fervent that the firm decided to move approximately 600 operational staff 1,200 miles away from New York City in order to nurture the team concept away from New York's highly individualistic culture. This was considered far enough away to allow the team concept to grow, but near enough to shuttle back and forth as needed.

The team concept was introduced in a new facility in the South. This was a pure greenfield operation, except that many of the managers who were transferred to the new facilities came from the old hierarchical, authoritative system. They became, for the next 3 years, the *relos*, or those who relocated, which should suggest how quickly they assimilated into the emerging culture.

The former New Yorkers in this firm were highly suspicious of this socialistic, team-based system emerging in the South. They were extremely concerned that this was the management's covert attempt at leveling individual bonuses. Some New Yorkers found the team concept intriguing; however, most were either annoyed by it or simply angry about it and were not reserved about expressing their dissatisfaction.

The difficulties this organization had in going to teams is a testament to preparing the context for such radical change. The relos had a difficult time dealing with the change in roles from being a manager and having all the technical knowledge and power to being a coach—a term that was actually used for their position. They now were supposed to facilitate more than manage. Yet, the immediate image I had after meeting the relos was a 300-pound football player being asked to ballet dance. Even if he can do it, it still looks a little funny.

It was typical for managers in New York to call down to their support staff in the South and ask for *who* is in charge of this or that. When the response came back that a team was in charge, often the person in New York went ballistic. For the entire 3 years I worked with this organization, there was a constant struggle between the team people from the South and the individualists from the North. Indeed, even though many people in the firm were pleased that their firm was doing something ahead of other Wall Street firms, when it came down to the practical day-to-day operations, they exerted constant resistance to going to a team-based system—especially one professing to be what I now would call *collective individualism*. For all intents and purposes, the team concept was evolving in a very hostile context and, over time, had achieved certain aspects of Ubuntu.

One humorous example of the resistance was relayed to me by the head of the OD team. Mike had asked to have his business card redone to label his position as senior coach, rather than something like vice president. Every time he sent in his corrected card to New York City, it came back the same old way. It took an intervention from the worldwide head of the firm's support operation to get the corrected card sent to him, after 6 months of trying. Certain cultures are sown deep.

In line with other events, the visionary who began the team process left the firm, along with the OD consultants who had championed the team concept. Also, some key coaches who had become converts subsequently left. Of course, they set up a consulting group to do with other companies what they attempted to do in this firm. I must add that it is unfair simply to say that the team concept no longer exists in the firm; it did before they were completely acquired a few years back and operations in the South were shut down.

My experience now with many organizations indicates that, at an organizational level, the organization must go through a crucial transition (the squiggly line, as shown in Figure 9.1)

To go from a team concept being driven by its founder to a belief that is fully identified by the workforce and its collective leadership. Like individuals, the organization must also be developmentally ready for the change. In this instance, the Wall Street firm was not ready, at least not in total.

Let me summarize some additional points raised above. First, the context is so crucial to the transformation process that often the context must be changed first or challenged if any real change is to take place and become rooted. Second, individuals we would evaluate as transformational do not accept the context as given. Indeed, they see opportunities in the context that others see as overwhelming obstacles that cannot be overcome through will or many options for change. Transformational leaders see the elements of the future in the current context and move to capitalize on what they see before others do, which puts them ahead of the competition.

Third, we used an example here of going to teams because, in discussing leadership systems, my colleagues and I see team or shared leadership as being one very important and distinct level of leadership in organizations. I said earlier that, in many organizations today and into the foreseeable future, one key challenge is to understand what constitutes the full potential of shared leadership processes in teams. This challenge is on the doorstep of all the organizations that are currently develing operations and moving toward a truly networked organization.

Following our tradition, let me leave you with one question to consider for further reflection. Take a look at the context in which you currently lead and follow. *What would you challenge or change to effect a true transformation in the way your organizational unit develops the full potential of its members?*

SOME THINGS WORTH REPEATING AND REFLECTING ON

- The context includes the people and the other operational, financial, and technical systems; thus, it must be changed if a full and successful transformation is expected.

- At the same time, leaders have to examine their personal identity about what constitutes leadership and what needs to be changed. Many leaders struggle with this transition as their identity is the source code for their behavior, and accessing the source code takes a lot of reflection and support.
- If you take the context as a given, then you are always limiting your ability to transform the organization.
- Know the part toward which you are directing the transformation of the people and the context. Do not ask the programmers to rewrite the code to make things as they were, because you are avoiding what those things can and should be.

BOX 10.4

Wofford, Goodwin, and Whittington (1998) examined a cognitive processing model to explain how transformational versus transactional leaders view the way to work with followers. In their field study, they tested whether transformational versus transactional leadership used different schemas and scripts to interpret events and interactions with their followers, which would then result in their choice of different leadership behaviors to those events. Wofford et al. reported support for transformational leader cognitions being related to their choice of how to act transformationally with their followers. What this early study showed was that we have to train not only the leaders' behaviors but also their thoughts about choosing those behaviors with followers.

A SHORT EXERCISE

We have noted that organizations have immunities to change, which lead to resistance and most organizational change processes failing. Take a look at your current organization and address the following questions:

- How do people typically resist change at the outset?
- What are some of the things that you do to resist change?
- How can you model a more positive approach in your own behavior to support change?
- What type of promise can you make and keep that could sustain change?
- Have you chosen something to measure to assure you are tracking the changes you have chosen? Have you been diligent in tracking change?
- What has been your most successful change promise? Why was it most successful?
- How can you reapply what you learned?

CHAPTER 11

CORE PRINCIPLES

Even if you're on the right track, you'll get run over if you just sit there.

Will Rogers

I will begin with the four principles that I have interwoven throughout my discussions about leadership in this book. Each of these principles can be applied to understanding individual-, team-, and organizational-level leadership.

The first principle pertains to managing one's *vulnerability*:[135]

Principle 1: *The most exemplary leaders, teams, and organizations are balanced in how they manage their vulnerabilities. Vulnerabilities are embraced, understood, dealt with, and certainly not avoided.*

The immediate reactions to this statement by many people in leadership positions typically range from disbelief to challenge. The reaction is so consistent that it appears to represent an archetype across many cultures. Many leaders are afraid to discuss their vulnerabilities. Ironically, our individual and collective strengths are typically tied to understanding and compensating for our core collective vulnerabilities. More importantly, if you are not feeling vulnerable at some point in time as a leader, you are likely not leading aggressively enough or taking enough risks with people challenging you or your goals.

Many people would like to believe that leaders are close to being invulnerable; however, throughout history this has been proved false, particularly concerning the ones described as charismatic. There are many examples cited in the leadership literature to support this conclusion, going back to Weber's foundation work on the emergence of charismatic leadership.[136] Weber argued that one precondition for charisma to emerge in organizations is a crisis—meaning people feel vulnerable and look for some center of gravity to move toward. Charisma was described as being crisis-induced, and some evidence supports Weber's position, although other evidence reported by Bass (2008) indicates it is not always necessary to have a crisis for a charismatic leader to emerge.

Weber's basic argument is that a leader comes along in crisis and shows those in desperate need the way out of their mess. Through the leader's direction and confidence, there are typically greater levels of hope and a promise of a better future. Examples such as Hitler are often used, depicting how he brought the German people out of the economic ruin and despair created after World War I. The same can be said, but for vastly different reasons, for Franklin D. Roosevelt around the Depression, for Winston Churchill in World War II, and perhaps in business for Steven Jobs with Apple because he returned to turn this company around to being a major force today in three industries—music, computing, and telecommunications.

Similar and less dramatic effects can be seen with Alan Mulally, the new CEO of Ford Motor Company, or Anne Mulchay, the CEO of Xerox. Both of these leaders came into their roles when their companies were on the brink of financial ruin. For many in those companies, these leaders offered the way out of hell, and we know from history that they may take them away from hell or plunge them directly into it as we see with the Hitlers, Pol Pot, Idi Amins, and other similar despots.

We can speak of countries, companies, teams, and individuals, and to a large extent our conclusions would be the same. Being cognizant of one's vulnerabilities and allowing for a sufficient level to be exposed to challenge by others is one basis for sustaining effective leadership over long periods. Lose touch with your vulnerabilities, and you run the risk of them overwhelming you. Simply face them head-on, and you may still fail. No guarantees. Facing them is necessary but not sufficient for success. This only provides the basis for the remaining three principles.

In the time the world knew of Mother Teresa, she always appeared so vulnerable. She was frail and typically ill, to some extent because of the lifestyle she chose and because of the very sick people she helped throughout her lifetime. Her vulnerability did not just attract the world to her; it created awe and reverence for her deeds and, ultimately, power. Being vulnerable made her all the more credible and trustworthy.[137]

This type of vulnerability has often drawn followers to leaders such as Jesus Christ, Ghandi, Martin Luther King Jr., Lech Walesa, Nelson Mandela, and Daw Aung San Suu Kyi.

> ### BOX 11.1   More on Visionary Leadership and Its Impact[138]
>
> Martin (1996) reported a strong positive relationship between visionary leadership, trust building, and follower attitudinal reactions with 4,454 executives. Setting the vision and building the context of trust were two crucial elements in achieving positive and supportive reactions from followers.
>
> Berson, Shamir, Avolio, and Popper (2001) examined the relationships between vision content and ratings of transformational leadership for 229 leaders. They reported a positive relationship between vision content that was optimistic and ratings of transformational leadership. Also, they reported that this relationship was moderated by organizational (size, for example) and personal (experience as a manager, tenure, for example) attributes. Specifically, transformational managers with high amounts of experience and low tenure produced the most optimistic visionary speeches. (Also refer to den Hartog, Van Muijen, & Koopman, 1996, for additional discussion on content analysis of visionary statements.)

Are we more willing to listen to leaders who are more vulnerable? I would say *no*, if the leaders did not exude a high degree of confidence, a clear set of values, a strong belief system, and a tendency toward self-sacrifice. Mother Teresa's case is probably the clearest example of how one's vulnerabilities represent the core of what constituted her inner and outer strengths. She said she was never worthy of the attention being given to her and surely not worthy of receiving the Nobel Peace Prize. Yet, the world thought she was worthy and granted her the respect that world-class leaders command. Several days after her death, the Catholic Church seemed to be searching for ways to expedite her sainthood. Even the Church was concerned about reducing cycle time for a worthy cause.

When asked 10 years ago about his father's accomplishments, Martin Luther King III indicated that his father would be pleased with the progress in our nation regarding racial integration and equity but not fully satisfied at all. Today, with the first African American U.S. president, I wonder how both Dr. King and his son would reply to the same question. Many top Black leaders, including the president of the United States, directly attribute their success to Martin Luther King Jr. and the sacrifices he made to make their successes possible.

We can contrast the individuals described above with Mobutu Sese Seko, Adolph Hitler, Pol Pot, Joseph Stalin, Ferdinand Marcos, Nicolae Ceausescu, Benito Mussolini, and Chairman Mao, who were ruthless in protecting their vulnerabilities, fearing exposure and other potential risks to their influence and control of others. Now, look at their institutions and their shadows. Who, in the end, was most vulnerable in terms of sustaining their causes throughout the course of history?

A few years back, I reviewed a training video produced by the Blue Angels, who are U.S. Navy pilots that fly exhibition shows, demonstrating their ability to fly very close in formation through many challenging routines and at extremely high speeds. A clear message from the interviews with each of the Blue Angel pilots is their keen sense of each other's vulnerability. Two of the pilots said they were just average pilots given an extraordinary opportunity to represent the Navy and their country. They said time and time again that each of them must know even the smallest weakness of each other in order to be successful. In their job, the line between success and failure is death. No one can be hesitant to point out either his own or another member's vulnerabilities. Through the examination and understanding of each of their vulnerabilities, the team creates a vital force that endures over time.

A portion of the Blue Angels video discussed the team's debriefing process. Now, imagine your management team sitting down and reviewing each member's weaknesses, mistakes, and hesitancies. Consider, now, that rank is irrelevant. This is the process the Blue Angels go through every day, and it requires generally twice the amount of time to debrief than it takes to fly the actual mission. Also, the Blue Angels conduct a predebriefing before they even execute the mission. This is actually pretty common practice among teams that perform in threatening contexts. We have seen similar types of debriefing with teams that protect nuclear facilities as well as police SWAT teams. To go through such debriefs requires a sufficient level of exposure to being vulnerable to get to ground truth, which is what everyone on these teams perceives happening.

I often suggest to a team to pick an event that is a significant performance event for the team and to go through the process of debriefing that event. It is a wonderful process for reflective learning if you are willing to place your vulnerabilities on the table. It helps groups and individuals explore very deeply where they have traveled in their process of working together. I came across a quote that symbolized for me the core of this process—reflective learning—which I keep coming back to in this book: T. S. Eliot, in his poem *Little Gidding V*, said that the outcome of exploration is "to arrive where we started, and know the place for the first time."

The former dictator of Romania, Nicolae Ceausescu, was so concerned about any threats or challenges to his power that he never allowed any questions to come from the audience during his speeches. At one rally, a brave individual stood up and began to question his policies. He got so unnerved that he could not speak. He finally had to leave the stage to collect his thoughts before he could return to the event. What these leaders miss are those people willing to say, "You are at the cliff's edge. Stop, before you fall." The question you might ask yourself is, What type of vulnerability do you want to characterize your leadership?

This vulnerability was clearly evident in the words of the Blue Angel aviators, who saw their mutual or collective role as being the advance team for the U.S. Naval Air Force. One of the pilots remarked that his role was to represent the guys out there on the carriers in the Gulf who make it possible for the Blue Angel pilots to be the kind of representatives they are for the soldiers and for our nation. They understood not only their own vulnerabilities but also their fellow pilots'.

Let me now move to a second principle, which is *identification.*

Principle 2: *Through identification, the greatest force for control is created between leaders and followers, and that force is called commitment, not compliance.*

Good people who have a strong set of core values choose things we can all identify with and come to support fully over time. Passion comes from identification; without identification, there is no passion and little, if any, commitment. Often, a leader must become adept at articulating a message to people in ways they can identify with that message. Steven Jobs accomplished this with Apple by conveying to his workforce that Apple, a renegade company, would design and produce computers for "everyone else." Other companies were producing computers for the engineers and techies, whereas Apple would produce computers for everyone else without the technical sophistication needed to run a typical computer. This, of course, was opposite to the image in most computer companies that a technical writer wrote code that only a technician could read. The company symbolized what Jobs was striving to get others to identify with by flying the skull and crossbones flag above the Macintosh lab.

We see this sort of identification in similar types of organizations that have created compelling missions such as Teach for America, Doctors Without Borders, The Red Cross, Google, and Mothers Against Drunk Driving (or MADD). The connection power created by the mission of an organization goes far beyond any other rewards that might motivate individuals who work for this organization.

Returning to Apple, ironically, its fear of being too vulnerable in the market likely created its greatest vulnerability, which was its failure to release its operating system. This strategy was in contrast to the DOS operating system, which was released to clone manufacturers of PCs back in the 1980s. Apple's fear of giving up that which was most cherished led to its loss in the race to be the standard operating system for all personal computers. The company, like the individual leader or team, failed to manage its vulnerability and in the end lost its identification in the market for at least a decade or more before trying quite a different strategy with its iPod. With the new strategy, they opened up the market to programmers to provide apps for their phone that Apple itself could not have created as quickly or as efficiently.

Today there are over 100,000 applications, and as Google readies to enter the smart cell phone market with Android, Apple's decision to open up to outside programmers may remain its distinct competitive advantage for some time to come.

All great leaders find a way to get their followers to identify with something that becomes so central to their values and belief systems that leader's and follower's values become inseparable.[139] In Mother Teresa, we saw an extreme version of commitment to beliefs and values. She was the prototype of what people believe should represent service to humankind or a servant leader.[140] Amid terrible scandals in which officials of the Catholic Church have been charged with taking advantage of their position and power, here stood this small and frail woman doing what she always believed was within her job description. She felt she did not deserve the recognition that was placed upon her, because she would say time and time again, she was just doing her job, which was simply an extension of God's work. That is the reward, and people of all faiths identified with her and the beliefs she showed through her sacrifices for humankind.

Similar types of identification can be seen with the current president of Brazil, Luiz Inacio da Silva. This president came from a very similar and humble background to many of his citizens and in 6 years has positioned Brazil to be one of the top economies in the world. Many Brazilians identified with his humble roots and he with theirs, which built enormous credibility for him to enact significant changes in the way Brazil's economy and political systems had operated over a century's time.

Once a leader like President da Silva has his followers' identification, most other things are relatively easy to accomplish, except one: getting people to question what is being done, to be sure the leader does not fail with spiraling successes. I guess we could rephrase a popular aphorism here: Be sure that as a leader, you do not wallow in your own success. People identify with the vision and mission and, therefore, are willing to put in the extra effort typically needed to accomplish great visions. If you ask members of the team or organization, they would likely say, "There is no question why we are doing this. There is only a question of how we are going to do what is the right thing to do." Teams that can identify with a central purpose can argue all they want because everyone knows in the end that each member is striving to achieve the same end. The Blue Angels do it for survival at the lowest end of motivation, but they also do it for the highest end of motivation in that we have labeled their identification with their mission of representing the entire U.S. Navy. They identify with representing the U.S. Navy and, more importantly, their country by displaying the very best of what they can accomplish. That is the power of identification, and it can be wonderfully taken advantage of and horribly misused by what I call *pseudo transformational leaders*.

Leaders such as the late Marshall "Bo" Applewhite of the Heaven's Gate cult, or other cult leaders such as Jim Jones and David Koresh, horribly misuse the power of identification. The same is true with more recent leaders such as Bernie Madoff, who stole billions from investors for years without anyone stopping his Ponzi scheme. Ironically, with Mr. Madoff, there had been several government teams called in to audit him over the years, but frequently the government sent in young consultants who were so taken with Mr. Madoff's charisma that they repeatedly failed to challenge his practices. In fact, many even asked to work for him after their audit was completed.[141]

People in the Heaven's Gate cult identified with Applewhite's vision of a better life beyond their current one. The Hale-Bopp comet, speeding past Earth in 1997, was seen as the sign that it was time to leave this life, according to Applewhite and the 39 out of 40 other cult members who agreed to commit suicide along with him. (Perhaps you are wondering about the last person. Why didn't he go with the group? In an interview following the demise of Applewhite, he said that he believed in the vision but was just not ready to go yet.) More than 900 did the same in a Jonestown, Guyana, jungle commune in 1978 for another cult leader, Jim Jones, leader of the Peoples Temple, a California-based religious cult. And then there was the disaster caused by the Branch Davidians, David Koresh, and the U.S. government in Waco, Texas.

These religious leaders simply abused the power of identification that people had in them and their vision and became messianic in their own minds of who they represented. They kept everyone from questioning their vision; unfortunately, in their own minds, they became way too invulnerable, as did their followers. Their sense of invulnerability reduced significantly what they were able to learn from others. And as often is the case, they preyed on the most vulnerable people from whom to gain commitment. God did not want David Koresh to be the only man having sex with very young women in his congregation. There is no gray area here; he used religion to leverage his power over others for his own gain, which was personalized power. So, I would not call it commitment demonstrated by followers. I think *coercion* and *compliance* are much more appropriate terms. For people who did not have a strong character and who needed continuous, positive recognition, cult leaders often gladly provided followers with what they needed to gain their absolute power. It was always for their selfish gain, but ironically, it usually resulted in their demise as well. You can rest assured that these types of leaders are out there today, some using religion, some using positions in government, and some using positions in business, who protect their own vulnerability at the expense of exploiting their followers' vulnerabilities.

I said earlier that crises can induce charismatic leadership because people are looking for those types of leaders who can help them feel safe and well again. We only hope, in these instances, that the right people come along; unfortunately, history shows that this is not always the case and that the best barrier to their emergence is to develop strong, independent followers.

BOX 11.2   Follower Self-Identity

Howell and Shamir (2005) identify some theoretical propositions regarding how follower traits might influence what we end up observing in leader and follower relationships (also see Dvir & Shamir, 2003). These authors identified followers' self-concept clarity and collective identity as important factors in determining how followers form relationships with their leader. To the degree that followers have a strong and personalized relationship with a charismatic leader, they are more likely to show blind loyalty, obedience, and deference to the leader.

Carsten, Uhl-Bien, Patera, West, and McGregor (2007) examined individuals' cognitive or social constructions of followership, reporting that the common attributes in people's heads were followers being passive or proactive in their roles. One can conclude that not all followers are created equal in the minds of leaders or followers. This pattern was reflected in the classic work reported by Kelley (1992), who conceptualized followers as falling into four quadrants based on whether they are active or passive followers and whether they are critical or noncritical thinkers.

In one case, a leader appears to have come along that most in the world can identify with: Nelson Mandela. Mandela has become a symbol for getting people to identify with his mission through inclusion in a society that has controlled, in the strictest sense, exclusion of one group from another. He has been committed to a vision of one South Africa and has sacrificed dearly as a consequence of his beliefs. His sacrifice, confidence, persistence, sense of fairness, and vulnerability have made his chance of success all the more possible.

Any leader willing to endure the type of treatment he endured in prison for 27 years is worth listening to and, arguably, identifying with in his efforts—particularly someone who has repeatedly said that together they will build the future, not re-create the past, now with Blacks in a superior position over Whites in South Africa. He has repeated over and over again that looking back to blame others will never create the "new" South Africa, a difficult thing to say when members of one's family have been grossly discriminated against for generations. One could ask, What makes South Africa different from the former Yugoslavia or Afghanistan or Lebanon or Iraq or Kenya? I am very biased in my response because I believe that Mandela is and will be one of the truly great leaders of the previous and well into the current century and beyond.

I had the good fortune to meet a young Zulu chief on one of my trips to South Africa. I was at a conference center outside Johannesburg that focuses on providing an environment where guests and residents can learn to appreciate each other's cultural differences. It is called a *cultural village*. I was assigned to stay that evening in the Zulu village. I met this man, who was apparently a respected king of the Zulu tribe. I spent time with him that evening, discussing various differences and similarities in our lives. He was about my age, yet our life streams were very different. I found him to be a very pure, positive force in life. He was so positive and warm to others, always smiling and embracing people with his words and his touch.

I heard from one staff member a story about this positive and optimistic Chief who brought me back again to what T. S. Eliot said: "Know the place for the first time." Apparently, before the end of apartheid, this particular chief had been arrested as a young man and put into one of the worst prisons in South Africa. Typically, when one was placed in this prison, one was never heard from again. For several weeks, this remarkable chief received one beating after the other. At the end of this period, he realized, lying on the floor of his cell, that he was nearing his death. Most major bones in his body were broken, including his jaw. He was preparing himself for his last beating, lying there on the cell floor.

One thing he had extreme difficulty with was the realization that his family would not know where he had died and could not prepare him properly for moving on to the next phase of his existence. Lying there on the cell floor, he heard, very faintly, voices coming through the drainpipe in the floor from another cell. He began to say his name, but it was almost inaudible because of his broken jaw. Somehow, however, he was able to be heard by the people in that next cell as he asked again and again for whoever was there to tell his family where he died.

One person who heard his pleas told a visitor what she had heard. When this visitor left the prison, she immediately went to the house of a friend who knew of a sympathetic and very wealthy White woman who had considerable influence in the apartheid-era South African government. On hearing her story, the woman went immediately to the prison to inquire about the chief's whereabouts. Now, having been publicly exposed, the police could not take the chance of killing him. So, for weeks they denied that he was in the prison; this gave the chief time to recover to an acceptable level to be released. Yet, this lady persisted until finally the chief was healed enough to be allowed visitors.

Through a fortuitous event, a great man's life was saved. And for me, it was a privilege to meet this person who exuded optimism, kindness, and good humor. He shared with me no sense of hatred or vengeance. I have met many Black South Africans, like this chief, who have moved from the past to create the future. One of them is General Mobuto, who spent several years on Robbins Island with Mandela. He, too, is one of the warmest and most gracious persons I have had the good fortune to meet in my life stream, and together they have made me realize how important it is to put the past where it belongs—in the past.

In many ways, like the Zulu chief I mentioned above, General Mobuto embraces life in such a positive way. He is revered by people in the military but not for being a military man; he was not. General Mobuto told me many interesting stories, but one I want to share is about how he and the other African National Congress (ANC) leaders imprisoned on Robbins Island dealt with their incarceration. He said the group of ANC leaders put on the island were all highly educated men. For example, he had a PhD, and Mandela was a lawyer. Their guards were very young men with little formal education. Over time, the ANC leaders came to label the prison Robbins University or Mandela U. Mobuto and Mandela decided they would teach their captors about the type of quality people imprisoned there, and ultimately, the world would also find out about their deeds. They also focused on their own education to prepare themselves for leadership roles in the postapartheid government.

General Mobuto said to me that these young guards knew little about life and often would consult with him and other ANC leaders in prison on how to deal with the normal life situations that a young man must confront. Over time, the guards became advocates for their prisoners. Once again, General Mobuto had assumed the role of professor, and he and his colleagues did so by questioning a basic assumption. They questioned that a prison could not be a center for learning and ethical conduct. They proved in their situation that this assumption was terribly wrong, and in so doing they gained the identification and trust of their captors (see Box 11.3).

BOX 11.3 Transformational Leadership in Correctional Institutions

Gillis, Getkate, Robinson, and Porporino (1995) examined the ratings of supervisors given by offenders within correctional service institutions. Those who rated their supervisors as more transformational had more positive work attitudes and greater work motivation. Nonleadership was related to lower work motivation and job involvement. The credibility of the leaders was related to whether they were seen as transformational.

Many of these leaders, along with Mandela, have been able to build a very strong sense of identification with the new South Africa. I have never met a White, Black, or colored person in South Africa who did not have a positive feeling for Mandela in general, even if he or she did not agree with the government's specific policies or initiatives. People respect this great man and realize the type of sacrifices he has made to transform South Africa into what could be the most highly diverse and integrated nation on earth as we turn into the next millennium (see Box 11.4).

> **BOX 11.4   Charismatic Leaders and Impression Management**
>
> Gardner and Avolio (1998) proposed a model of impression management to help identify the strategies used by charismatic or transformational leaders to influence followers. Specifically, they provided an explanation of the linkages between a leader's motives, values, vision, and desired identity images and the type of impression management strategies used by the leader to create with followers a charismatic relationship.
>
> Charismatic leaders are described as using impression management (IM) strategies such as framing to position their vision in ways that their words amplify audience values and stress the vision's importance to followers so that they will come to identify with it overtime. "How the vision is communicated thus becomes as important as what is communicated" (Westley & Mintzberg, 1991, pp. 43–44).

By the way, those prison guards from South Africa did grow up. I heard General Colin Powell speak recently in Minneapolis, and he described an experience he had at President Mandela's inauguration. General Powell said that when Mandela ascended onto the stage to give his acceptance speech, he was seen waving enthusiastically at a small group of men sitting in the first row. Powell observed this group of White men smiling with pride as their new president took over the highest office in their country. You may have guessed they were Mandela's correctional officers on Robbins Island.

Let me move to the third principle, which is *trust* and has been implied in our discussions of vulnerability and identification:

Principle 3: *Our highest trust is typically afforded to those we identify with and to those who often appear to be or are vulnerable.*

I said "appear to be or are vulnerable" purposefully above. Let me try to explain. Some leaders set up the *common-enemy strategy*. They are saying, *I* and *we* are all vulnerable to "evil" forces if we do not work together, and of course they mean also, "If you don't follow me." Some such leaders are quite elaborate in their use of impression management techniques that get followers to think that everyone else is out to get them and that only through their unquestioning support will the result be favorable. Recall former President Ronald Reagan's call to contain and defeat the "evil empire," referring to the former Soviet Union. Former President George W. Bush did the same in creating what he called the "axis of evil," including in that North Korea, Iraq, and Iran. Similar strategies are oftentimes used by leaders, including in the countries labeled the axis of evil, to gain the support for their leadership from citizens who fear the consequences if actions are not taken. Some people come to trust them because often their descriptions of threats contain some validity. Unfortunately, the trust is usually misplaced, and such leaders, depending on how deeply troubled they are, will take advantage of that trust until there are no more credits to offer from followers.

We see this level of misguided trust in the former televangelist, Jim Bakker. He continually lied to his congregation and took advantage of their sacrifices to enhance his wealth and satisfy his extravagant desires, all in the name of God. He was a symbol of the church and, indirectly, of God. Through his affiliation with the church and his position, along with his ability to be identified with his constituency, he was able, with then-wife Tammy Faye, to steal repeatedly from his congregation. Yet, when he violated a core aspect of what people identified with in the church—Thou shalt not steal—he was summarily thrown out. Another televangelist, Jimmy Swaggert, was thrown out for another sacred violation—Thou shalt not commit adultery.

BOX 11.5   Credibility, Trustworthiness, and Leadership

In a 1997 survey conducted by the Society for Human Resource Management (*HR News, 1997*), a national sample of respondents indicated that the number one attribute they look for in managers is credibility and trustworthiness. More recent surveys of trust, authenticity, and leadership continue to show that it is one of the most, if not the most, valued characteristics in leaders (Avolio & Luthans, 2006). According to a Watson Wyatt 2002 survey, total return to shareholder (TRS) over a 3-year period was 186% higher for those companies that had high levels of trust compared to those with low levels of trust. In an update to this study reported in 2006, found that 72% of employees believe their immediate bosses act with honesty and integrity in their business activities, but only 56% believe that about top management total return to shareholder (WorksUSA, 2002).

Based on a 2004 U.S. poll of working adults cited in Avolio and Luthans (2006), approximately one third of the respondents indicated that the leadership in their organizations exhibited authentic leadership, frequently, if not always. Being trusted shows up continuously as the top attribute associated with exemplary leadership as shown by the meta-analytic results of Dirks and Ferrin (2002). Dirks and Ferrin's meta-analysis summarized 40 years of research on trust and produced the following results: Trust in leadership had a significant relationship with job performance ($r = .16$), organizational citizenship behavior (altruism, $r = .19$), turnover intentions ($r = -.40$), job satisfaction ($r = .51$), organizational commitment ($r = .49$), and a commitment to the leader's decisions ($r = .24$).

Time after time, study after study has shown that the most important attribute a leader can have is trust, or integrity (see Box 11.5).[142] With high levels of trust, one can almost rule the world, and unfortunately destroy it as well.

Mother Teresa gained the trust of millions worldwide. Anyone willing to sacrifice for so many people had to be trying to do the right thing. When the choice was to do something for someone else, for herself, or for her own organization, she chose others over herself. The world came to trust her and to identify with her cause.

Another example is Sam from the Canadian correctional system mentioned earlier. Sam was a technology supervisor in a unit that repaired damaged government cars, among other metal products. His unit had one of the lowest recidivism rates in the correctional services. I first met him on a tour of a high-security prison in northeastern Canada. I was contracted to train leaders to be more transformational, with the hopes of translating this alienated workforce into productive members of Canadian society. Sam was one of the supervisors who attended this workshop, and in many ways he was already a highly transformational leader in terms of leadership style and impact on inmates.

It was apparent to me from the start that Sam treated inmates as real people: He gave them respect, he was tough on them, and he worked very hard not to have to see them again and again and again. He realized that these people needed no further instruction on how to fail, nor did they need to be reminded they had failed themselves, their families, and their society. They were in his shop because they had failed at most everything they did, including crime.

Sam identified with their situation. He worked to build their confidence and self-efficacy, and he treated them as he would expect them to be treated once leaving the institution, with respect and dignity. He was attempting to create their future in the present and showed that, with support, they could make it out there on their own. Years after leaving prison, many wrote Sam, many called, and some even named their children after him. And, unfortunately, some came back to visit for extended periods. Even Sam could not transform everyone.

Sam was trusted, and he put trust in others. In his shop were people guilty of manslaughter and murder, and Sam put his back to them, realizing full well his vulnerabilities. Yet, his controls were probably far greater than in most other supervisors' workshops. His group of inmates demonstrated a commitment to him, along with the controls that existed in the system. I believe that if anyone were to have harmed Sam, and certainly many could have, the reaction would have been swift and uncompromising. That person's future would have been very limited in that society, and as in any organization, appropriate controls would have been activated for anyone who needed it—by one's peers.

Sam was an extraordinary teacher, and like Stacey and Madeline, he got people to do things we are amazed any individual could accomplish. Amazing things happen when people are committed. Predictable things happen when people are controlled through compliance.

BOX 11.6   More on Mediation: Self-Efficacy and Transformational Leadership[143]

Shamir, House, and Arthur (1993) were one of the first to propose a link between transformational leadership and self-efficacy, suggesting that self-efficacy is a potential mediating mechanism through which transformational leadership impacts followers' performance. The rationale for this prediction is based on the idea that transformational leaders' success in working with followers is in part based on their ability to connect a follower's self-concept or identity to the mission of their unit or organization (Kark & Shamir, 2002; Shamir, 1995). Carless, Mann, and Wearing (1995) obtained MLQ ratings of 695 middle-level branch managers employed by a large Australian bank who were rated by their direct reports. The focus of the study was to examine whether self-efficacy predicted transformational leadership and whether, in turn, group cohesion mediated the relationship between transformational leadership and performance. The authors reported that self-efficacy was a significant predictor of transformational leadership and performance. Group cohesion was a significant mediator of leadership and performance.

Walumbwa, Avolio, and Zhu (2008) provided the most direct test examining the links between transformational leadership and the self-efficacy levels of followers. Walumbwa et al. reported that transformational leadership was positively related to follower identification with one's work unit and self-efficacy. They also reported that these meditational effects interacted with followers' estimates of means efficacy in terms of predicting performance. Means efficacy was the confidence rating that followers gave to the tools, people, processes, and resources that they had available to successfully perform their work.

The perspective of some leaders drives them to see the future in current events. It helps them consider and understand how one crazy idea can make a business innovation, a new medical breakthrough, a completely new direction, or a cause to pause and reflect (see Box 11.6). The leaders' perspectives can drive the leaders to see the merits of investing in people versus viewing them as a cost on the balance sheet. It helps some leaders to wonder why someone is not doing so well on a particular day. It provides leaders with the understanding to be empathic toward others. Yet, at another extreme, it influences leaders to say things like, "That will never work," "I don't get paid to develop people, so just make do," or "Don't you ever do anything right?"

The fourth principle is the most abstract, but I discussed it with you earlier. It pertains to a person's *perspective*.

Principle 4: *The leaders demonstrate a perspective or frame of reference or both that they can put themselves in those situations that others endure that maybe are different from their own, which enables them to fully appreciate how others feel and react.*

This perspective, which I have now introduced at several points in this book, represents the lens through which leaders look at the world. Behind the lens is the person's "software," which interprets what is focused on and perceived.

By the way, those second in command and below have lenses and software, too, and if they are built like the leaders, then asking them about the organization when the leader is absent should result in the same answer, and often does. A large part of the institution left behind by a leader is the perspective-taking capacity developed in followers. Variations in perspective-taking capacity lead some people to protect themselves from an intrusion into even their slightest vulnerabilities; others will fully expose themselves, knowing that they are doing the right thing. They deeply believe that it is worth the risk for the good of their group.

I introduced Mort Meyerson, the former CEO of Electronic Data Systems (EDS), earlier in the book. Recall that, after retiring from EDS, Meyerson was called on by Ross Perot to run his new organization called Perot Systems. Although hesitant at first to come out of retirement, he took the position and never looked back. In a follow-up interview, he indicated that nearly everything he did at EDS in his leadership role changed in his new role. He discovered that the needs and requirements of his workforce at Perot Systems were completely different, and at first he felt quite vulnerable. It took time for his perspective to shift, but it apparently did over time. Many returning CEOs, however, do not have this perspective shift and stay fixed in the model that used to work for them.

In the interview, Meyerson described the types of controls EDS placed on its employees. Yet, when he began working at Perot Systems, he could see that the new workers were different from the ones he had led at EDS. First, they knew many things that he had no idea how to do. They were technical specialists who had knowledge that went way beyond his capabilities, as well as those of other managers at Perot Systems. Second, they sought development and were not content simply to receive what the corporation decided to provide them in terms of responsibility and training. Third, he quickly realized that a control mentality completely underestimated the employees' ability to achieve their full potential. He had to change his perspective and style to accommodate a change in their needs, capabilities, and desires. Things changed, and to be successful, so would his perspective about the needs of employees and his role as a leader. He became the coach versus the commander, the facilitator versus the foreman, and the teacher versus the tormentor.

Meyerson's story has been repeated again and again throughout the United States and in other countries that are developing organizations representative of more advanced social systems. Here, I mean that members of the organizational community are well equipped to take more responsibility for the direction it chooses. A tremendous perspective shift is occurring in the way managers control people and work processes, which is now coming to fruition as we enter the period of social networking. We see that entire communities can be created over night to accomplish something and to work together with little or no formal hierarchy, such as with open source computing. This was recently tested where a group of scientists did an experiment in which they positioned 10 weather balloons around the United States within undisclosed locations. They then announced a $40,000 prize to anyone who found all 10 balloons. The team that won the prize did so in less than 9 hours. This team literally had to coordinate thousands of people it never met to achieve this task in less than one day. This is the age in which we are all leading and following, which does not discard heroic leadership; it adds to it.

Going back to an interview with Steven Kerr, the former Vice President for Corporate Leadership Development at GE, Kerr described Jack Welch's direct involvement in the development and coaching of leadership in GE. He described Welch's passion for getting his senior managers to honor the initiatives, not to control them.[144] He described Welch's intimate knowledge of the career paths of more than 1,000 GE employees in their succession-planning program. He argued in the interview for critical reflection, as we have described in the debriefing or After Action Review (AAR) process. As I suggested earlier, to reflect critically requires being comfortable with one's level of exposure and vulnerability. One also has to believe in what one is doing and where an even better idea can make a better contribution to performance. It requires trust to feel safe to offer and receive critical ideas. And, it requires a shift in perspective that coordinated conflict around ideas is a very good process for the acceleration of change and the unearthing of insightful ideas.[145] Thus, we need to build the perspective-taking capacity of leaders in order for them to be adaptive to the changes they will certainly confront throughout their careers and lives.

A deep perspective, once developed in individuals, provides them with a frame of reference that guides their actions to a point where we describe their behavior as being self-sacrificing, being solidly committed to others, being trustworthy, and having a high level of integrity. James McGregor Burns said that transforming leaders sacrifice their own gain for the gain of others. They are morally uplifting.[146] To paraphrase Nelson Mandela, let's not look back to right the wrongs; let's look forward and not forget the wrongs but ensure that the system we build won't allow them to ever happen again. And the system he is referring to is based on core values and beliefs to guide exemplary behavior.

Prior to the 1994 World Cup rugby games held in South Africa, many of Mandela's advisors had asked him not to open the games. Rugby was what many in South Africa identified as a White man's sport. The national rugby team had never had a Black player. If he opened the games, many would say he would be indirectly supporting the legacy of apartheid. On the day of the opening ceremony, President Mandela opened the games by holding hands with the captain of the rugby team while also wearing a jersey with his number on it. Not only that, but the national airline of South Africa flew a 747 jet, painted in the national colors of the new South Africa, several hundred feet above the stadium. Mandela rose and said that there was one South Africa and one national rugby team, and on the field that day was the team representing the new South Africa.

If you have traveled in any country that plays rugby seriously, you realize the importance of his actions and this statement to the identification that people have with their country. It was a profound, and some said very courageous, step forward to building the new South Africa, which everyone must be a part of for it to succeed. Mandela could have read the political winds to decide what his choice should have been that day. Fortunately, he appears to be a leader who demonstrates a deep belief and inner perspective that guides his actions in even the most difficult circumstances.

We, too, here in the United States have had such leaders—in Abraham Lincoln, for example, who abolished slavery, knowing full well that he would throw the nation into civil war. Yet, he did so because he knew, without law or guidance of external rules or procedures, the difference between right and wrong. Leaders who make such difficult decisions take action based on their inner beliefs and values, and over time, people come to trust those leaders to do the right thing. We trust their perspective; it provides us and them with very predictable courses of action and a basis for framing the problems we must eventually confront together. Moreover, their perspective becomes the shadow of their institution, which is left behind. We strive as a nation to provide justice for all.

Now, one question you might have is, do these leaders exist in business? I would say that recent evidence might suggest otherwise as greed and unethical behaviors seem to dominate the business headlines. However, I think in fairness to business, there are leaders who are genuinely authentic and set a high standard for moral and ethical conduct. For me, those leaders include the current richest man in the world, Warren Buffett. Mr. Buffett is known as an uncompromising, ethical leader, who many business leaders turn to for advice and counsel, including the second richest man in the world, Bill Gates.

Today, Mr. Buffett says he does not have to seek many proposals, because they typically end up coming to him. The story is generally consistent in that people who have built a company from scratch but realize to grow it they will need more capital come to Mr. Buffett with their proposal. What they are looking for is someone who can not only support them but also leave them to continue to grow a business they love. Indeed, Mr. Buffett typically asks them what they will do with all of the money once he buys their company. He looks to invest in those who say, "Continue working, because I love what I do." By the way, his retention rates of CEOs after buyouts are near perfect, as opposed to many leveraged buyouts where the first thing the owners do is fire the top management team.

Having now reviewed these four very important leadership principles, let me conclude this chapter with a question for you to reflect on. *If you have known anyone with the type of perspectives I have described above, what type of influence did that person have on your perspective, and how does he or she still influence the growth of your perspective even today?* Although often one is enough, some people are fortunate enough to have had more than one individual in their lives who had this type of impact on their development. It is my belief that, all other things being equal, those people emerge as our best leaders.

SOME THINGS WORTH REPEATING AND REFLECTING ON

- The four principles discussed in the chapter are necessary, but not sufficient, for achieving the full range of leadership.
- Showing one's vulnerabilities, building identification, and gaining trust make up the highest form of control. It is called commitment.
- What may appear at first to be a liability may very well provide the basis for an individual's, team's, or organization's greatest strengths.
- What makes the best leaders predictable is the breadth and depth of their perspective.

Let me break with the past tradition and tell you about one more leader who did not accept her context and who demonstrated through her actions a deep and profound perspective to care for others. Her name was Amy Beatrice Carmichael. She was born on December 16, 1867, in Belfast, Ireland. Amy's father died when she was quite young. Following his death, she threw herself into serving others. When she was barely 20 years old, Amy took off for missionary work in Japan. Following her work in Japan, she traveled to China and then to Sri Lanka. She returned to Ireland briefly for the funeral of the head of her mission. Soon afterward, however, she went to Bangalore, India. She remained in India for the next 55 years. In India, Amy created an organization to protect the children of the temple. One tradition among the Hindus was that a girl child was promised to the gods before birth in order to curry their favor. The girl would then be delivered to the temple women and be prepared to be the prostitute of the priests by age 5. Amy created the Dohnavur Fellowship. She was affectionately called Amma, or *mother* in Tamil, and worked to protect thousands of little girls from being sacrificed for the good of the church. Perhaps what is more remarkable about Amma is that, after a tragic accident, she spent the next 20 years bedridden but still led her missionary organization in an exemplary fashion. When I personally feel that things are getting too difficult in my organization, I am reminded of people like Amma, Stacey, Sam, and Madeline.

A SHORT EXERCISE

I would like you to choose something about yourself that you feel inhibits your leadership and that you feel you need to be more transparent about. Once you have chosen some aspect of your leadership, sit down with a small group of trusted colleagues, and ask them for feedback on the area you have chosen. The goal is to be more vulnerable and to pick something, going forward, you can display more transparently with them and others. Set that as a goal, and explain it to others who do not know you.

CHAPTER 12

PERFORMANCE

Every team that wants to move toward significance and greatness has to decide what truths it will hold to be self-evident and to get those values circulated through the organization.

Pat Riley, former head coach of the New York Knicks

A guiding principle about leadership that I try to keep in mind is that if a leader has a direct impact on performance, she or he is probably too directly involved in what the other person or group is doing. This point goes back to some of our earlier discussion of control systems and effects of identification in organizations. Controlling someone at work is not necessarily leading someone at work, and it is especially not working to develop a sense of identification and ownership in what he or she is doing. Leaders cannot directly control commitment; it comes through building trust, identification, and a willingness to support the leader, group, organization, and ironically enough, the leader managing his or her vulnerability.[147,148,149]

What we really need to explore is exactly how both leaders and leadership can indirectly and positively influence development (see Box 12.1). Some authors have called this substitutes or surrogates for leadership.[150] I really do not think they are always substitutes for the leader, but rather they can be extensions of the leader that through leader and follower interactions have become engrained aspects of the leader's style and perspective now embedded in the follower. Indeed, James McGregor Burns, who coined transforming leadership, specifically focused on explaining how leaders transform followers to be leaders. In his view, the ultimate job of the leader was to develop followers into leaders who could carry on and continue to advance performance—taking, in my view, a rather indirect view of leadership impact.

> **BOX 12.1 Transformational Leadership and Bank Financial Performance**
>
> Geyer and Steyrer (1998) reported that, in a large-scale study of German banks, transactional leadership was more predictive of short-term performance, whereas transformational leadership was predictive of longer term financial performance of bank branches. What subsequent research has shown is that transformational leadership is mediated in its impact on longer term performance through such variables as commitment, trust, efficacy, identification, potency, collective efficacy, and cohesion (Avolio, 2005; Bass & Bass, 2008; Bass & Riggio, 2006). For example, Kark, Shamir, and Chen (2003) reported in a sample of Israeli bank managers that transformational leadership was positively related to follower efficacy ($r = .13$) and collective efficacy ($r = .31$). This relationship was mediated by the followers' level of identification with the leader.

Recall my earlier comments regarding the importance of focusing on the second in command and whether you could discern the leadership of the organization from meeting those individuals. What information would you get if you talked with the second in command? I argued that you would get the message from the second that was originally communicated by the first but in her or his words, filtered through that individual's identification with what the leader had set out to accomplish in the mission or vision.

Of course, without a clear mission and vision, you usually get many, many different stories, because there is no one script that is followed (see Box 12.2). The second in command translates what the leader's intentions, aspirations, and vision are, and those translations become part of the script he follows in his role as a leader. However, like most stories, as it is passed down the line, it gets interpreted by each individual, but as long as it stays true to its core message, those interpretations may help to forward the message throughout an entire organization and community, if not society.

Let's explore the indirect effects of leadership by examining how the articulation of a leader's vision may impact followers and the direction he or she chooses to lead. A leader articulates a vision of some desired future state, for example: All children in this nation will someday grow up in an environment where the full range of opportunities is available to them solely on the basis of their ability. The articulation of this vision creates numerous examples in people's minds that relate to their own circumstances. My children and your children can all compete for the same jobs, for the same colleges, for the same homes, and for the same communities, and the competition is based on merit, not on gender, race, or ethnicity. This was the type of vision I was hearing on a national level during the 1960s in the United States, and it was at that point only a vision. For example, there were no CEOs of *Fortune* 500 companies that were women or any senators or Supreme Court justices that were women.

The elemental ideas comprising the vision will affect each of our willingness and desire to make a difference in how we contribute to a nation's progress and how we translate that desire into action. For example, the vision could lead human resource professionals to design selection systems that are culture fair and based on merit. Community leaders might exercise the vision by developing programs to uplift the disadvantaged through training and special education projects. Still other advocates might take a stand in the courts on what constitutes fair treatment of people at work, in education, and in the broader community. The leaders of the country would develop and support legislation such as the Civil Rights Act, and now the vision is reinforced by the power of law, in case the law or external controls have to substitute for internal commitment (see Box 12.3).

BOX 12.2   Leading at a Distance

Howell, Neufeld, and Avolio (2005) reported that the relationship between charismatic leadership and business unit performance varied, depending on whether followers were close to or at a distant from their leaders. Charismatic leadership had a positive impact on bank financial performance where followers were rating the charisma of a leader who was at a distance.

Shamir (1995) reported that distant charismatic leaders were viewed as expressing more ideological positions and visions, showing less fear of being criticized for voicing their opinions. Close charismatic leaders were seen as being more considerate and open with others, setting higher performance standards, using more original and creative thinking, and having a greater impact on task-related motivation.

Ultimately, if it is successful, a leader's vision will have a positive impact on people's identification with the cause or core focus of the vision, and the identification may lead to a myriad of different actions and behaviors that reinforce the core vision. Leaders indirectly affect others through the picture of the future they create via a vision, and it is the individual's interpretation of that vision that results in how he or she chooses to commit and behave. One of the challenges for any visionary leader is to figure out how to align followers' efforts around a shared purpose that allows for enough individual freedom without losing the potential for coordinated effort.

> ### BOX 12.3   Attributions to Social Close and Distant Leaders
>
> Yagil (1998) reported that the attribution of charisma to socially distant leaders was related to the level of acceptance of the leader's ideas and ability to perform the mission as perceived by the followers. Attribution of charisma to socially close leaders depended on personal modeling and confidence expressed in followers' personal ability.

Here is a very different example of an indirect form of leadership that links to what I call *individualized consideration*. A young employee is hired by an organization. At the outset, she is not very confident in her abilities, which are considerable, according to everyone else's judgment. Her initial manager spends the first several months of her tenure trying to identify the source of her poor self-concept before considering taking developmental steps. After learning about her strengths and weaknesses, he comes to some conclusions about which developmental opportunities could enhance this individual's self-concept. He tries to boost her confidence by saying she is capable of taking on more challenging tasks and by providing specific examples to reinforce his points. Through the confidence and support he transparently expresses to her, he builds confidence in her to try some more challenging tasks with adequate support to reduce the probability of failure.

In the beginning, the leader sacrifices a great deal of his time without any apparent short-term gain or benefits for bottom-line performance. Over time, the employee's confidence grows, and it starts to effect a change in her judgments about herself. This is seen in her providing new information and data when presented with the same old question: Who am I, and what am I now capable of doing? If fully successful in this transformation, the leader is able to build in his employee some internal controls and standards of what she is now capable of doing or choosing not to do in the event he is not around to coach her through future challenges. Hopefully, someday she will do the same for others who eventually report to her. And at this level, we can say that the manager's influence would have cascaded like falling dominoes to new employees with whom he would never have direct contact.[151] The eventual shadow of this leader is being institutionalized through his developmental efforts with his follower.

To initiate the developmental process, we can go back to Figure 8.2. The leader depicted a future different from the person's conception of what she felt she was capable of fulfilling. This different scenario created some positive tension for her to consider changing and the support from her leader for her to try new directions. As Albert Einstein once said, "a happy man [person] is too satisfied with the present to dwell too much on the past." The leader was able to convey the positive sense of that future to his follower and over time to get her to believe in it and to believe in herself. The believing in herself represents the transformation in perspective from "He tells me I can do this" to "I know I can do this" to "I know I can help others do this." She takes actions and decisions that stretch her and those around her. She challenges her own thinking and that of others she would never have previously questioned. She begins to expand her boundaries of vulnerability and moves to positions of increasing challenges. Eventually, she can get others to identify with things that are important and to delay her self-gratification for the good of others when needed.

One day, her manager moves on and she must take over his leadership responsibilities. She is alone physically, but she retains the cell of her leader throughout her life in terms of the model or theory of leadership she has learned through his mentorship. And like falling dominoes, his influence has continued to influence her, and she, in turn, has a positive influence on the next person, and so on down the line. Each of their theories of leadership, or perspectives on how to develop, become more aligned and significant to developing the next person in line to assume a leadership role.

In large part, the leader can sustain his influence to the extent that the model that guides his behavior is transferred to followers, reinterpreted, and shared. The model can contain the leader's philosophy on how to treat others, or it may be specific to a particular initiative or agenda constituting a vision. Then someday in the future, the initial follower is met by another follower, and for all intents and purposes she appears to be the one in charge, yet the influence of the former leader remains in the way she thinks about leadership and the way she behaves. In some ways, she has become a partial substitute for her mentor. Perhaps, others will see her as a born leader, because they do not know the history of her prior relationships. It is easier to attribute leadership to being born versus going back through the developmental events that shaped the leader.

Interestingly, one can see the same process occurring in the evolution of highly developed and high-performing teams. When groups get together and are out of alignment, this usually means members have conflicting views or no views at all on who will do what. As group members interact over time, a sharing of perspectives and understanding occurs that, if properly led, can result in an alignment among group members' thinking and behavior—referred to in the teams literature as a *shared mental model*. This alignment ultimately can be around the team's shared values, common vision, central purpose, leadership method, and so forth. Many authors now talk about groups building a shared mental model that becomes the basis for a group becoming a team and that team fully sharing in its leadership responsibilities (see Box 12.4). For groups starting from very diverse points, the achievement of this type of alignment is indeed a great accomplishment.[152]

BOX 12.4   Groups Becoming Teams

Current empirical research on teams indicates that exemplary leadership can have a positive impact on group orientation, efficacy, and performance (Hackman, 1990; Kumpfer, Turner, Hopkins, & Librett, 1993). The type of leadership that we believe differentiates groups from teams can be labeled *transformational*.

Returning to our earlier example, a young man is now working for the woman we described above as the follower. He appears very capable but lacks the drive and self-concept to succeed fully. She studies him to learn his weaknesses and strengths. She takes the time to build his confidence and efficacy. She cares about him and articulates a future he never would have considered on his own. Over time, he expands his boundaries of vulnerability and takes on more difficult challenges and opportunities. He begins to make a positive difference with others in terms of their development. At one point, he tells a friend that his new manager is a born leader.

In the descriptions of both individuals, we have outlined what constitutes the developmental core of transformational leadership—the higher end of the full range of leadership. It is represented in the behavior of the leader who works to develop others to their full potential. The foundation for those behaviors is the leader's deep perspective, understanding, model of life, core values, and sense of right and wrong. These qualities make up the idealized and inspirational components of transformational leadership. The leader develops herself or himself and then develops others to exceed current development and performance capacities. This begins to focus on the individualized consideration component of transformational leadership and intellectual stimulation to the extent that the follower's basic ideas and assumptions are challenged. This can occur in a leader–follower relationship or in a group or team between one colleague and another. Such transformations may even occur with the follower developing the leader, which is even more common today, given the develeling going on in organizations and the fact that managers typically do not have the full slate of advanced technical skills of people who report to them.[153]

The indirect and sustainable effects of leadership are what my colleagues and I are striving for in our work on extending the full range of leadership development. We must help leaders understand their indirect effects on others and where their legacies can make a positive difference, albeit indirectly and often with no direct credit given to them. This is where we begin to get at the deep processes of leadership that wrap around the four principles discussed in the previous chapter. It is where we go from talking about leadership styles to deep perspectives and philosophy surrounding leadership development. It is not always noticeable or apparent in the second and third in command to even a very discriminating eye, but we can conclude that it is there through the constellation of actions taken by a leader and her or his followers over time. It is also there to the extent that the organization has developed a sufficient cadre of leadership to sustain itself and grow.

I recall being in Saudi Arabia working with a large Toyota distribution company. One of the top managers in that company was asked about his goal for investing in leadership development. Without hesitation, he said it was to develop a sufficient number of leaders at all levels to continuously grow his organization. Many of his actions were directed at developing followers sometimes 3 or 4 levels below him in the organization to assume leadership roles above their current positions. He was the ideal person to be leading a transformational leadership program and frequently had to take a lot of risks to sustain the investment the organization was making in this effort.

Now, let's consider a very different example. The new CEO of an organization wants to build among his staff an authentic organizational learning system. In my view, if organizations were designed to be learning systems then most of the development work we do with them would occur through natural learning. Natural learning means that what can be learned in moments at work can develop the type of leaders you need to advance the organization. Given recent evidence on how people learn leadership, which is usually through real events on the job, designing organizations to be incubators for development makes a great deal of sense to me. It also eliminates the problem of transferring what is learned in workshops back to work.

To create that type of learning incubator, the leader might say, "Challenging each other is a great thing, and we must fully support peoples' learning initiatives. Conflict is okay over ideas; it stimulates better and more creative insights." He conveys his beliefs and principles, which are based on a very high moral character. He gets down to the business of running the organization, and the response is not so good. People do not offer ideas. What he said is okay with all of them, and they are very willing to implement new initiatives. They say in actions and sometimes words, "You're in charge and we're not, so if it's what you want, sure we will be happy to do it." They are passive, dependent followers. They do not want to take risk, they do not want to feel vulnerable, and they do not want to act independently from given orders On the surface, all may look well, but the lack of transparency and authenticity between the leader and follower diminishes each of their capabilities in the short and long term.

These followers may be an ideal match working for a more direct or, in the extreme, autocratic leader. Unfortunately, this type of leader is always a heartbeat away from complete system failure. If a major problem is there and noticed by such followers, the chances are low that they will tell the leader what they know to be true. They may have been developed to be risk-adverse when working with previous leaders, and since feedback to leaders requires taking some risk, they may choose not to rock the boat. This type of behavior is the opposite of what we hope to see in highly developed followers, which is taking ownership for what they see and telling what they know.

Unfortunately, bad leaders leave legacies, too, that typically outlast their time in office. I would define such bad leaders here as not being morally uplifting, inspiring, intellectually stimulating, individually considerate, or even positively transactional in the contingent reward sense. These bad leaders may only manage by exception, cueing followers to avoid mistakes at all costs. And perhaps contradicting what I said earlier, the effects can be deep but rarely positive. I say *rarely* because sometimes they do become examples of what you do not want people to do, which could also be viewed as a powerful form of training leaders about what not to do as leaders.

These leaders, like in the positive examples described above, also indirectly affect the people around them even after they are long gone. Followers have come to doubt themselves, to not take risks, and this can bleed over into new leaders working with these followers. The leader's indirect impact is as palpable as that of the former, more positive leader I described above. Now, we must work them out of the system to go from a state of learned helplessness that currently exists to being willing to exercise ownership for leadership.

I recall one incident where the director of a medical association was meeting with one of his vice presidents. Each time she met with him, she was visibly nervous. The director tried to go out of his way to reassure her and provide his support for her development. After months of these types of interactions, he finally asked why she was so nervous in their weekly meetings. She said it was the office, the same furniture, the same rug, and the same feelings she had when she came in with the former director who was downright abusive. The director was shocked, as his style was absolutely the opposite of the former director who had stepped down over 2 years earlier and had subsequently passed away. So here he was sitting in the office of a former director, now dead, and his very qualified follower was apoplectically sitting in the office because it reminded her of all the bad meetings she had participated in with the previous director. The director then said he would start by doing one thing. By the next week, he would have all the furniture out, and they would start fresh. He did just that, but it took nearly a year before she was completely comfortable with the director's intentions. A long and very bad shadow had been left by the former director.

The mental models that bad leaders develop in their followers' perspectives must be abandoned and retired for progress to take hold, but as shown above, this may take a considerable amount of time and energy on the part of the new leader. This is a huge chasm to cross and is often underestimated by new and inexperienced leaders, as well as by some old and more experienced ones. You will always lead in what was left behind by other leaders, including yourself.

BOX 12.5   Air Force Cadets and Transformational Leadership

Over a 2-year period, nearly 12,000 cadets from the Air Force Academy rated 160 U.S. Air Force officer leaders by using the MLQ survey. Other survey measures were also collected, tapping into motivation, organizational climate, reward and discipline policies, and performance (Clover, 1988). Positive relationships were reported between transformational leadership and organizational climate in air force squad units.

BOX 12.6   Intellectual Capital and Organizational Transformation

Nearly two thirds of managers and hourly workers responding to a national survey of employees reported that they believe their organizations are operating on 50% or less of their intellectual capital. Many workers believe that they are undervalued, that their thinking is unimportant (*HR News*, 1997).

Some Specific Indirect Effects

A lot of attention has been paid lately to looking into the indirect effects of leadership in areas such as innovation and performance (see Box 12.5). Below, I list some of the more important ones that have been uncovered. Taking these effects into consideration should help build in your mind a system-level model of what constitutes genuine leadership development. This is crucial to your fully understanding the process of leadership, in that at its highest level of analysis, we are trying to develop and embed a full range leadership system throughout an organization (see Box 12.6).

- Leaders who are more transformational increase the commitment and trust levels of people who work around them. The increase in trust and commitment, in turn, has been shown in several independent studies to affect individual and unit performance. For example, and as noted earlier, the transformational leadership of Singaporean school principals increased their followers' trust, which, in turn, predicted school performance.[154]

- Leaders who are more transformational affect positively the efficacy levels of those people who report to them. Their raised levels of efficacy have led to higher individual performance.[155]

- Leaders who are more intellectually stimulating get followers to generate a wider range of ideas, which, in turn, leads to greater product innovation, designs, and patents.[156,157]

- At a group level, members of teams that exhibited more transformational leadership also exhibited higher levels of potency and efficacy, which, in turn, predicted higher levels of group performance.[158]

- A study on communication processes found that leadership affected unit performance indirectly through the style and content of communication. Transformational leadership had a positive impact on communication content and style.

- Managers who used more individualized consideration had more personal interactions with employees, which, in turn, predicted bottom-line unit performance.[159]

- In the Avolio et al., paper titled "A Funny Thing Happened on the Way to the Bottom Line" (see Box 12.7), leaders who were seen as more transformational used humor in more constructive ways, which, in turn, predicted bottom-line unit performance.[160]

Many more studies show the merits of transformational and positive transactional leadership having an indirect impact on performance. I reviewed these research findings here to have you consider where you might target your efforts as a leader. For example, do you target your efforts on building trust, so that followers take greater ownership and in turn step up and provide exemplary service to customers? Getting leaders to think in this manner gives them an opportunity to see from a process perspective how they can transform individuals, units, and entire organizations to higher levels of leadership potential. Herein is the essence of transforming followers into leaders.

BOX 12.7 Transformational Leadership and the Use of Humor

Avolio, Howell, and Sosik (1999) reported on a study of directors of strategic business units in Canada, indicating that those who were seen by followers as more transformational also used humor in a way to build morale, reduce stress, and enhance creativity, which, in turn, positively affected bottom-line performance. Sense of humor exhibited by the leader moderated the impact of leadership on performance.

Consider the Situation or Context

You have certainly heard people ask, "Under what conditions or situation will a particular style of leadership work?" This is a crucial question in that almost all styles of leadership can be effective in one situation, but not in another. Let's explore some extreme views on this statement. Punishment that is arbitrary and capricious has been used for years by the military in training basic recruits to help them adapt to military discipline and command. By using arbitrary punishment, you can break people down, make them dependent on you, and then gradually put the pieces back together in the way you see them fit. This is one way to develop unit cohesion, to give the unit a common enemy. Yet, in most other contexts, this is a very ineffective form of leadership, particularly where you want followers to take ownership.[161]

Being avoidant as a leader is almost always ineffective. Yet, in many instances, a leader may choose to be avoidant, which could be seen by others as a contribution versus shirking in one's responsibilities. For groups being led, a leader may avoid making a decision until the issue has had time to sink in, or until all of the facts are available. In another case, leaders often avoid engaging in conflict until the time is right.

In a context where the cost of mistakes is very high, leaders find it very difficult to be intellectually stimulating and creative in their dealings with others. They may think, "Why should I think out of the box if it will only get me or us into trouble? We operate in a no-mistakes culture, which means simply stay within the established rules and don't rock the boat."

In a very different context, my colleagues and I measured support for innovation in the organization's culture. We found that, in units where support for innovation was high, the unit's performance was more positively predicted by the leader's level of transformational leadership. Support for innovation was found to be a potent factor in determining the relationship between transformational leadership and performance.[162]

The conditions under which leadership is observed can have a considerable effect on how that leadership impacts the individual's or group's performance. In crisis, a determined and persistent leader may be seen as achieving the difference between success and failure. We also indicated earlier, based on Weber's work, that charismatic leaders typically emerge in situations where the context is uncertain and the followers seem lost. In a more stable setting, charismatic characteristics might be seen as being too overwhelming and unnecessary by followers.

The context also shapes how the leader will actually be described by others. For example, Michelle Rhee, who is the current superintendent of the Washington, D.C., school system, took over the position at a time when the school system was literally failing. Many of her constituents who were fed up with the performance status of the schools see her as a savior. Others who have a vested interest in seeing the school system remain the same revile her and say she is becoming a dictator. How could one honestly examine her leadership without analyzing the context in which she is leading? Leadership is, therefore, never contextually neutral, although in some weak contexts (where rules and standards are very unclear) the effect the context has on the interpretation of leadership is expected to be minimal.[163]

I met with the CEO of a large European organization to discuss a leadership training intervention being planned in conjunction with his human resources staff. When I first walked into his office, I realized pretty quickly that he wanted, perhaps needed, to control the next hour-long discussion. He appeared to be very concerned about losing control in allowing his followers to take actions on their own based on the goals of the training. One symbol of his concern was his reaction to the HR officer's suggestion to conduct 360° survey feedback with him and his staff. He clearly was uncomfortable making himself vulnerable to feedback from followers. He did not see the value in such feedback.

This CEO was adamant that the 360° survey should not be used in his organization because it was too much effort for very little payoff. He did not feel the need for such surveys because he was sensitive enough to problems that were bothering his staff. He could go to a workshop and simply sense what his staff was thinking. I found his comments rather curious, in that he showed very little awareness of how the HR staff member and I felt at our first or subsequent meetings.

The main purpose of the meeting was to have him take us through his vision and how to involve all of us in its implementation. He kept saying that he wanted training that was not "in the clouds." He wanted something that was very tangible and would have bottom-line impact, and he was quite afraid of having one of those process-type sessions that generated more confusion than light. Ironically, we had fully intended to lay out some specific issues to be included in the training workshop that could result in the specification of concrete goals for our work together. He did not stop to consider, however, that this was the direction we had already set.

The CEO demonstrated a very clear perspective of his leadership style and philosophy in that first meeting. He wanted to be the focus of everyone's attention. If we could stay away from process and clouds, then, he thought, we would have a chance of getting something tangible accomplished. He was a very bright and clever man but did not get the essence of the situation he was confronting. Let me explain. He tended to exaggerate the need for his control and influence over others to the point of generating high levels of fear among his associates.

If he ventured toward a cliff, his followers would be the last to inform him of his peril. This was in part out of unquestioning respect for him and, for most, fear of being wrong.

The company this CEO headed had come through a disastrous 4-year period. It was a 100-year-old manufacturing company that had gone rapidly downhill before he took command. When he came in, he replaced nearly three fourths of the senior management, many of whom had started their careers with the firm. He and *his* management team then proceeded to destroy the century-old culture, replacing it with a very hard and driven management system—the type I often hear described as "our culture is to build shareholder wealth." He described his involvement with metaphors, such as being in a war for survival in which he was the general and *they* were the soldiers. In his view, he needed to get the system under complete control before he could again relinquish control. His ideas were probably right for the earlier points in the crisis period, but he was naive about how he was going to change a control-oriented system to an involving and commitment-oriented system with followers that assumed ownership.

His behavior in our first meeting suggested to me that he was completely unaware of the impact of his style on the ultimate transformation he himself desired. Yet, I saw a ray of hope in that when he was confronted, he often said that it was only one man's opinion and that we would have to get input from others. I am not sure he always did, but there was a crack in the wall to look through.

I was reminded in our discussion of something another leader had once said. General Colin Powell said that his most important leadership lesson came through his work with his commanding officer when he was a lieutenant. His commander taught him that leadership was where people were willing to follow you because they were curious about where you were heading. Imagine the trust it takes to follow someone willingly just because you are curious, as opposed to scared. People do not fully follow in the sense of an independent follower when they are scared.

The other thing this CEO did not realize was that he had picked a whole new level of direct reports that were not much different from himself, and their directive and unrelenting style became part of the new culture in the organization. Perhaps without knowing it, he was at a very significant turning point in this organization's long history. He and his management team had destroyed the old values and had made no attempt in 4 years to institute a new set of core values. Other managers at lower levels yearned for a value system that provided clear indicators of what it takes to be successful in this organization. The timing was ripe for change; however, the approach he was taking was highly problematic. He was not yet convinced of the relevance of leadership training, although he appeared to understand it on an intuitive level. His embedded leadership model concerning prior training interventions was not a very positive one. Thus, we needed to get him to relinquish some old assumptions to move forward to develop a new framework and deeper perspective.

Around the world, many managers like the one I described above are successfully leading their organizations. Yet, when they see the need to move their firms toward high-performance systems and teams that take full ownership in what they do, they suddenly realize they must change their styles and cultures. Yet, it is most interesting to witness that, although wanting to move toward a more inclusive culture, they are modeling again and again that they are still partly stuck in an embedded system they themselves created—a command and control system. And they are typically shocked to realize, well into the change process, that *their* people are not getting *their* change message across to followers. "We are saying change: Take responsibility for decisions" . . . and then comes this huge silence, when no one steps up to make a decision even when requested again and again by top leadership.

The above conundrum became evident at country level when the leadership of Singapore realized that it had to move away from a security-minded, control-based culture to one that was more innovative and entrepreneurial in order to move up to the next stage in its economic development. The country started national campaigns to create what they called *a thinking and learning nation*, one that would spark many innovations and new directions for business. Unfortunately, many of the Singaporeans who were brought up in a more control-oriented culture had a difficult time thinking of themselves as independent thinkers. In fact, in a national poll that I conducted on leadership, we found that the government leaders, who are typically handpicked early on in schools for being the best of the best, were the most entrepreneurial. So here you had a case where the government, over time, had populated its workforce with ethical and entrepreneurial leaders pleading with other sectors to step up and change.

There are three things one needs to do in order to influence changing a control-dominated system. First, to change from a control to an ownership culture requires that the leaders become the cells for the type of behavior they want to see in others, which was happening in Singapore, and today is even more widespread in part due to the exposure Singaporeans have to other cultures through expatriates, technology, and travel. To be the cell that propagates in others, leaders must be the first ones to go ahead and model the changes for others. This requires being vulnerable and taking risks.

Second, they must understand the needs of their followers and try gradually to move those who are most prepared into a position of greater independence. These would be followers that are more developmentally ready for the change. Similar to the way I defined developmental readiness earlier, they must have the capability to think about the way to change how they interact with others, as well as to have the motivation to do so. This thinking about thinking provides them with the capability to question their own internal mental models and to see ways to change them. To be developmentally ready also means you have to have the confidence to make such a significant change in the way you think and behave.

Third, such leaders wanting change do not have to convince everyone all at once, just a few well-placed, respected champions of the change process, who can then model the new ways of thinking and behaving for their peers. If you are emphasizing more discretion in decision making, then make it as visible as possible by pointing to areas where the people must take ownership for making decisions and where exemplars and champions are indeed taking ownership. Here is where a little bit of avoidant leadership can go a long way. Specifically, wait long enough, and someone is bound to fill the gap and make a decision. So you will have to work at suspending judgment and allowing others to lead, and again you have to be willing to be vulnerable.

The leadership training that goes on in autocratically run organizations takes more time to work out. Yet, there are certainly some success stories where this training has occurred, and the changes have been dramatic. Nevertheless, it takes persistent effort, and it has to be done in a very consistent and strategically redundant way until people finally believe that you are serious. It takes this amount of time because you are changing not only behavior but also the rules and regulations that have become embedded in the fabric of the culture and your followers' shared mental models (see Box 12.8).[164] If you spent several years institutionalizing this way of thinking to create a dependent followership, then expect it to take at least half the time to consciously undo what was embedded, to replace it with something new. Followers will look for contradictions, and just one can derail a change initiative as not being for real, because so many are not.

BOX 12.8 Transformational Leadership and Total Quality Management (TQM)

Horine and Bass (1993) reported a positive relationship between the transformational ratings of three top CEOs and the achievement of the Malcolm Baldrige National Quality Award in those respective companies. Those who won this prestigious award created continuous improvement cultures and processes in their respective organizations.

So, what should you take away from this chapter to think about in terms of advancing your leadership development? Many people are under the misconception that leaders directly influence performance. I say *misconception* because often a leader's influence is indirect through his or her immediate and indirect followers, through the context or culture, or through some interaction of each of these elements over time.[165,166] By thinking in this way, you are beginning to think as a strategic leader with strategic thinking.

I would like for you to consider a roundabout way to having an impact on those people you are attempting to influence. For example, you can first concentrate your efforts by reestablishing a climate and culture in a way that will provide people with more degrees of freedom to take ownership over decision making. Recall Bill and Hanover Insurance and how long it took him to get followers to assume local ownership in a firm that was led as a command and control system. To develop ownership, you can provide them with more autonomy and discretion, along with facilitation and coaching in line with their readiness to assume such ownership. This will take the type of individualized consideration that was portrayed above in the leader working with his follower that had a poor self-concept.

To change the organization, you can build trust as the foundation step for building teams. You can gain commitment or loyalty before attempting to uncover and promote innovation. In all of these actions, you are attempting to influence others indirectly, and in doing so you can take advantage of the full range of leadership development, including the target individual, the follower, and of course the changes in the context and culture that are manifested over time.

Think about when you have been in a situation where you have had a very indirect and positive influence on someone's performance or development. Did you start by changing the context first or the individual's behavior? What did you do to start the process? What worked, and what did not work? How long did it take? How did you know you were successful? How did you feel when the other person got the credit for your indirect influence? Now, look at something you went about changing directly and see what you could have done differently in perhaps a more indirect way.

SOME THINGS WORTH REPEATING AND REFLECTING ON

- To have a sustainable impact on followers, leaders must consider the systemic cultural and structural changes required for long-term and deep change.
- A leader can build her or his legacy by developing followers into leaders, who, in turn, have similar effects on their followers over time.

- Most likely, if a leader continuously has a direct effect on performance, she or he is probably not leading very well, or as we described in terms of the 4 Is of transformational leadership.
- What you leave behind in followers in terms of your leadership model may have very well started by how you changed the context in which your immediate followers led and assumed ownership.

A SHORT EXERCISE

I want you to select one condition that you feel can indirectly impact others to improve their performance. For example, you might choose to keep your ratio of positive to negative comments at 3 to 1 in your meetings. By keeping your comments at a positive ratio of 3 to 1, you can reinforce others who will be more comfortable speaking up and questioning the direction you set. Look back over the past week, and see how your ratio fared as well as the ratios exhibited by others. Now, keep track of your positive ratio in the meetings you attend over the next week.

- For those meetings closer to a 3 to 1 ratio, how would you describe the meeting dynamic?
- What impact did the meeting dynamic have on the team's performance?

CHAPTER 13

LEARNING FULL RANGE LEADERSHIP DEVELOPMENT (FRLD)

True merit is like a river, the deeper it is the less noise it makes.

R. Atkinson

Throughout my discussion of leadership, I have from time to time inserted some unique places where leadership can be observed developing. This included Sam's shop in the correctional services system, among other venues. Let me expand the domain of places where one can observe leadership by saying that, in every organization and in every culture, some form of leadership can be observed and, I would argue, also developed. In fact, a recent project involving over 62 countries suggests not only that leadership can be observed but also that characteristics and attributes can be universal and likely span all cultures, such as transformational leadership (see Box 13.1).

I would like to share a few unique places with you where I have observed the type of leadership discussed in this book that underscores some of the key points that have been discussed. I use these examples more or less as points for encouraging reflective learning—in some cases, my own learning. And the people that I frequently refer to were often like the deep river described in the quote above, who made little noise but did make a tremendous difference in people's lives.

BOX 13.1   The GLOBE Project

There is a growing interest in research and theory that focuses on the role of leadership across global or cultural contexts. This interest is driven in part by the globalization of organizations that requires leaders to work from and across an increasingly diverse set of locations.

(Continued)

(Continued)

The net effect is an increased focus on cross-cultural leadership research (Gelfand, Erez, & Aycan, 2007; House, Hanges, Javidan, Dorfman, & Gupta, 2004). Extensive reviews also exist for cross-cultural research that is more tangentially linked to leadership (Hofstede 2001; Kirkman, Lowe, & Gibson, 2006; Leung, Bhagat, Buchan, Erez, & Gibson, 2005).

There have been numerous critiques and discussions of work in this area (see *Journal of International Business Studies, 37*[6]). The work of Global Leadership and Organizational Behavior Effectiveness (GLOBE) constitutes the most ambitious and influential cross-cultural of leadership studies to date. The study, detailed in an edited book by House et al. (2004) involved a group of over 160 researchers working in 62 societies. The results indicated that certain leadership factors appear to transcend cultures. The eight global leadership factors identified included styles such as Team Builder, Charismatic, and Nonparticipative Leadership.

Further channeling research on cross-cultural issues, Walumbwa, Lawler, and Avolio (2007) examined the effects of allocentrism (collective orientation) and idiocentrism (individual orientation) on the relationships between transformational versus transactional leadership with both organizational commitment and satisfaction with supervisors. Allocentrics reacted more positively to transformational leaders, while idiocentrics had a more positive reaction to transactional leaders.

In the early 1990s, my colleagues and I received a large army research institute contract to study the development of leadership at a 4-year military college. The college chosen to participate in this study was an all-male military academy with a 150-year history with deeply embedded traditions. Over this time span, this institution had created a very complex culture for developing its leaders. Even though everyone we met said this was one of the best training programs for leadership, no knew why it worked, and often said so, in so many words. But this is quite common at other such institutions that are highly branded for leadership development—everyone says they do it, but no one really knows how it is done.[167]

Our overarching goal for this project was to meet the freshman class at orientation as they were saying good-bye to their parents and then to follow them through to graduation, which we actually accomplished. In this institution, freshmen were affectionately called *rats*. For nearly a year, the first-year cadets were treated with complete disrespect by their upperclassmen who saw as their mission in life to mold these rats into human beings the entire world would be proud of. And like many other similar "bonding" programs, often actions were taken to the extreme. Yet, I hasten to add, the commandant at the time of this study did everything in his power not only to support our research program but also to bring a sense of enlightenment to the leadership development process in the institution.

The commandant, Marty (not his real name), had been a rat himself many years ago and had served in the military, as well as worked in a very responsible leadership role in industry before returning to take over the commandant's position at this institution. He saw many positives in the bonding process brought about by having rats walk the *ratline*, which literally meant that for one year, the cadets would have to walk the farthest distance between two points throughout the academy. Marty worked hard to raise the cadets' focus higher up on the range of leadership to be more progressive in their views regarding the development of each cadet's full potential. This was an admirable goal, but it was thought to be rather strange by the hard-core academy types within the institution. Indeed, in some ways, the resistance to his initiatives cost him his health and his job, although some might say he was modestly successful in changing some ways of this 150-year-old institution.

During freshman orientation session, I thought the processes used by the upperclassmen were often cruel and extreme. Once they found a weak cadet among the group of 400+ rats, they would work on him day and night until he broke down and complied with their every wish. Alternatively, if someone seemed to emerge as a leader, they went after him with a vengeance, often breaking him down as well over time as an example for others to toe the line. The pressure to perform was extreme, and the constant harassing by the upperclassmen made life for the first several months quite unappealing. This leveling process continued for most of the first year, and the message was clear to cadets that they were to comply.

On the surface, anyone might ask, "What really can be learned about leadership in this type of institution?" You browbeat the cadets until they submit, and then you build them back up if they had the tenacity to stick around for a year. In the first year of our study, more than 150 out of the 400+ cadets left the institution. I really had to reflect on what was going on to understand the depth of the leadership system that I was privileged to observe in this academy. I revisited this issue in my mind many times. Let me point to some examples that I think have some universal application and also fit with the concepts I have already mentioned in previous chapters.

As I compared this institution to my own university at the time, and in fact many other organizations, I came to realize that what the institution's leaders were doing was gradually giving students more responsibility, although day to day it did not seem that way. Each and every year, cadets would take a significant jump in the level of responsibility afforded to them, and it began with developing the next generation of followers (new rats) into leaders within the institution. In this role alone, the seriousness by which the upperclassmen approached their task was truly remarkable and quite reflective of the high levels of identification they had with the overall mission of their institution. Of course, some of it was driven by the joy of getting back at the next class, which would lower one's own suffering, in the form of cognitive dissonance reduction with the cruel experiences of the year before. (*Cognitive dissonance reduction* explains how people restore a sense of fairness in their minds after being treated unfairly. In this instance, a cadet may think his entire first year was unfair. Yet, when it is his turn to lead, a sense of justice regarding the issue of fairness is restored in his mind by doing the same to others that was done to him.)

I believe that, in the United States, there are very few institutions where the students are able to kick out another student for cause, and in this case, a violation of the honor code. At this institution, if a student violated the honor code, he was drummed out of the corps. This meant a full review and trial largely run by students in what they called their honor court. Although the institution's administration had considerable input into the decision, the students largely drove the process. I was told that in the 150 years of the institution's history, only one case was reversed, and in that case the administration had screwed up, not the students. I have rarely seen anything comparable to this decision-making authority at other U.S. or foreign institutions of higher education.

The first year was clearly geared toward making the rats feel vulnerable, building a sense of identification in each other (becoming a *brother rat*), developing trust based in part on the honor code and in large part through fear, and developing the deep perspective in the rats that now you know what really bad followership is so that when you are a leader you will be much more aware of your followers' needs and how you choose to address them. Certainly, for some cadets, this was implosive therapy for developing confidence and self-discipline. For some who chose to leave, it was too much too soon that they were not developmentally ready to address. It was an either–or model, meaning you can take it like a man, assimilate it, and identify with it, or just leave. Given its extreme focus on building discipline, I am not at all surprised that leaders emerged in this institution repeatedly over time. As I have noted earlier, leaders oftentimes emerge in times of crisis and stress.

To address the severe nature of the system, many very interesting facets had naturally emerged in this institution's culture and structure over the past 150 years. For example, each rat was assigned an upperclassman who would harass him, but the rat also had a *dyke* (term used for a mentor), whom he could go to for advice and counseling. This was someone he could choose or who sought him out for help and advice. Over time, it led to an elaborate array of leadership relationships because one's dyke's dyke became your uncle dyke, and so on, and so forth. This form of diagonal mentoring provided a counterbalance to the harsh realities of the ratline. In my view, what seemed to emerge over time somewhat spontaneously were systems of checks and balances. The dyke is one such example.

> ### BOX 13.2   A Key to Xerox's Competitiveness
>
> Xerox Corporation has set up a friendly battle between its optical scanning and electronic imaging groups. The purpose was to put pressure on the old products to be either improved or gotten rid of to make way for new products. By creating such internal tension, Xerox hopes to beat its competition to the destruction of their best products. Systems based on conflict can produce interesting developments. Microsoft is similarly known for an internal culture that is highly aggressive. At Microsoft, it is expected that you do combat with other employees so that the battle of intelligences produces the best ideas. Putting the most intelligent people in the room and letting them go at it has been at the basis of Microsoft's corporate culture regarding leadership and product development.

Another interesting feature of the institution was the overlap between the class and military systems. Each of these systems had different levels and ranks, so to speak. So, it was possible to find someone who was senior to you in the class system but junior with respect to military rank. This required constant attention by the cadets to potential conflicts of interest between the two sometimes competing systems. In fact, it built significant tension or conflict into the system's structure, similar to the example above for Xerox (see Box 13.2).

It is also possible to view the institution's processes as an elaborate assessment center for leadership development and emergence. Because all cadets lived on campus within the same housing complex, they were all almost always under constant review by their peers. The seniors lived on the first floor, the juniors on the second, and so forth on up to the rats, who received the least desirable quarters on the top floor. Throughout each year, your classmates got to observe you dealing with the most difficult stressors, persisting at tasks for which others had accepted defeat, and coming up with quick ideas under duress; and of course, they observed the type of credibility and integrity you exhibited throughout the entire day. Cadets would often say they knew very well who the good and bad cadets were.

In our study, my colleagues and I were interested in how moral development and perspective-taking capacity developed over time, among many other facets of leadership. We used several measures of perspective-taking capacity, including an interview designed by Robert Kegan (Lahey et al., 1991). In this projective interview, people are asked to respond in any order they choose to a series of words typed on 10 index cards. The first card might be *fear*. The general idea is that people at different levels of moral development or perspective-taking capacity have the ability to frame fear in different ways. One expects the individuals at lower levels to frame fear in terms of protecting self-interest, whereas at higher levels it may be fear of what others think of you or, even higher, fear of what you think of yourself in terms of the internal standards that guide your behavior toward others (for example, Did I live up to my values and standards with the action I took?).

As we set out to conduct this study, our expectation was that people who had a higher moral perspective-taking capacity would be able to think about the conflicts that others have and help extend themselves to resolve them; they could have their assumptions challenged without fear of losing their self-image, and in fact, it would be reinforced; they could go out in advance of others in what they thought and how they acted without fear that others would not follow; and they would have a set of ideals that could provide them with an internal guide for their behavior and decisions, by definition, regardless of the situation. At the most basic level, they could put themselves in another's shoes and understand how that person viewed a problem.

In the process of conducting the interviews, something happened that I believe conveys the deep meaning of what we are trying to grasp in this perspective-taking/moral capacity construct, which lies at the base of building the individual and collective forces in organizations (see Box 13.3). Perspective-taking capacity is what differentiates the leaders we associate with the term *idealized* with other leaders who might be referred to as *idolized*.[168,169]

We had interviewed several cadets one morning when, during the fourth interview, a cadet asked us whether we had heard of an incident that occurred earlier that morning. The incident was about a cadet who came out for what the upperclassmen call a *sweat party*. A sweat party involves waking up the rats for a 5-mile run at 5 a.m., usually with the cannon going off that is placed strategically in the barracks courtyard. That morning, one cadet came out of the dorms, limping very badly. He had a doctor's note excusing him from any physical exercise. After presenting the note, he was excused from that morning's "party." And then, off went the several hundred cadets running up the hill. Halfway up the hill, someone looked back and noticed the injured cadet limping well behind the group, obviously in a great deal of pain. Some of his fellow rats called to him to go back, showing appreciation for his efforts, but he continued throughout the morning until he finished. Inspiring, yes, but that is not the real value of this story.

BOX 13.3   Moral Development and Transformational Leadership

Lucius and Kuhnert (1997) examined the relationship between the perspective-taking capacity of cadets attending this 4-year military institution and the ratings they received on the MLQ survey. The authors reported that scores generated from using Kegan's subject-object interviews (Lahey et al., 1991) correlated positively with ratings of transformational leadership. Those cadets judged to be higher in moral development were also rated as being more transformational. Turner and Barling (1998) confirmed these results, reporting positive correlations between the level of moral reasoning and the ratings of transformational leadership of managers.

The first cadet described the incident as it had occurred based on other reports but was completely clueless as to why this cadet had attempted the run in the first place. He kept saying things like: "He had the excuse, a written excuse. Why would he do such a stupid thing? I don't get it. . . . I really don't get it."

In a subsequent interview, another cadet brought up the same incident. He, too, described it in detail, yet his perspective on the event was quite different. He judged the reason this cadet limped the 5 miles was peer pressure. He said the injured cadet would rather suffer the physical pain caused by the run than the psychological pain caused by the condemnation from his peers.

Then there was a third cadet who mentioned the incident. He did not bring up the event right away but shared another one with us. He recounted an event for us that occurred at the end of the previous academic year when he had been a senior in high school. Apparently, a group of his friends were out drinking, and on the way back, his best friend was killed in a car accident. He discussed the weeklong drinking binge in which he participated with his buddies and how the friend had been the first person in his life he was really close to who had died. He then said that after a week of drinking, he looked at what he was doing with his friends and decided it was of no real benefit to his departed friend or himself to keep drinking. Although many of his friends condemned him for not being loyal to the cause, he simply chose not to go out and drink another night. He said that at that point, he made a choice that he would try to learn as much as he could from the incident to improve himself and his relationships with others, and in his mind, this would be a much better way of honoring his fallen friend.

We then asked him about the incident that had occurred that morning, which he, too, had heard about. We asked him for his perspective on the event. He said that he was surprised the cadet continued the run but that he was nevertheless proud of the cadet's choice to do so. He thought the cadet's behavior had compelled him to ask himself: Was I doing everything I could do to be the best at what I am capable of doing in this place? He said it was something to which he was giving quite a bit of reflection to see what could be learned from the events and the cadet's example.

In our study, the third cadet was one of the highest-rated cadets in terms of leadership by his peers and was considered for top leadership positions in the institution. He also scored very high on Kegan's interview, suggesting that our observations of his perspective-taking capacity were confirmed by the results of the interview. Perhaps we had a future manager here who would reflect before acting and be courageous enough to take a high ethical stand when needed. We will have to wait for the sequel to determine whether this supposition will come true.

Another individual I came to respect highly at this institution was Marty, who I referred to earlier. Marty, the commandant, tried tirelessly to enhance the leadership culture in the institution. His goal was to make these cadets the best leaders and followers possible and to do so by providing them with more than one model for leading others. The one model he wished to expand perspective on focused only on maintaining the command and control over others with periodic bursts of inspiration. The cadets, both new and old, saw Marty as an outsider who had gotten soft over time and was trying to submarine a system that had worked well for more than a century. He was fought at every turn, and some might say he tried to change this institution too deeply and too quickly.

The institution has one of the strongest and most well-articulated cultures I have ever witnessed. It was no easy task for any leader to transform it to a more enlightened system. But Marty tried, and he worked to enlist the support of students and colleagues in his efforts. Unfortunately, a heart attack shortened his tenure in the commandant position, along with his 3-year effort to alter the culture. The person who came in after Marty was a Special Forces guy who was very tough and fit very nicely with the prior culture. I should add one thing about Marty: He had the vision to move the institution forward for all the right reasons, but he cared a bit too much about what others thought of him and his efforts. Karl Kuhnert called this type of person a team player,[170] the individual who is too preoccupied with what others think about him or her. Marty had this tendency in his perspective that ended up causing him a great deal of pain, but he did survive to go on and do other good things at this institution.

The Special Forces guy had a big picture of himself behind his desk, working his way through some jungle, with eyes blackened and a maniacal look on his face. Near the end of our project, many in the institution seemed to think it was finally returning to normalcy after a long period of insanity. I guess what is normal and insane all depends on one's perspective and goals. I often think, in terms of leadership development, that if it is too comfortable, then it is probably not developing or evolving. As Max Depree, former CEO of Herman Miller, once shared what a mentor of his used to say, "Leaders don't inflict pain, they bear it." I do not mean necessarily pain, just a sufficient level of healthy tension that they create and bear for the good of their group or organization" (p. 44).[171]

Like other military organizations that spend a great deal of time on leadership development, this institution of higher learning was not much different. Perhaps most striking to me was that, in many ways, the students were running the institution, and to some degree it was working. Even more important, the whole institution was involved in leadership development, not just trainers, not just managers, not just peers, but the entire institution.

ANOTHER INTERESTING PLACE

I turn our attention again to South Africa. My colleagues and I were working for a research and development agency that was attempting to move toward being fully privatized. This former government agency still was seen as being very closely tied to the previous government, the last government to enforce apartheid. Members of this agency were particularly proud in that, during the years that most of the world had an economic embargo against South Africa, they continued to develop and design weapons system that were used in the war against Angola or, indirectly, Cuba and the former Soviet Union.

Unfortunately, since the fall of President de Klerk's government, this agency had been seen as a holdover from the apartheid years, with members sympathetic to the old system. At that time, most of its funding came from President Mandela's government, which was not only dominated by Blacks but also interested in cutting defense expenditures. All in all, the future looked very dim indeed for this proud group of engineers and scientists, whom I would say was sort of like NASA, the space agency in the United States.

Our first meeting with the senior management team took place in an African game reserve lodge where a lot of management training takes place in South Africa. Surrounding managers with these natural and sometimes threatening environments is perceived as good for opening up discussion, an irony I still smile about from time to time. Here we are, surrounded by animals that could, without remorse, eat your young for lunch, talking about leadership development—the enlightened approach—a full range.

It is probably fair to say that the senior management was suspicious of our presence and of what they referred to as the *American model* we were going to present to them on that first day of the retreat. At the outset of the first day of our workshop, the CEO took a very aggressive stance and was obviously impatient with our process. It probably did not help the situation any when I questioned whether his management team was a group or a team. He was adamant that it was a team, NOT A GROUP. (That is the way he said it to me, to emphasize his point.)

We found out later in our intervention that these senior managers were clearly not a team and barely a functioning group. This became readily apparent to us all when we spent nearly half a day creating what we called their *team compact of understanding* and what they called a *freedom of information act*. Some had worked together on this leadership team for nearly 10 years, and rarely had they had an open exchange of views with each other. Adaptive conflict was by no means the highest level of interaction within this team, unless it was described as being completely internalized and not shared. And it was typically avoided with the senior manager in charge, making him and his decisions highly vulnerable, as he rarely knew when he was heading straight for a cliff. He clearly did not know what he did not know.

As we usually do in our training workshops, we first asked participants to discuss their ideal models of leadership and followed with a presentation of the full range model and cases regarding its application in their context. We proceeded to provide feedback on the MLQ survey, and it became apparent that some managers on the team were a little more than surprised with their results. It is fair to say that they were shocked and angry. In such a closed organizational system, the managers had little, if any, feedback of how others perceived them in their leadership roles. This lack of knowledge made them very exposed because, like the senior manager, the entire team really did not know what they did not know. And given the dismal context and future in which they were and would be embedded, they simply could not afford to close any doors to useful ideas and information.

When they evaluated the team in terms of its leadership and culture, the CEO again took the bold and often strong stance that consistent values underlaid his team's behavior. Unfortunately, the data we collected on the organization's culture looked like someone had fired a shotgun at the flip chart in terms of what each team member felt was the culture. Absolutely no convergence or alignment was found among their scores. They were so disparate on their evaluations of the team and its culture that they finally stopped blowing smoke and began to accept the fact that they were definitely not a *team*.

We had finally reached a point where we could begin to reconstruct the group and organization—a significant point of honest reflection. The CEO was struck by the disparities in his team's view of its leadership and culture, and I was struck by his lack of awareness. He simply did not see them because the script for his organization had been written very differently by him. The script dictated that one should not dare to bring bad news to the boss. This was bad, bad news.

From that point of breakdown or tension (with respect to the feedback on their cultural data in the workshop) to a year later, some remarkable shifts had taken place in their perspectives about the purpose of the team, the businesses in which they should or should not invest, the type of organization they desired to be, and their intentions for future organizational enterprise. A vast amount of intellectual resources had been released to address some really productive endeavors. Ironically, it started with a common point of tension for the group, which led to an exploration, and in their case the exploration required the development of a compact of understanding. After working together for so many years, they needed to rebuild trust and develop greater openness. For nearly half of one day, they focused on building a set of agreements that would allow them to talk more directly and openly with each other and to be more transparent. This was a discussion a team was having that had worked probably more than a decade together. The compact was revised periodically over time, and things changed in the right direction and by many accounts were beginning to take hold in the culture.

Certainly, this group still had many external forces to overcome, but their energy had been renewed in large part by a leader who allowed them to discuss their opinions more freely. What would seem like a very simple gesture to an introductory organizational behavior class was a huge step forward for an organization and society that had lived under such intense control conditions as were in force with the system of apartheid. It had become a culture of never saying what you really thought, which had been one of the few color-blind principles of the society for more than 40 years.

> *Know ye by these present that as a member in good standing of the Pitney Bowes Shipping and Weighing Systems Engineering Organization, you have the inalienable right to whatever information you need to do your job.*
>
> John Manzo of Pitney Bowes,
> "Freedom of Information Act"

ONE LAST STORY

I was asked to develop a senior level leadership training program for a large bank in Southeast Asia. This particular bank had a very high profile in its country and was seen as a bellweather of how the financial system was working in its society. There was a lot of pressure on the bank and its leadership because its position in the market had been deteriorating over the years, and the board of directors felt that the senior management did not have the wherewithal to address the decline.

As my first step into the bank, I decided to interview all the top managers. What I typically find when I conduct these interviews is that the stories of what is going on in the organization can differ dramatically. The chairman of the bank, who had been brought in by the board of directors to reenergize it, had a very clear idea of what he wanted to accomplish over the next several years. This bank was languishing in its markets, and his charge was to reenergize its leadership to move the bank forward again to be at the top of its game. At the same time, he said that he wanted to give the bank's leaders sufficient time to get their act together so that the changes would be ones they implemented, not ones forced by him on the organization.

The CEO of the bank felt like the organization was generally in good shape and all it needed was a little tweaking. He had some very clear ideas of how the bank should move forward, but unlike the chairman, his ideas were largely transactional fixes. The chairman's ideas were mostly transformational. When the CEO would present his ideas to the board and chairman, he was typically frustrated with their lack of understanding of what he was presenting. Many were not bankers like him, and he had little tolerance for explaining what he was trying to accomplish.

Other senior managers had equally different views of the bank and its future. The CFO was a very skilled and capable financial analyst. She frequently saw herself as the heir apparent to being CEO, although many of her colleagues felt she was not ready for that position. She conveyed to me that she was not sure others saw her as a leader and that her goal was to lead a bank like the present one, whether here or somewhere else. She had a lot of raw potential but was receiving little if any mentorship from the CEO. She was frequently aghast at how little many of her colleagues knew about banking, and she would not hesitate to lecture them on the proper ways of doing banking.

The COO ran his own group and was seen as being quite charismatic. He had a very loyal following in the bank but only among *his* people, which he frequently referred to them as in discussions with them and, oftentimes, in larger groups. He also had some clear ideas of what he wanted to accomplish, but getting him to talk about them was difficult, and it appeared to me that as long as it benefited his group, he would be okay with the new direction. If it did not benefit his group, he would find some way to subvert the direction being pursued. The problem for the bank was that he had very deep relationships with some of the more powerful clients, thus retaining him was key, but he felt he was being stretched too far in his work and wanted to trim back his responsibilities to something more in line with his interests and available time.

One of the formidable challenges in working with this bank was the fact that most of the top management team were out of alignment with each other, and for those below them, everyone knew it. Thus, it was not uncommon to get a *no* from one leader in top management and simply go across the hall to get a *yes* from another. In fact, the more I worked with the top management team, the more evident it became that they were aware of what they were doing wrong, but they were unable to change. This was clearly a point of frustration for the chairman who was quite disciplined in his approach to management, and I would add somewhat controlling. He frequently would tell me about a previous organization that he had run and how exacting the operational efficiencies were under his leadership. He felt the bank was very sloppy in its execution and that had to be changed.

I found that it took an enormous amount of effort to try to get the senior leaders to see a common enemy that was not themselves. As time passed in our working together, other banks were moving up in their markets, and the chairman was becoming increasingly impatient with the progress being made regarding the bank's turnaround. Although many of the senior leaders were ready to change, the CEO continued to see that the bank only needed a little tweaking here or there to improve. He felt that he was firmly in charge, and he wanted to lead the bank in his way. His colleagues marveled at the level of details the CEO was involved in and felt that he was not leading but simply managing details. He clearly was not leveraging the full talent of his staff, and I felt he was naïve about how he could change the bank's direction to a great extent on his own. I saw very little strategic leadership in his style. He was doing his work and would oftentimes say that he got done what he needed to get done and the problem was with the others.

In our second retreat, we had some real breakthroughs occur. As I oftentimes find myself doing, I was pressuring the top managers to be more transparent with each other and to open up their dialogue. This was clearly not occurring until one more senior manager from a group of about 40, who was retiring in the near future, started to lay out the issues he observed and began to name names. He did so in a way that was very respectful, which got others to start opening up, including the CEO. He was one of the most respected managers in the company and had a lot of credibility with his fellow leaders. In this session, the chairman himself did not disclose a lot, but he was the least tenured in the group, so he mainly observed and, at times, tried to mentor the group and encourage it to move forward. He was not shy on stepping in and mentoring, oftentimes offering his views like a young schoolboy who had the right answer and could not wait to be chosen by the teacher. There was no doubt he was likely the brightest in the room, but being bright and leading sometimes get into conflict with each other.

Toward the end of the retreat, we had each manager make a commitment on video to make one change in how they led. The CEO was the first to step up, and he really laid out his weaknesses in terms of being too focused on managing the details. He committed to backing off and leading more strategically and would expect the same from his top management team. Others followed suit in their commitments, and over the next 6 months, progress was clearly being made, but unfortunately not quick enough for the chairman. Also, friction between the CEO and the chairman grew more intense as the CEO began to take more decisive and strategic action. At one point, the chairman finally asked the CEO to step down, which he did, leaving the bank to be run by the chairman. In some ways, I think the CEO had reached his ceiling of strategic leadership, but I will never know that given the timing of his termination.

In this case, as in others in my career, I saw that if you could gain the leadership group's trust, you could eventually get them to work together to achieve better performance. I would deem commitments that were made in many, if not all, cases as being genuine and doable with the proper developmental supports in place, including follow-up. However, the realities of the market and the relationship between the chairman and the CEO derailed the direction that was being pursued and, ultimately, the objectives of the intervention. I suspect, as I look back on this situation, that if there had never been a training workshop, the CEO would not have lasted as long as he did. Frankly, I will never know if that would have been the case, and it points to not only making sure individuals are developmentally ready to change but also making sure the overall organization and, probably in this case, the chairman are ready as well.[172]

NEW DIRECTIONS

When I first started getting involved in leadership development with companies like IBM, most of the design work took place with trainers who were internal staff working for the host organization. We would sit down and map out our strategy, goals, instructional design, modules, time, and resources needed and would build this idealized program. The more I engaged in these types of developments, the more I realized I was missing something very key to leadership development—the leaders to be developed. I even recall saying at an IBM meeting that we should perhaps include the followers in our design so they get the type of leaders they truly desire. I recall the head of training looking at me very strangely and not reacting to my suggestion. Today, we find many top companies now pursuing leader-driven leadership development.

SOME THINGS TO THINK ABOUT

As work on leadership development has progressed over the past 25 years, it has taken on a number of different directions. Let me group these directions into 3 categories: solid foundations, shifting sands, and promising futures.

Solid Foundations

- In my view from the start and until this moment, leadership development must have a well-validated model guiding it. I encourage people who get involved in leadership development to ask a simple set of questions. What validated model underlies the development work you are doing? By validated, I mean a model that has been proven effective in terms of predicting performance. I know a lot of trainers and human resources professionals think having a model or theory pertains to academics. This is largely because they do not understand model building and validation. A model or theory is like the schematics for a house, which help to guide the way you expect the house to be built. Of course, you will adapt the building of the house along the way, but without a model, how would you end up with what you expect? The same is true for leadership, so every leadership development effort should have some model underlying it that you are trying to develop in those going through leadership development. A validated model is one that has been proven to predict performance outcomes.

- The measures you use to assess whether you are actually developing leadership should also be validated. Why organizations pay consulting firms to use their measures with no proven validity is simply beyond me. All you need to do is to ask a simple question: Has this measure ever predicted any performance outcomes? I can assure you that more than 90% have no proven validity, so in my estimate you are using a drug that was never tested. You are the pilot test.

- It is incumbent upon any leadership developer to demonstrate the return on development investment (RODI) of the leadership intervention. What manager does not look at return on investment (ROI)? Why do we expect managers to be accountable to supporting development if they do not know the ROI? We should not estimate the RODI simply to make us look credible in the eyes of managers. We should do so, because it is what managers expect when they are asked to invest time and resources in some initiative.[173]

- You need to know your stakeholders, audience, and context. Ask yourself, whom will this intervention benefit most, other than the participants? How could you work with those stakeholders to reduce their immunity to change to support the success of the proposed intervention? In terms of the audience, I would simply ask how developmentally ready are they to engage in the leadership intervention. If they are not ready, how can you assist each individual in getting ready?

- The context is that which you are embedding the leadership intervention into overtime. I would ask, how receptive is the context to the model you are attempting to develop in the participants. For example, if you are developing leaders to be more individually considerate and developmentally focused, does the organization provide any support or resources for doing so? To the extent the climate and culture of the organization are immune to change, it is likely they will challenge even the most effective leadership interventions.

Shifting Sands

- Many organizations have been convinced by consultancies and their own internal staff to adopt competency models to guide their leadership initiatives. Unfortunately, most if not all of these models have never been validated, and more importantly, most of what are called competencies are simply not competencies. I have seen long lists of competencies, sometimes more than 20, that are being advocated, and generally what happens is that there is no focus in these initiatives on key areas for development. The measures used have been developed for each organization and generally have never been proved valid. Now, I am not suggesting that managers should not develop competencies at work. Rather, I am saying the strategy that has been used does not work. If it does work, ask whoever is selling you the model to show you the evidence.[174]

- I am amazed at how much organizations will pay to listen to someone else's story about leadership, or what I like to call the *me on me* approach. These approaches include the Steven Covey models to the famous leader's lectures. Now, again I am not saying these could not or are not useful, but generally they are not what I would call leadership development, but rather they can typically be considered in the category of entertainment. I would add that if the messages in these programs resonant with people, there is likely to be something of value. However, I am not sure what it is because very few interventions actually examine their impact on leadership development or RODI. Again, simply ask whoever is selling you leadership development the following question: Do you have any evidence that at least one leader has been developed with your intervention? About 95% will not be able to answer that question honestly in the affirmative.

- I believe the rapid growth in executive coaching is a consequence in part of organizations being dissatisfied with prior leadership development efforts. It is also part of a trend described below to individualize training delivery. Yet, like most programs, there is no evidence demonstrating that coaching actually works. It may work, but most executive coaches would not take the time nor are they trained to assess the impact of their efforts. This is unfortunate because, eventually, if you do not demonstrate its worth, it too will be thrown on the junk heap of leadership development attempts.[175,176,177]

Promising Futures

- As we move forward with leadership development, there are some intriguing trends that are emerging on the horizon that are quite promising. The first trend relates to natural learning. More and more leadership development evidence suggests that using natural events at work to trigger and sustain development is going to be a core element of what I have called authentic or genuine leadership development. [178,179] Thus, events that occur on the job that can be used to foster development around which we can wrap our training and coaching will likely become the foundation for future development efforts.

- The world has become so customized in terms of products that I expect the same to occur for leadership development. The concept of developmental readiness will become more relevant to the extent that we can ideally tie natural learning events to the readiness of individuals to develop. It is likely that each individual's course and trajectory for development will be unique and different, and the way to maximize development is to be customized in our approach.

- With advancing mobile technology, a lot of how we support the learner over time and how he or she accesses information will come from these mobile devices. These devices and the apps developed for them will provide the means to truly customize leadership development to the developmental readiness of each learner.

- There will be far more effort put into translating models and theories of leadership development so that they become the structure upon which development and, indeed, accelerated development is based. The better able we are to show the relevance of valid models, the more likely we will be to accelerate development based on something that is proven to have worked in the past.

- Linked to the natural learning strategy, the organization itself will become the incubator for leadership development. Increasingly, more of what managers do will be to focus on development, and more of what they get rewarded for will depend on how successful they are in developing future leaders.

- I can see in the very near future that we will be using virtual simulations that are so real and dynamic that the participants will have a difficult time discerning what is and is not real. This will include automated actors who will adjust to the readiness of each participant in such a way that can optimize the acceleration of leadership development.

SOME THINGS WORTH REPEATING AND REFLECTING ON

- Leadership development, to have a sustainable impact, must be built upon validated models and methods.
- The highest levels of leadership correspond with the highest levels of perspective-taking capacity.
- To fully change leadership in a large corporation there must be sufficient tension to challenge the existing models.
- More and more, leadership development will occur in organizations taking advantage of natural learning events.

A SHORT EXERCISE

Choose a very specific goal for yourself to change your leadership style. Select one of the styles along the full range of leadership, and identify a very specific behavioral action (for example, work every day in every interaction to assume a positive intent in other people's actions). Select and monitor one behavior over time, and by exhibiting it more frequently, consider how others are reacting to your change in leadership style.

CHAPTER 14

ADVANCES

To teach is to learn twice.

Joubert J. Pensees, 1842

As I look back over the past decade, there is a great deal that we have learned about how leadership impacts performance and how it is developed. I have also moved my research beyond examining the full range of leadership to include an emphasis on two new areas: authentic leadership development and what my colleagues and I have called *positive forms of leadership* (for example, psychological capital). I would like to briefly share with you some of the insights that have been learned from this work that inform how you might develop leadership.

I chose the term authentic leadership development to emphasize two important points. The first point was that most leadership development initiatives were not close to being genuine in the sense of how life's program or stream develops leadership. Making up what should be in training programs frequently does not approximate the level of challenge and emotional engagement that typically occurs when an individual is developed in terms of his or her leadership.

The second point was that genuine leadership development occurs more often in natural environments, such as one's organizational setting versus in a training workshop. In fact, what we have found is that what might even appear to be an inconsequential trigger moment, or an event lasting less than a minute, can actually grow over time in terms of its impact on leadership development. I really do mean a moment here. I have found, from extensive in-depth interviews of leaders at all levels and across cultures, that a moment's interaction with a trusted advisor can impact leadership development years into the future.

For example, one school leader told me that when she asked her previous mentor what was the one thing she could do to develop her leadership in her new role, he simply said for her to consider that every conversation matters. This simple statement led to her, over the next 10 years, developing a discipline around being mindful of the importance of every single interaction, whether with students, teachers, parents, board members, community members, or other administrators. Moments need to be added to the discussion of accelerating leadership development. Certainly, dramatic transitions or crises can shape leadership development, but what we may have missed when focusing on the crucible events are the events that seem so inconsequential that we keep coming back to over time.

The focus on psychological capital came from the work that my colleague, Fred Luthans, and I were exploring at the University of Nebraska. We wanted to look for areas to link my interest on leadership development with his interest on motivation and positive psychology, and we came to focusing on psychological capital. Psychological capital, or PsyCap, is a resource (like intellectual or financial) that leaders and followers have that helps energize them through challenges. There are, so far, four components that make up what is defined as psychological capital. The components include optimism, hope, efficacy, and resiliency.

These four concepts had certainly been examined in the clinical psychology literature; however, we were the first group of researchers to explore them in the world of work organizations. What we have found is that the four PsyCap components in combination provide synergistic value in creating the energy in individuals and leaders to predict higher levels of engagement, commitment, and performance. We have also shown that the PsyCap of leaders can, over time, relate to the levels found in followers, potentially uncovering what might be referred to as a cascading or spreading contagion effect. Perhaps most importantly, these four components are states, not traits, and that distinction means that they can be developed, for which we have preliminary validation evidence.

BOX 14.1   Evidence for PsyCap Predicting Performance

There is growing empirical evidence that this core construct of PsyCap is significantly related to a broad range of very desirable employee outcomes (Luthans, Norman, Avolio & Avey, 2008; Luthans, Youssef & Avolio, 2007). Moreover, recent evidence shows that it can be developed with very short micro-interventions. Results from two separate field studies have indicated that such short (micro) training interventions can be used both to develop participants' PsyCap, as well as to improve their on-the-job performance (Luthans, Avey, Avolio & Peterson, in press).

Returning to authentic leadership development, my colleagues and I have spent the past 7 years focusing on what constitutes authentic leadership. Part of the motivation for doing so came from conversations I had with Bernie Bass, who did the foundational work on transformational leadership. We discussed that there were likely two types of transformational leaders—the genuine type and pseudo-type. I was concerned at the time of these discussions that we may be developing leaders who wanted to look like transformational leaders but who did not have the moral perspective needed, and therefore, we were developing them not to grow followers but to take advantage of them.

This led to a concerted effort in our work in Nebraska to both define and model what constituted authentic leadership. Authentic leadership was defined early on as

> a pattern of leader behavior that draws upon and promotes both positive psychological capacities and a positive ethical climate, to foster greater self-awareness, an internalized moral perspective, balanced processing of information, and relational transparency on the part of leaders working with followers, fostering positive self-development. (Walumbwa, Avolio, Gardner, Wernsing, & Peterson, 2008, p. 94)

Based on several years of work, my colleagues and I concluded that there were at least four key components comprising authentic leadership that dovetailed with notions of ethical and transformational leadership but were also unique in defining what constituted exemplary leadership. We set out to develop a measure of these constructs, to show how that measure differed from other similar constructs, and to determine how that measure augmented those other measures in predicting performance. At this point, there have been numerous studies that have shown that authentic leadership is a unique construct made up of the four components described below.

The first component of authentic leadership is exhibiting high levels of *self-awareness,* which represents leaders' deep understanding of their self-concept[180] and provides for the lens through which leaders derive meaning from their leadership and their leadership's impact on others.[181]

The second component is called *relational transparency,* and this is defined by leaders' presentation of their thoughts, beliefs, and emotions in an open and transparent manner. It was suggested that leaders who were more open and authentic in terms of their behaviors and interactions with their followers would encourage their followers to also be more open with disclosures, leading to the formation of a more authentic relationship between leader and follower.[182]

The third component of authentic leadership is *balanced processing,* which reflects leaders' openness to and nondefensive orientation toward including all aspects of relevant information before making decisions. Authentic leaders solicit and regard outside views, even when those views challenge their own convictions and positions.[183]

The fourth and final factor comprising authentic leadership is leaders' more highly developed *moral perspective*, where they rely upon guiding internal values and beliefs to drive their actions.[184] This component links most directly to the base for what constitutes transformational leadership. Because of their high moral perspective, authentic leaders are more likely to resist external pressures and to act in line with their values and beliefs.[185]

An implication of this research for practicing authentic leadership is only at the very early stages of development.[186] What we have seen in the accumulated research so far is that authentic leadership measures add to transformational and ethical leadership measures in predicting performance. What this means is that we are measuring something unique that is important to assessing leaders above and beyond the other measures we have used in the past to gauge exemplary leadership. The measures similar to the ones assessing PsyCap represent styles or states that can change or be developed. This has led us to explore the types of trigger moments that impact one's self-awareness and the potential training interventions that could support authentic leadership development.[187]

As we have begun to focus more on these moments, we have come to realize that not all development actually needs to occur through negative events. A lot of the leadership literature traditionally focused on events that were major life crises or transitions that future leaders survived and became a better leader as a consequence. I would hear story after story about how some major life crisis, health or otherwise, brought the true leader out in someone. Although I do not necessarily disagree that leadership is developed through these trials-by-fire, I would suggest that the evidence we collected over the past several years indicates that a lot of authentic leadership development also occurs through experiencing positive moments in life, some really being *moments*. In the comprehensive Asian city study discussed earlier, when asked about life events that contributed to their leadership development, 21% of the CEOs discussed events that were positive (see Figure 14.1).

Can you think of a positive trigger in your life that has shaped your thinking about leadership? Here are a few examples to trigger your trigger:

My father always told me to assume positive intent in others.

There is nobility to business, and when you realize that, it makes leading much more rewarding.

The true mark of success is how many people would hide you in life.

Never grow up as you grow old, so you continue to see life through the eyes of child.

You only go through parenting once, so get it right the first time.

Figure 14.1 Trigger Events for Asian CEOs

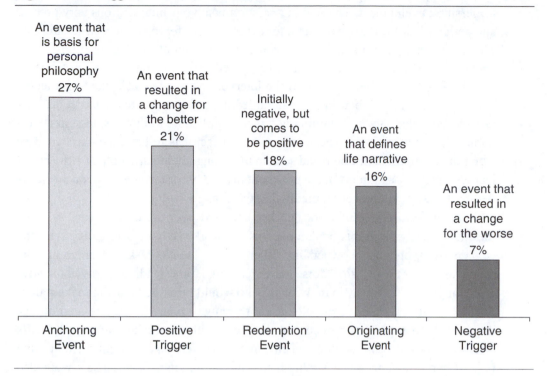

The research on authentic leadership is now expanding into other areas that we have called micro-interventions. We have selected the term micro-interventions because we believe the direction that leadership development will be taking over the next decade and beyond is to embed leadership interventions in short dosages in the flow of work. We have also moved to adopt the lean philosophy that less may be more impactful in terms of leadership development. Consequently, we see even 5-minute interventions distributed over multiple points in time and focused on such things as enhancing self-awareness having more beneficial impact than a full day's worth of training.[188]

There is already some evidence my colleagues and I have collected that shows that by simply getting managers to focus on distinguishing adaptive versus mal-adaptive self-awareness or reflection, we can get them to enhance how they view themselves as leaders. In a preliminary study, using online, short micro-interventions, the degree to which a manager's self-awareness was enhanced was shown to be significant with very short intervention times, spanning no more than 15 minutes at a time. Having a manager ask, *Am I in a reflective mode, thinking about adaptation and change versus simply ruminating on what went wrong?* can in and of itself positively impact leader development.

There are several key factors that we are learning that are essential to authentic leadership development. The first factor is to make your interventions very precise and perhaps just focused on one area for development, for example, self-awareness. The second factor is to make sure you have appropriate follow-up boosters to enhance whatever initial effects you have created in the foundational microtraining. The third factor is to help show how the intervention is relevant to the target learners. This goes back to focusing on natural learning events where the target learners can see that what they are learning is directly applicable to their leadership development and performance. The fourth and final factor is to have the contextual or situational support to promote and sustain the change being attempted by the target learners. If the situation is not developmentally ready for the changes you are seeking in others, it will be very unlikely that the changes will endure.

Another fruitful area of work that has emerged over the past 5 years, which I introduced early on in this book, concerns the work we have been doing with the concept of psychological ownership. When I moved to Nebraska, I learned that the state was one of the first to endorse homesteading. Homesteading involved the government giving land away to individuals who would farm the land and make it their own. To initially survive in Nebraska farming, given its austere conditions, required that people work together to help each other succeed. Nearly 100 years after the onset of homesteading, when I moved to Nebraska, I could see that same type of homesteading, or ownership mentality, among its citizens. There were also some interesting examples that I came across that reflected that taking-ownership orientation in local company culture. For instance, there were a number of organizations that were employee owned in Nebraska, similar to the farming example I shared above. This represented people working together to help each other succeed.

I recall teaching a class with one of the most renowned Nebraska football coaches named Tom Osborne. When he talked about his leadership as a football coach, he relayed the idea that each year he asked everyone involved with the football program to write down what he or she thought the mission should be. It did not matter if you were an assistant coach or a person who cleaned the towels; everyone was asked to take ownership for the mission.

It was based, in part, on my observations above that we started our work on what constituted psychological ownership, which I now consider to be one of the most important interim outcomes of leadership effects. Specifically, transformational leaders develop followers into leaders. However, one might extend this notion and say they are also developing them to take greater ownership. So, what constitutes ownership in our definition and measures? There are two forms I will discuss below. One form is called prevention-oriented psychological ownership and the other promotion based.

My colleagues and I have now distinguished prevention-based ownership from promotion-based ownership, proposing that territorial ownership involves an external reference (us versus them) and is a more defensive orientation. Specifically, "feelings of territoriality are heightened when individuals fear their objects of ownership may be influenced by external entities" (Avey et al., 2008, p. 176). For example, if you think back to a time where someone was infringing on your territory, which could be what you thought you owned at work, what actions did you take against that individual, if at all? Did you try to protect your territory or defend it from being infringed upon? Did the defense of your territory lead to destructive versus adaptive conflict? Generally, we have seen throughout history that much of the ownership debate underlying conflicts and wars is related to feelings of territoriality.

Now, turning to promotion-oriented psychological ownership, there are four components that I suggested earlier and briefly defined that include self-efficacy, accountability, belongingness, and identity. Let me revisit those and expand on the definitions.[189]

Self-efficacy represents your beliefs about your ability or capacity to produce the required levels of performance in order to be successful.[190] If you do not have sufficient levels of personal efficacy, you likely will have a limited amount of motivation to feel or take ownership in some task or activity, which in the context of our discussions could mean not taking a leadership role.

Accountability has been defined as, the "implicit or explicit expectation that one may be called on to justify one's beliefs, feelings, and actions to others" (Lerner & Tetlock, 1994, p. 255). Accountability represents the second dimension composing promotion-oriented psychological ownership. Higher levels or feelings of accountability enable individuals to hold themselves, as well as others, responsible for certain activities or tasks. Individuals feel the right to know information about and hold others accountable for influence and, in turn, come to hold themselves accountable for a specific area or target of responsibility, feeling an increased sense of responsibility for doing so.

Belongingness is the third component and refers to an attachment to certain referents (places, objects, ideas, among others). For example, in the workplace, an individual's need to belong may be satisfied by public recognition or relationships in and around one's job, work unit, or the entire organization. I recall one union leader telling me how proud she was to belong to the organization she had worked for over her 25-year career until it was acquired. When the name changed and other aspects of her former organization changed, she no longer had that same sense of belonging. It was lost, and she was ready to disengage and take less ownership in her work.

The fourth dimension of psychological ownership is identity. Identity refers to an alignment between the view you have of yourself and a particular referent or target. Such referents of ownership are often used by individuals to describe their individual identity. For example, individuals may experience a sense of identity being an elite member of a first-responder team. Over time, they cannot separate the identity they have to this unit from how they view their personal identity. We see with such units a very high level of identity that is translated into sacrificing one's life for being a member of the team. As it moves to the very highest levels of such identity, we can even label it ethos. In the United States and other militaries, there is what is called the warrior ethos or identity. What it means on the ground is that a soldier will never leave another solider behind. At this level of identity, the level of trust and cohesion that is exhibited is enormous.

In the early work on ownership so far, we have found that leaders who are evaluated by their followers as being more transformational also have followers, over time, who say they have higher levels of promotion-oriented ownership. Conversely, those leaders seen as less transformational tend to have followers who lean more toward a "what's in it for me" attitude that typically corresponds to higher levels of territorial ownership.

BOX 14.2 Psychological Ownership and Relationships to Performance

Preliminary studies that have assessed the level of psychological ownership experienced by employees have found it to be related to job satisfaction, organizational commitment, involvement, turnover intentions, organizational citizenship behaviors, employee deviance, and self-perceived changes in attitudes and work-related behaviors (Avey et al., 2008). Subsequent research has also shown that transformational leadership predicts higher levels of promotion-oriented psychological ownership.

The last area of work I would like to briefly share with you is the work we are doing on extreme environments. When we hear dramatic stories about leaders, they are usually about how the leader addressed some very difficult and challenging event that may have put the leader or his or her team or organization at extreme risk. The extreme stories are so common that one would expect that the field of leadership studies should have a lot to say about how leaders function in extreme contexts. Unfortunately, that is not the case. As the world becomes a riskier place to travel, to do business, and to govern, this will be an area that all leaders will have to learn more about: leadership operating in extreme contexts.[191]

Extreme contexts are environments in which events occur, or have a higher probability of occurring, that can result in severe physical, psychological, or material consequences (for example, death, physical harm, devastation, or destruction) to organizational members or others served by these types of organizations. The types of extreme context I refer to above are commonplace in many professions, including military, medical, law enforcement, fire and rescue, and crisis-response organizations. For example, the SWAT teams that protect nuclear facilities may have to be deployed without warning to thwart a determined terrorist group from causing a catastrophic meltdown of a nuclear reactor. How can we prepare you if you are in that situation now? How does what constitutes the leadership systems and processes in these settings differ in these contexts?

An extreme context means that an extreme event either has occurred or has some level of probability that it could occur in the future. These extreme events can occur in any organization. What is important for us to consider, and for you as well, is how your leadership will differ depending on the event and for periods before, during, or after an extreme event. The event must (1) have potential for massive physical, psychological, or material consequences for organization members; (2) have consequences that are considered unbearable by those organization members; and (3) exceed the organization's capacity to prevent such an extreme event from actually taking place.

An extreme event is

a discrete episode or occurrence that results in an extensive and intolerable magnitude of physical, psychological, or material consequences to—or in close physical or psycho-social proximity to—organization members. Whereas, an extreme context as "an environment where one or more extreme events are occurring or are likely to occur that may exceed the organization's capacity to prevent and result in an extensive and intolerable magnitude of physical, psychological, or material consequences to—or in close physical or psycho-social proximity to—organization member.[192]

The work that is now being undertaken in this area of research has just begun. However, I would suggest that much of what we discussed in this book so far will likely be relevant to leadership in extreme contexts. For example, building a deep sense of trust among your followers will be even more essential to get those followers to support you when addressing extreme events. It is also in those situations that more individuals will have to step up and take leadership and ownership. Consequently, if you have developed a dependent following, it will likely be ill equipped to deal with the rapidly changing dynamics of extreme contexts. In fact, it is difficult for me to consider a more important area for developing followers into leaders than for extreme contexts.

Also, I suspect that coming to know yourself, being authentic in every sense, and being willing sometimes to make the ultimate sacrifice for your mission will facilitate others working with you over time. These are not trivial requests, and people will have to feel you always have their best interests in mind when you ask them to move forward. I recall one fire chief from New York City indicating to me that he was so proud after one of his new recruits indicated to him that if he was asked to run down a high-rise hallway he would do it without hesitation. Apparently, the hottest flash point in a high-rise building is the hallway, so the recruit being willing to run down it said a lot about the fire chief's leadership in the eyes of the young man.

Related to the trust required, everyone will feel some sense of vulnerability in an extreme event or context. It is how the leaders and their units work to manage those vulnerabilities that may be the deciding factor between life and death. Not being transparent with each other potentially puts everyone at risk, so making sure that each and every unit member has situational awareness is a must-have in these situations.

In sum, my intent was to give you just a glimpse at some of the new and ongoing work my colleagues and I are involved in that has stretched our focus in terms of assessing leadership, its indirect effects, and its development. I would like to now turn to the last chapter for some final thoughts and reflections on my learning and on leadership and what I hope you have derived from reading this book.

SOME THINGS WORTH REPEATING AND REFLECTING ON

- You have control over the level of PsyCap you exhibit with others.
- Building ownership is a way of transferring leadership to others.
- Most leadership development occurs through natural learning events.
- Positive triggers can accelerate leadership development.

A SHORT EXERCISE

Take a look at your current job, and try to identify natural learning events that can shape your leadership development.

- What impact has those events had on accelerating your development?
- What impact could you have on developing others using these events?
- Are there events that are not yet wired into your job that would enhance your development?
- What events should you look for in your next job to accelerate your leadership development?

CHAPTER 15

THE END AND THE BEGINNING

Again, I have come back to the same place, for the first time.

I began this book in a small town called Destin over 10 years ago when I worked on its first edition. Destin is in the panhandle of Florida on the Gulf of Mexico. I have returned there several times during the course of writing the first edition of this book to do my "Ernest Hemingway thing" of writing portions of this book on the beach. Back then, on many early mornings, I sat at my laptop, typing away while watching people on the beach, inspired by the waters in front of me and Destin's pure white sand that squeaks when you walk on it. I am usually more reflective at the beach, and to write a book about leadership in this situation was truly inspiring for me.

Today, I am sitting in my office in Shoreline, Washington, having moved to the University of Washington and the Seattle area. I am still fortunate enough to be looking out a window to see the water, this time the Puget Sound, and to reflect on all that I have learned from my colleagues and from people who have worked with me on leadership development. Although there is a lot I did not change in this version, maybe 50% to 60%, I did change quite a bit in what I wanted to say, how I wanted to say it, and why I said it. The experience of going back to revise this book (which I resisted, as I had never done that before and did not feel it would be very interesting) has been a great experience in my own leadership development. Why? I see that in many ways my perspective on leadership development has changed. It is much more based on the situation than on the individual in terms of balance as suggested in the first edition. I also realized that some of the things I said a decade ago, I would not change as they made perfect sense to me today, given what I have learned. There were other things that were not wrong, but just did not seem relevant anymore. And finally, there was how I said things and how I have changed the way I wanted to express myself that led to a number of revisions.

By stepping back and looking at what I wrote, I was given the chance to reset and come out with version 2.0, so to speak. I still believe that you have to go inside yourself, and then by stepping back in and reflecting, you have a chance of moving forward. I encourage leaders to do this quite often to enable them to understand the past, function in the present, and begin to create the future. And, it is no different with following, except it is likely to be more difficult. Why?

In the United States, we do not tell our children on the way out to school, "Now listen, be the best follower you can be, okay?" To reflect on what it takes to be an exemplary follower will require much deeper reflection because we have very little practice in this area. Yet, it is so fundamental to building the vital force in you, in your leadership, in your teams, and in your organization. Followers allow leadership to happen and as I hope I have shown, make it happen.

Of course, leaders have their role in this process, too. Yet, the sine qua non of leadership is reflected in the profound accomplishments of the follower. Every great leader knew this and worked to achieve it through her or his own behavior and what she or he encouraged in others. In James McGregor Burns's terms, the transforming leaders were those people who uplifted followers to lead themselves. The leader can only assume a bit part in this life play, although too often she or he is given much more center stage than deserved.[193] I would add that my thinking has not changed at all on this point, as I still believe one of the best reflections of leadership is the shadow leaders create through their followers.

I believe that at the core of leading others is a solid and complete understanding of one's vulnerabilities and a comfort level to allow them to be exposed. Followers are often asked without forethought to allow themselves to be vulnerable, to listen to the leader, to do their best to make the leader successful, and so on. I suggest that some of the vulnerability rests with the leader. Recall that we have defined the level of leadership you will see in others (second in command) as being based, in part, on your own behavior. This statement applies to so many things, including how you treat your own failures; how you address criticisms of your most central beliefs, ideals, and values; how you respond when someone challenges your absolute best ideas; and how willing you are to get out of the way to let those who should lead, lead.

The sense of vulnerability I have described here can only come through a profound understanding of who you are and your best self. We are all constantly going through in vivo, or natural leadership development events, so what are you deriving from those experiences? What types of boosters do you build in for yourself to sustain your momentum toward changing, and how to you personally track development? What types of life experiences are you consciously trying to add to your life stream now, and which in the past had the biggest impact on your leadership development? How do you address the ones that come along in your life stream that are unplanned and very difficult to assimilate? How are you triggering development in others for whom you have responsibility to develop?

I am reaffirmed in my belief that leadership is one of the most profound forces in the universe for good and evil. We must challenge ourselves to make it right in ourselves, in others, and in those we choose to be led by over time. Leadership can be on the order of Jesus Christ, Mahatma Gandhi, Nelson Mandela, Mother Teresa, Herb Kelleher, Eleanor Roosevelt, Golda Meir, Eva Perón, Albert Einstein, John F. Kennedy, Abraham Lincoln, Amy Carmichael, and on and on. We should honor the very best leaders and their followers through our own efforts to be exemplary in our efforts to develop leadership.

The first message I wish to leave with you is to achieve in yourself a level of confident vulnerability. This will provide others with the space to enter into your reflections, ideas, actions, and accomplishments. It is the space that both leaders and followers require to be successful and to enhance their vital forces over time. It is also something that will be trusted in you and in others you lead.

Confident vulnerability may seem an oxymoron, but exemplary leadership, insights, great discoveries, and adventures are often based on paradoxical thinking. I wonder if that is why Microsoft's former CEO and chairman, Bill Gates, tried to create at his company a learning culture based on what they called an *armed truce* among leaders, among followers, between leaders and followers, and between peers. Getting people to say *no* may be more important than giving an initiative, the easy *yes*, without forethought.

Now, let's address this issue of vulnerability from another angle. Allowing yourself the space to be vulnerable defines the areas that you may want to develop most. It is not just being vulnerable, it is defining the parameters within which you want to achieve your next level of potential, and then the next. Vulnerability is a profoundly beautiful thing in children, in the loving relationship between husband and wife, and in high-performing teams. Thus, working on vulnerability seems a very worthwhile goal to enhance your leadership potential and performance.

No coin should be more profoundly coveted and rewarded in the realm than when we get others to identify with something we and they truly believe in. You have met those people who so firmly identify with what they are doing that you are drawn to them by their example. Their efforts are so deeply rooted in what they identify with that it is almost insulting to them to add in rewards of trivial consequence. Thus, if you really want to ring the bell on leadership, find something you want to identify with and need to accomplish, and then develop the reasons that are required to bring others to your way of believing. So many individuals lack this sense of identification and come to work each and every day leaving their brains on hooks outside the door. This requires that you model your own beliefs and ideals, that you energize others to put in the effort required to achieve those ideals; that you amend your basic ideas when new insights are brought to the fore-ground; and perhaps most important, that you understand what each follower will need from you to identify with the cause or mission you have chosen to pursue. What will motivate them to be like you and still be willing to disagree for the common good of your group and vision? This is one of the ultimate leadership challenges, particularly as you gain more power and influence in a leadership role.

Once the doors for greater vulnerability are open, finding the right hooks on which to build identification is a crucially important task of leadership. Yet, it is not a lonely task at all, in that you must know what people can identify with for them to be fully committed to your mission. If you listen and observe very carefully, in many cases, you will learn what will bring people together. Sometimes it may not always be so obvious, and sometimes people will need to be pushed toward this realization, but in the end, if you know where you want to go, you will get there through their identification with your ideas and, of course, your demonstration of commitment to them over time. It takes a little bit of individualized consideration to find out what connects them to identify with the mission or vision. For some, it may be the thrill of the challenge, for others what they will learn, and for still others, a sense of accomplishment. Connecting to each individual's sense of what is important is where you need to go to optimize the leadership system in your organization.

Please consider that nothing profoundly unique and interesting is ever fully adopted at the outset without either question or conflict. It probably should not be, in that beliefs are something we develop in ourselves and others over time, with some individuals taking more time than others. You have to identify with something yourself, and then you can persist in bringing others to that level of identification at the truly deep levels where transformational change occurs in perspectives and in shared mental models.

Once you identify with something, you must convey it to others in a thousand different ways, all nested in your enthusiasm and expressed desire to accomplish something profoundly important. Too often, leaders spread themselves thin and want to identify with the next flavor of the month. The greatest leaders throughout history could not do it, and I suggest we use them as a starting point for role modeling. You will know that people identify with what you are trying to present when they come up with examples that are beyond the ones you have been presenting to them to clarify the mission or vision. At that point in their understanding, a true shift in perspective has occurred, and you can now rest a bit easier that your leadership legacy, as well as your shadow, is well on its way to being formed in your second in command and beyond.

No higher control exists in the universe than that based on complete and absolute trust in someone. You will stop and wait, you will never question, you will follow absolutely willingly, and you will place your most precious secrets with those people you trust. It is a battleground in organizations that is won and lost almost every day by leaders, followers, teams, and entire organizations. You certainly feel the impact of its absence in those organizations with profoundly obvious organizational structures that are supposed to ensure that employees comply with doing the right thing. In those situations, so much energy is dissipated in a system that requires commitment to controls.

At the opposite end, it is an amazing feeling to be part of a relationship, team, or organization based on trust. It is nice to have trust; it is part of the fundamental framework required for achieving the vital force in any organization, team, relationship, and individual. It is a must have to sustain success and reinvention of one's self, a group, an organization, a community, and a society. If it is not there, you will expend a lot of time and resources assuring compliance.

Trust is as fragile as vulnerability, but unfortunately, it is too often taken for granted until it is lost. As a leader, you must know where you are in the process of building trust. At times, you first have to clear the land, so to speak, before you can build the foundation for trust. The more mistrust that pervades a system before you start your good work, the more likely the clearing process must be put in place. It will take time to take out the immunities that will kill any initiative you attempt in a leadership role. Also frustrating to many leaders is that trust requires continuous replenishment as new people get on board, but it is never as difficult as the first time, because over time you will have advocates.

Trust is part of the essential foundation for accomplishing one's leadership legacy over time. No one carries into the future such things as ideals, principles, and beliefs from someone she or he does not trust. So, in the end, if you have a long-term, personal vision for leadership success, the choice to build trust is a simple and profoundly meaningful one for everyone, including for your own aims and aspirations (see Box 15.1).

BOX 15.1   Visionary Leadership and Its Impact via Impression Management

Holladay and Coombs (1994) examined the contribution that context and delivery make to how effective a leader is seen in delivering a visionary statement. This experimental study examined how the leader delivered the vision (strong versus weak) and the vision content, including such things as emphasis or mission, core values, and optimism. Both vision style and content positively affected the leader's charismatic image and perceived effectiveness, although delivery was weighted by raters as far more important to these judgments. Your commitment should determine the quality of your delivery; otherwise, it is just impression management, which is not sustainable.

A few years ago, I interviewed a CEO who said he had been implementing a team-building program in his factory for 2 years. When I interviewed his staff, no one had heard of a team-building program. At the end of the day, I asked him about this discrepancy. To paraphrase what he said, "I have spent the past 2 years building trust around here. That's Module 1 in my team-building program."

And now, we end where we began, with our discussion concerning perspective. This whole journey together has been about developing, shifting, and reinforcing aspects of each of our perspectives, or you can call it your implicit model of leadership and its development. Leaders, who we may also consider exemplary, have developed a lens and frame of reference through which they view the world that we write about and discuss with colleagues. These leaders viewed the world in a way no one else considered, and in so doing, they took small steps that contributed to huge steps for humankind. In both leader and follower, the transformation my colleagues and I have studied is fundamentally about a shift in perspective, which ultimately leads to a shift in behaviors, actions, and accomplishments.

Development in its purest sense involves the planned evolution of people's perspectives and the capacity to enlarge those perspectives to understand the needs, abilities, and aspirations of all those around you and those you will meet in the future. In this journey, your perspective will often have to continue to evolve for others around you also to advance and develop to their full potential. Your continuous personal improvement (CPI) leads to their CPI, which in turn ignites the continuous process improvement (CPI) for the organization. It is always a work in progress with never an end point, just a process sustained by the vital forces we have created in each other. So, you do not get to spike the ball but just continue to improve.

Before closing, I need to mention one other person. Early on in this book, I talked about the importance of the parent as leader and how the teacher picks up where the parent left off, and the manager picks up the rest in terms of developing the full potential of individuals. I tend to see the trainer as being the last in the food chain for developing leadership. Everything I have said about leadership at the high end applies to exemplary parenting.

In our research on life streams and their development, my colleagues and I have discovered that one of the most important factors is the ethical standards set by the mother as a role model for her children (see Box 15.2). Recalling that Martin Luther King Jr., Mahatma Gandhi, and Nelson Mandela were all primarily raised by their mothers, I often joke with people that my best contribution to the leadership potential of my children would be to die young in order to get out of their mother's way. Their mother, Beth, represents one of the most principled people I have ever known, and in every sense, she exemplifies all the finest aspects of transformational leadership with our children. She sets for them a very high moral standard, she works with them to do their best, and she challenges the way they think, while also supporting them in all their needs. Every day, I see their respect and admiration for her, and her leadership in our family has convinced me that everything I study about leadership and followership links directly to the family team.

My highest compliment is to say that the teachers and managers who will work with our children in the future will probably have to afford less time to our children's leadership and followership development. And without any evidence from experiments, meta-analyses, or correlation studies, most of what others will see in our children will be a direct consequence of Beth's long shadow of influence. And for that, I will always be grateful. You cannot imagine how profound an experience it is to see such exemplary leadership in one's home every day. What I said nearly 10 years ago is truer even today, so I guess I can now say that I have a longitudinal study of her positive impact on our children, and the evidence will speak for itself over time. To develop leadership means to cover all aspects of the context, including the family and community's contribution.

Okay, a final thought for you to reflect on: If all of this leadership stuff still seems overwhelming to you right now, then you may want to take the approach suggested in the story in Box 15.3 from President John F. Kennedy. It applies as well today as it did a decade ago.

And now, my journey again with you has come to an end. I would like to express my appreciation to you for your willingness to work with me and listen to me, for some again, for others for the first time. I have never taken that for granted, and I would not have done a revision if I thought no one out there was listening. Yet, in the end, if you have gotten this far, you must have read something you liked, and for that I have a deep sense of satisfaction. Go forward, do great things, and make sure you leverage your vulnerabilities.

BOX 15.2   Female and Male Leadership Styles

A commonly asked question is whether men and women lead differently. A number of studies encompassing a broad range of leadership theories have focused on examining this question (Eagly, 1991, 2005; Eagly & Carli, 2003a, 2003b; Eagly & Johannesen-Schmidt, 2001; Eagly, Johannesen-Schmidt, & van Engen, 2003; Eagly & Johnson, 1990; Eagly & Karau, 2002). For example, Eagly (1991) and Eagly and Johnson (1990) concluded, based on a comprehensive meta-analysis of differences in female and male leadership styles, that on average, women leaders tended to be more democratic and participative than their male counterparts. "Women evidently proceed with more collaboration and sharing of decision-making" (Eagly, 1991, p. 16). Yet, the actual differences were rather small and varied at times, depending on the role held by the leader.

(Continued)

(Continued)

Hackman, Furniss Hills, and Peterson (1992) reported that both feminine and masculine factors were positively correlated with evaluations of female and male leaders' transactional and transformational leadership. The pattern in these results might suggest that to be optimally effective requires that leaders be both feminine (for example, empathic) and masculine (for example, decisive) in their behavior and style. Thus, a balance between the two over time may provide the basis for the highly effective transformational leader.

Bass, Avolio, and Atwater (1996) examined female and male differences in leadership style by using the MLQ survey. Generally, the differences across three separate studies between female and male leaders were rather small, although there was a consistent tendency for female leaders to be rated more transformational than their male counterparts by both female and male raters. The mean differences were stronger for managers from larger *Fortune* 500–type organizations as compared to MLQ data for female and male leaders in not-for-profit, small health-care, social service, government, and other local agencies, as well as in small businesses. In a fourth sample of leaders who were from educational organizations and held positions such as superintendents, principals, and staff from public school districts, again the differences in leadership style were not very large between female and male leaders rated by their direct reports.

Avolio, Mhatre, Norman, and Lester (2009) conducted a comprehensive meta-analysis to examine if there were gender differences associated with different types of leadership interventions. For example, does the impact of a developmental intervention vary for male versus female participants? Comparing the overall effect sizes for the impact of leadership interventions with all male versus all female groups, Avolio et al. reported that the effect sizes were nearly equivalent. However, the authors did report evidence for moderator effects depending on the nature of the intervention, focus of intervention impact, leadership theory, sample characteristics, and study setting.

Overall, the leadership and gender studies have produced some consistent but relatively small differences between men and women's leadership styles. The largest gender differences actually are associated more with differences in beliefs that individuals hold for male versus female leaders or managers. For example, Schein (2001) reported in her research on sex stereotypes associated with managerial or leadership roles that if someone was asked to think about a managerial role, they typically thought more about males and stereotypical male attributes than about females.

BOX 15.3 Reflections on John F. Kennedy

John F. Kennedy liked to tell about a French marshal who assumed control of France's North African territories: Looking around at the barren hillsides, the marshal said to an aide, "We must plant trees." The aide objected, "In this environment, it will take 100 years for a tree to grow to its full height." "In that case," the marshal said, "we have no time to lose. We must begin this very afternoon."

NOTES

1. Christie, P., Lessem, R., & Mbigi, L. (1994). *African management: Philosophies, concepts, and applications.* South Africa: Knowledge Resources.

2. Avolio, B. J. (1995). Integrating transformational leadership and Afrocentric thinking management. *Human Resource Management Journal, 11*(1), 17–21.

3. Hofstede, G. (1991). *Cultures and organizations: Software of the mind.* New York: McGraw-Hill.

4. Bass, B. M., & Avolio, B. J. (1994). *Improving organizational effectiveness through transformational leadership.* Thousand Oaks, CA: Sage.

5. Avolio, B. J. (1995). Leadership: Building the vital forces in highly developed teams. *Human Resource Management Journal, 11*(6), 10–15.

6. Kelley, R. (1992). *The power of followership.* Garden City, NY: Doubleday.

7. Bass, B. M. (1997). Does the transactional-transformational leadership paradigm transcend organizational and national boundaries? *American Psychologist, 52,* 130–139.

8. Avolio, B. J. (2005). *Leadership development in balance: Made/Born.* Hillsdale, NJ: Lawrence Erlbaum.

9. Avolio, B. J., Walumbwa, F. O., & Weber, T. J. (2008). Integration of leadership theory, research and practice: What's next? *Annual Review of Psychology, 60*, 421–449.

10. Dragoni, L., Tesluk, P. E., Russell, J. E. A., & Oh, I. (2009). Understanding managerial development: Integrating developmental assignments, learning orientation, and access to developmental opportunities in predicting managerial competencies. *Journal of Applied Psychology, 32,* 731–743.

11. Avey, J. B., Avolio, B. J., Crossley, C. D., & Luthans, F. (2008). Psychological ownership: Theoretical extensions, measurement and relation to work outcomes. *Journal of Organizational Behavior, 29*, 1–19.

12. Hannah, S. T., Uhl-Bien, M., Avolio, B. J., & Cabarretta, F. (in press). A framework for examining leadership in extreme contexts. *The Leadership Quarterly, 20*(6), 897–919.

13. Matusek, L. (1997). *Finding your voice: Learning to lead anywhere you want to make a difference* (p. 17). San Francisco: Jossey-Bass.

14. Cascio, W. (1995). Whither industrial and organizational psychology in a changing world of work? *American Psychologist, 50,* 928–934.

15. Hamel, G., & Prahalad, C. K. (1994). *Competing for the future: Breakthrough strategies for seizing control of your industry and creating the markets of tomorrow.* Boston: Harvard Business School Press.

16. Manz, C. M., & Sims, H. P., Jr. (1991). *Super leadership: Leading others to lead themselves.* Upper Saddle River, NJ: Prentice Hall.

17. Gardner, W. L., Avolio, B. J., & Walumbwa, F. (2006). *Authentic leadership theory and practice: Origins, effects and development.* Amsterdam: Elsevier JAI Press.

18. Avolio, B. J., & Luthans, F. (2006). *High impact leader: Moments matter in authentic leadership development.* New York: McGraw-Hill.

19. Salas, E., Mullen, B., Rozell, D., & Driskell, J. E. (1997). *Effects of team building on performance: An integration.* Paper presented at the annual meetings of the Society for Industrial and Organizational Psychology, St. Louis, MO.

20. Manz. C. M. (1986). Self-leadership: Toward an expanded theory of self-influence process in organizations. *Academy of Management Review, 11,* 585–600.

21. Avolio, B. J. (2007). Promoting more integrative strategies for leadership theory building. *American Psychologist, 62,* 25–33.

22. Avolio, B. J., & Hannah, S. T. (2008). Developmental readiness: Accelerating leadership development. *Consulting Psychology Journal, 60,* 331–347.

23. Lord, R. G., & Hall, R. J. (2005). Identity, deep structure and the development of leadership skills. *The Leadership Quarterly, 16,* 591–615. Also see Lord, R. G., & Brown, D. J. (2004). *Leadership processes and follower self-identity.* Hillsdale, NJ: Lawrence Erlbaum.

24. Popper, M., & Liphshitz, R. (n.d.). *Organizational teaming: Mechanisms and feasibility.* Unpublished manuscript, Haifa University, Haifa, Israel.

25. Shamir, B., House, R. J., & Arthur, M. B. (1993). The motivational effects of charismatic leadership: A self-concept based theory. *Organizational Science, 4,* 577–594.

26. Fukujama, F. (1995). *Trust: The social virtues and creation of prosperity.* New York: Free Press.

27. Waldman, D. A., Bass, B. M., & Yammarino, F. J. (1990). Adding to the contingent-reward behavior: The augmenting effect of charismatic leadership. *Group and Organizational Studies, 15,* 381–394.

28. Avolio, B. J., & Bass, B. M. (1988). Transformational leadership, charisma, and beyond. In J. G. Hunt, B. R. Baliga, H. P. Dachler, & C. Schriesheim (Eds.), *Emerging leaders' vistas* (pp. 29–50). New York: Pergamon.

29. Bass, B. M., & Avolio, B. J. (1993). Transformational leadership: A response to critiques. In M. M. Chemers & R. Ayman (Eds.), *Leadership theory and research: Perspectives and directions* (pp. 49–80). New York: Academic Press.

30. Bass, B. M., & Avolio, B. J. (1997). *Manual for the Multifactor Leadership Questionnaire.* Palo Alto, CA: Mindgarden.

31. Bass, B. M. (1990). *Bass & Stogdill's handbook of leadership.* New York: Free Press.

32. Frost, P. J. (1997). Cross-roads. *Organizational Science, 8,* 332–347.

33. Bass, B. M., & Bass, R. (2008). *The handbook of leadership* (4th ed.). New York: Free Press.

34. Judge, T. A., & Piccolo, R. (2004). Transformational and transactional leadership: A meta-analytic test of their relative validity. *Journal of Applied Psychology, 89,* 755–768.

35. Bass, B. M. (1998a). *Transformational leadership: Industry, military, and educational impact.* Hillsdale, NJ: Lawrence Erlbaum.

36. Kuhnert, K. W., & Lewis, P. (1987). Transactional and transformational leadership: A constructive developmental analysis. *Academy of Management Review, 12,* 648–657.

37. Lord, R. G., & Maher, K. J. (1991). *Leadership and information processing: Linking perceptions and performance.* Boston: Routledge.

38. Atwater, L. E., Ostroff, C., Yammarino, F. J., & Fleenor, J. W. (1998). Self-other agreement: Does it really matter? *Personnel Psychology, 51,* 577–598.

39. Avolio, B. J., Waldman, D. A., & Yammarino, F. J. (1991). Leading in the 1990's: Towards understanding the four I's of transformation leadership. *Journal of European Industries Training, 175,* 571–580.

40. Bass, B. M., & Riggio, R. (2006). *Transformational leadership.* Hillsdale, NJ: Lawrence Erlbaum.

41. Heifetz, R. A. (1994). *Leadership without any easy answers.* Cambridge, MA: Harvard University Press.

42. Peck, M. S. (1993). *A world waiting to be born: Civility rediscovered.* New York: Bantam.

43. Day, D. V. (2000). Leadership development: A review in context. *The Leadership Quarterly, 11,* 581–614.

44. Day, D. V., Harrison, M. M., & Halpin, S. M. (2008). *An integrative approach to leader development: Connecting adult development, identity, and expertise.* New York: Psychology Press.

45. Kark, R., & Shamir, B. (2002). The dual effect of transformational leadership: Priming relational and collective selves and further effects on followers. In B. J. Avolio & F. J. Yammarino (Eds.), *Transformational and charismatic leadership: The road ahead* (Vol. 2, pp. 67–91). Oxford, UK: Elsevier Science.

46. Kark, R., Shamir, B., & Chen, G. (2003). The two faces of transformational leadership: Empowerment and dependency. *Journal of Applied Psychology, 88,* 246–255.

47. Tichy, N., & Devana, M. (1986). *Transformational leadership.* New York: John Wiley.

48. Bass, B. M. (1985). *Leadership and performance beyond expectations.* New York: Free Press.

49. Bennis, W. G., & Nanus, B. (1985). *Leaders: The strategies for taking charge.* New York: Harper & Row.

50. Storm, H. (1994). *Lightning bolt.* New York: Ballantine.

51. Kark, R., Shamir, B., & Chen, G. (2003). The two faces of transformational leadership: Empowerment and dependency. *Journal of Applied Psychology, 88,* 246–255.

52. Judge, T. A., & Piccolo, R. (2004). Transformational and transactional leadership: A meta-analytic test of their relative validity. *Journal of Applied Psychology, 89,* 755–768.

53. Avolio, B. J. (2005). *Leadership development in balance: Made/Born.* Hillsdale, NJ: Lawrence Erlbaum.

54. Avolio, B. J., Sosik, J. J., Jung, D. I., & Berson, Y. (2003). Leadership models, methods, and applications. In I. B. Weiner (Ed.), *Handbook of Psychology* (pp. 277–307). Hoboken, NJ: John Wiley.

55. Bass, B. M., & Bass, R. (2008). *The handbook of leadership* (4th ed.). New York: Free Press.

56. Avolio, B. J., Zhu, W., Koh, W., Puja, B. (2004). Transformational leadership and organizational commitment: Mediating role of psychological empowerment and moderating role of structural distance. *Journal of Organizational Behavior, 25,* 951–968.

57. Colbert, A. E., Kristof-Brown, A. L., Bradley, B. H., & Barrick, M. R. (2008). CEO transformational leadership: The role of goal importance congruence in top management teams. *Academy of Management Journal, 51,* 81–96.

58. Burns, J. M. (1978). *Leadership.* New York: Free Press.

59. Bass, B. M. (1985). *Leadership and performance beyond expectations.* New York: Free Press.

60. Sergiovanni, T. J. (1990). *Value-added leadership: How to get extraordinary results* in schools. Orlando, FL: Harcourt Brace.

61. Dirks, K. T., & Ferrin, D. L. (2002). Trust in leadership: Meta-analytic findings and implications for organizational research. *Journal of Applied Psychology, 87,* 611–628.

62. Dumdum, U. R., Lowe, K. B., & Avolio, B. J. (2002). A meta-analysis of transformational and transactional leadership correlates of effectiveness and satisfaction: An update and extension. In B. J. Avolio & F. J. Yammarino (Eds.), *Transformational and charismatic leadership: The road ahead* (pp. 35–66). Oxford, UK: Elsevier Science.

63. Waldman, D. A., Javidan, M., & Varella, P. (2004). Charismatic leadership at the strategic level: A new application of upper echelons theory. *The Leadership Quarterly, 15*(3), 355–380.

64. Waldman, D. A., Ramirez, G. G., House, R. J., & Puranam, P. (2001). Does leadership matter? CEO leadership attributes and profitability under conditions of perceived environmental uncertainty. *Academy of Management Journal, 44*(1), 134–143.

65. Shamir, B., House, R. J., & Arthur, M. B. (1993). The motivational effect of charismatic leadership: A self-concept based theory. *Organization Science, 4,* 577–594.

66. Bass, B. M., & Avolio, B. J. (1998). *Manual for the Multifactor Leadership Questionnaire.* Redwood, CA: Mindgarden.

67. Avolio, B. J., Bass, B. M., & Jung, D. I. (1999). Reexamining the components of transformational and transactional leadership using the Multifactor Leadership Questionnaire. *Journal of Occupational and Organizational Psychology, 72,* 441–462.

68. Antonakis, J., Avolio, B. J., & Sivasubramaniam, N. (2003). Examining the contextual nature of the nine-factor, full range leadership theory using the Multi-factor Leadership Questionnaire. *The Leadership Quarterly, 14*(3), 261–295.

69. Sivasubramaniam, N., Murry, W. D., Avolio, B. J., & Jung, D. I. (1997). *A longitudinal model of the effects of team leadership and group potency on performance.* Unpublished manuscript, Binghamton University, Center for Leadership Studies, Binghamton, NY. Also see Sivasubramaniam, N., Jung, D. I., Avolio, B. J., & Murry, W. D. (2002). A longitudinal model of the effects of team leadership and group potency on group performance. *Group and Organization Management, 27,* 66–96.

70. Howell, J. M., & Avolio, B. J. (1993). Transformational leadership, transactional leadership, locus of control, and support for innovation: Key predictors of consolidated-unit performance. *Journal of Applied Psychology, 78,* 891–902.

71. Avolio, B. J., Howell, J. M., & Sosik, J. J. (1999). A funny thing happened on the way to the bottom-line. *Academy of Management Journal, 42,* 219–227.

72. Arvey, R. D., Zhang, Z., Avolio, B. J., & Krueger, R. F. (2007). Developmental and genetic determinants of leadership role occupancy among women. *Journal of Applied Psychology, 92,* 693–706.

73. Arvey, R. D., Rotundo, M., Johnson, W., Zhang, Z., & McGue, M. (2006). The determinants of leadership role occupancy: Genetic and personality factors. *The Leadership Quarterly, 17*(1), 1–20.

74. Day, D. V., Harrison, M. M., Halpin, S. M. (2008). *An integrative approach to leader development: Connecting adult development, identity, and expertise.* New York: Psychology Press.

75. Eden, D. (1990). *Pygmalion in management: Productivity as a self-fulfilling prophecy.* Lexington, MA: Lexington.

76. Eden, D., & Shani, A. B. (1992). Pygmalion goes to boot camp: Expectancy, leadership, and trainee performance. *Journal of Applied Psychology, 67,* 194–199.

77. Rose, R. J. (1995). Genes and human behavior. *Annual Review of Psychology, 46,* 625–654.

78. Gal, R. (1981). *A portrait of an Israeli soldier.* Westport, CT: Greenwood.

79. Vernon, T. (1996). Personal communication on results concerning the heritability of self-ratings of leadership using the Multifactor Leadership Questionnaire (MLQ).

80. Avolio, B. J., & Hannah, S. T. (2008). Developmental readiness: Accelerating leadership development. *Consulting Psychology Journal, 60,* 331–347.

81. Kuhnert, K. W. (1994). Developing people through delegation. In B. M. Bass & B. J. Avolio (Eds.), *Improving organizational effectiveness through transformational leadership* (pp. 10–25). Thousand Oaks, CA: Sage.

82. Avolio, B. J., & Gibbons, T. C. (1988). Developing transformational leaders: A lifespan approach. In J. A. Conger & R. N. Kanungo (Eds.), *Charismatic leadership: The elusive factor in organizational effectiveness* (pp. 276–308). San Francisco: Jossey-Bass.

83. Avolio, B. J., & Wernsing, T. S. (2008). Practicing authentic leadership. In S. J. Lopez (Ed.), *Positive psychology: Exploring the best in people* (pp. 147–165). Westport, CT: Greenwood.

84. Avolio, B. J., Bass, B. M., Atwater, L. E., Lau, A. W., Dionne, S., Camobreco, J., & Whitmore, N. (1994). *Antecedent predictors of the full range of leadership and management styles* (Contract MDA 903–91–0131). Binghamton, NY: Binghamton University, Center for Leadership Studies.

85. Yammarino, F. J., & Bass, B. M. (1990). Long-term forecasting of transformational leadership. In *Measures of leadership* (pp. 151–169). West Orange, NJ: Leadership Library of America.

86. Avolio, B. J., & Gibbons, T. C. (1988). Developing transformational leaders: A lifespan approach. In J. A. Conger & R. N. Kanungo (Eds.), *Charismatic leadership: The elusive factor in organizational effectiveness* (pp. 276–308). San Francisco: Jossey-Bass.

87. Avolio, B. J., Reichard, R. J., Hannah, S. T., Walumbwa, F. O., & Chan, A. (2009). A meta-analytic review of leadership impact research: Experimental and quasi-experimental studies. *The Leadership Quarterly, 20*(5), 764–784.

88. Frankl, V. E. (1963). *Man's search for meaning: An introduction to logo therapy.* New York: Pocket Books.

89. Gardner, W. L., Avolio, B. J., & Walumbwa, F. (2006). *Authentic leadership theory and practice: Origins, effects and development.* Amsterdam: Elsevier JAI Press.

90. Walumbwa, F. O., Avolio, B. J., & Zhu, W. (2008). How transformational leadership weaves its influence on individual job performance: The role of identification and efficacy beliefs. *Personnel Psychology, 61,* 793–825.

91. Carsten, M., Uhl-Bien, M., Patera, J., West, B., & McGregor, I. (2007). *Social constructions of followership.* Presented at Academy of Management conference, Philadelphia, PA.

92. Berson, Y., & Avolio, B. J. (2004). Linking transformational and strategic leadership: Examining the leadership system of a high-technology organization in a turbulent environment. *The Leadership Quarterly, 15*(5), 625–646.

93. Bono, J. E., & Judge, T. A. (2003). Self-concordance at work: Toward understanding the motivational effects of transformational leaders. *Academy of Management Journal, 46*, 554–571.

94. Kark, R., & Shamir, B. (2002). The dual effect of transformational leadership: Priming relational and collective selves and further effects on followers. In B. J. Avolio & F. J. Yammarino (Eds.), *Transformational and charismatic leadership: The road ahead* (Vol. 2, pp. 67–91). Oxford, UK: Elsevier Science.

95. Kark, R., Shamir, B., & Chen, G. (2003). The two faces of transformational leadership: Empowerment and dependency. *Journal of Applied Psychology, 88,* 246–255.

96. Avolio, B. J., Jung, D. I., Murry, W., & Sivasubramaniam, N. (1996). Building highly developed teams: Focusing on shared leadership processes, efficacy, trust and performance. In M. M. Beyerlein, D. A. Johnson, & S. T. Beyerlein (Eds.), *Advances in interdisciplinary studies of work teams* (pp.173–209). Greenwich, CT: JAI Press.

97. Avolio, B. J. (2007). Promoting more integrative strategies for leadership theory building. *American Psychologist, 62,* 25–33.

98. Avolio, B. J. (2005). *Leadership development in balance: Made/Born.* Hillsdale, NJ: Lawrence Erlbaum.

99. Avolio, B. J., Jung, D. I., Murry, W., & Sivasubramaniam, N. (1996). Building highly developed teams: Focusing on shared leadership processes, efficacy, trust and performance. In M. M. Beyerlein, D. A. Johnson, & S. T. Beyerlein (Eds.), *Advances in interdisciplinary studies of work teams* (pp. 173–209). Greenwich, CT: JAI Press.

100. Kazenbach, R. (1998). *Teams at the top.* Boston: Harvard Business School Press.

101. Cohen, S. G., Chang, L., & Ledford, G. E. (1997). A hierarchical construct of self-management leadership and its relationship to quality of work life and perceived group effectiveness. *Personnel Psychology, 50,* 275–308.

102. Avolio, B. J. (1997). *The great leadership migration to a full range leadership system.* College Park: University of Maryland.

103. Avolio, B. J., Kahai, S. S., & Dodge, G. E. (2000). E-leadership: Implications for theory, research, and practice. *The Leadership Quarterly, 11*(4), 615–668.

104. Hyatt, D. E., & Ruddy, Y. M. (1997). An examination of the relationship between work group characteristics and performance: Once more into the breech. *Personnel Psychology, 50,* 553–585.

105. Sheff, D. (1996, June/July). Levi's changes everything. *Fast Company,* p. 65.

106. Kotter, J. L. (1992). *Corporate culture and performance* (p. 44). New York: Free Press.

107. Bass, B. M., & Avolio, B. J. (1993). Transformational leadership and organizational culture. *International Journal of Public Administration, 17*(1), 112–122.

108. Miller, D. (1990). *The Icarus Paradox: How exceptional companies bring about their downfall.* New York: Harper Business.

109. Avolio, B. J. (2004). Examining the full range model of leadership: Looking back to transform forward. In D. V. Day, S. J. Zaccaro, & S. M. Halpin (Eds.), *Leader development for transforming organizations: Growing leaders for tomorrow* (pp. 71–98). Hillsdale, NJ: Lawrence Erlbaum.

110. Cascio, W. (1995). Whether industrial and organizational psychology in a changing world of work? *American Psychologist, 50,* 928–934.

111. Berson, Y., Shamir, B., Avolio, B. J., & Popper, M. (2001). The relationship between vision strength, leadership style, and context. *The Leadership Quarterly, 12*(1), 53–74.

112. Bass, B. M. (1990). *Bass & Stogdill's handbook of leadership.* New York: Free Press.

113. Deming, W. E. (1986). *Drastic changes for Western management.* Madison, WI: Center for Quality and Productivity Improvement.

114. Tapscott, D. (1995). *The Digital economy: Promise and peril in the age of networked intelligence.* New York: McGraw-Hill.

115. Bass, B. M. (1998b, March–April). Leading in the army after next. *Military Review,* 46–57.

116. Avolio, B. J., & Luthans, F. (2006). *High impact leader: Moments matter in authentic leadership development* (p. 47). New York: McGraw-Hill.

117. Hannah, S. T., Uhl-Bien, M., Avolio, B. J., & Cabarretta, F. (2009). A framework for examining leadership in extreme contexts. *The Leadership Quarterly, 20*(6), 897–919.

118. Hackman, J. R. (1990). *Groups that work (and those that don't): Creating conditions for effective teamwork.* San Francisco: Jossey-Bass.

119. Jehn, K. A. (1997). A qualitative analysis of conflict types and dimensions in organizational groups. *Administrative Science Quarterly, 42,* 530–557.

120. Gersick, C. J. G. (1988). Time and transition in work teams: Toward a new model of group development. *Academy of Management Journal, 31,* 9–41.

121. Kazenbach, J. R., & Smith, D. K. (1993). *The wisdom of teams: Creating the high-performing organization.* Boston: Harvard Business School Press.

122. Seltzer, J., Numerof, R. E., & Bass, B. M. (1989). Transformational leadership: Is it a source of more or less burnout or stress? *Journal of Health and Human Resources Administration, 12,* 174–185.

123. Burgess, K. A., Salas, E., Cannon-Bowers, J. A., & Hall, J. K. (1992, October). *Training guidelines for team leaders under stress.* Paper presented to the Human Factors Society, Atlanta, GA.

124. Avolio, B. J., & Bass, B. M. (1995). Individualized consideration is more than consideration for the individual when viewed at multiple levels of analysis. *The Leadership Quarterly, 6*(2), 199–218.

125. Bass, B. M., & Avolio, B. J. (1997). *Platoon readiness as a function of transformational/transactional leadership squad mores and platoon cultures* (Army Research Institute contract #DASW01–96K-008).

126. Avolio, B. J., Jung, D. I., Murry, W., & Sivasubramaniam, N. (1996). Building highly developed teams: Focusing on shared leadership processes, efficacy, trust and performance. In M. M. Beyerlein, D. A. Johnson, & S. T. Beyerlein (Eds.), *Advances in interdisciplinary studies of work teams* (pp. 173–209). Greenwich, CT: JAI Press.

127. Howell, J. J., & Higgins, C. A. (1992). Leadership behaviors influence tactics and career experience of champions of technical innovation. *The Leadership Quarterly, 1*(4), 249–264.

128. Most, R., & Avolio, B. J. (1997). Utilizing Web-site technology in developing the full potential of organizations. *Industrial Psychologist, 34*(4), 11–13.

129. Bass, B. M., & Riggio, R. (2006). *Transformational leadership.* Hillsdale, NJ: Lawrence Erlbaum.

130. Avolio, B. J. (2005). *Leadership development in balance: Made/Born.* Hillsdale, NJ: Lawrence Erlbaum.

131. Dvir, T., & Shamir, B. (2003). Follower developmental characteristics as predicting transformational leadership: A longitudinal field study. *The Leadership Quarterly, 14*(3), 327.

132. Avolio, B. J., Avey, J. B., & Quisenberry, D. (in press). Estimating the return on leadership development. *The Leadership Quarterly.*

133. Avolio, B. J., Reichard, R. J., Hannah, S. T., Walumbwa, F. O., & Chan, A. (2009). A meta-analytic review of leadership impact research: Experimental and quasi-experimental studies. *The Leadership Quarterly, 20*(5), 764–784.

134. Hesketh, M. (1997). Dilemmas in transfer of training. *Applied Psychology: An International Review, 46,* 317–386.

135. Avolio, B. J. (2005). *Leadership development in balance: Made/Born.* Hillsdale, NJ: Lawrence Erlbaum.

136. Weber, M. (1947). *The theory of social and economic organizations* (T. Parsons, Trans.). New York: Free Press. (Original work published 1927)

137. Dirks, K. T., & Ferrin, D. L. (2002). Trust in leadership: Meta-analytic findings and implications for organizational research. *Journal of Applied Psychology, 87,* 611–628.

138. Berson, Y., Shamir, B., Avolio, B. J., & Popper, M. (2001). The relationship between vision strength, leadership style, and context. *The Leadership Quarterly, 12*(1), 53–74.

139. Shamir, B., House, R. J., & Arthur, M. B. (1993). The motivational effects of charismatic leadership: A self-concept based theory. *Organizational Science, 4,* 577–594.

140. Greenleaf, R. K., (1997). The servant as leader. In R. P. Vecchio (Ed.), *Leadership: Understanding the dynamics of power and influence in organizations.* Notre Dame, IN: University of Notre Dame Press.

141. Bass, B. M., & Bass, R. (2008). *The handbook of leadership* (4th ed.). New York: Free Press.

142. Kouzes, J. M., & Posner, B. Z. (1991). *Credibility: How leaders gain and lose it. Why people demand it.* San Francisco: Jossey-Bass.

143. Walumbwa, F. O., Avolio, B. J., & Zhu, W. (2008). How transformational leadership weaves its influence on individual job performance: The role of identification and efficacy beliefs. *Personnel Psychology, 61,* 793–825.

144. Frost, P. J. (1997). Cross-roads. *Organizational Science, 8,* 332–347.

145. Quinn, J. B. (1997). *Innovation explosion: Using intellect and software to revolutionize growth strategies.* New York: Free Press.

146. Burns, J. M. (1978). *Leadership.* New York: Free Press.

147. Bass, B. M., & Bass, R. (2008). *The handbook of leadership* (4th ed.). New York: Free Press.

148. Bass, B. M., & Riggio, R. (2006). *Transformational leadership.* Hillsdale, NJ: Lawrence Erlbaum.

149. Bass, B. M., Avolio, B. J., Jung, D. I., & Berson, Y. (2003). Predicting unit performance by assessing transformational and transactional leadership. *Journal of Applied Psychology, 88,* 207–218.

150. Meindle, J. R., Ehrlich, S. B., & Dukerich, J. M. (1985). The romance of leadership. *Administrative Sciences Quarterly, 30,* 78–102.

151. Bass, B. M., Waldman, D. A., Avolio, B. J., & Bebb, M. (1987). Transformational leadership and the falling dominoes effect. *Group and Organizational Studies, 12,* 73–87.

152. Cohen, S. G., Chang, L., & Ledford, G. E. (1997). A hierarchical construct of self-management leadership and its relationship to quality of work life and perceived group effectiveness. *Personnel Psychology, 50,* 275–308.

153. Drucker, P. (1993). *Managing for the future: The 1990s and beyond.* New York: Truman Tally Books.

154. Koh, W., Terburg, J. R., & Steers, R. M. (1992). *The impact of transformational leadership on organizational commitment, organizational citizenship behavior, teacher satisfaction, and student performance in Singapore.* Paper presented at the Academy of Management, Miami Beach, FL.

155. Shea, C., & Howell, J. H. (1995). *The effects of charismatic leadership and task feedback on self-efficacy, performance quality, and attributes.* Doctoral dissertation, Richard Ivey School of Business, London, Ontario, Canada.

156. Thite, M. (1997). *Relationship between leadership and information technology project sources.* Unpublished doctoral dissertation, Swinburne University of Technology, Melbourne, Australia.

157. Howell, J. M., & Higgins, C. A. (1990). Champions of technological innovations. *Administrative Science Quarterly, 35*(2), 317–341.

158. Avolio, B. J., Jung, D. I., Murry, W., & Sivasubramaniam, N. (1996). Building highly developed teams: Focusing on shared leadership processes, efficacy, trust and performance. In M. M. Beyerlein, D. A. Johnson, & S. T. Beyerlein (Eds.), *Advances in interdisciplinary studies of work teams* (pp. 173–209). Greenwich, CT: JAI Press.

159. Howell, J. M., Neufeld, D. J., & Avolio, B. J. (1998). *Leadership at a distance: The effects of physical distance, charismatic leadership, and communication style on predicting business unit performance.* Unpublished manuscript, University of Western Ontario, London, Ontario, Canada. Also see Howell, J. M., Neufeld, D. J., & Avolio, B. J. (2005). Leadership at a distance: The effects of physical distance, charismatic leadership, and communication style on predicting business unit performance. *The Leadership Quarterly, 16,* 273–286.

160. Avolio, B. J., Howell, J. M., & Sosik, J. J. (1999). A funny thing happened on the way to the bottom-line. *Academy of Management Journal, 42,* 219–227.

161. Atwater, L. E., Camobreco, J. F., Dionne, S. D., Avolio, B. J., & Lau, A. N. (1997). Effects of rewards and punishment on leader charisma, leader effectiveness, and follower reactions. *The Leadership Quarterly, 8*(2), 133–152.

162. Howell, J. A., & Avolio, B. J. (1993). Predicting consolidated unit performance: Leadership behavior, locus of control, and support for innovation. *Journal of Applied Psychology, 78,* 891–902.

163. Weick, K. (1991). Educational organizations as loosely coupled systems. *Administrative Sciences Quarterly, 21,* 1–19.

164. Winston, M. G. (1997). Leadership of renewal: Leadership for the 21st century. *Business Forum, 22,* 4–7.

165. Balthazard, P. A., Waldman, D. A., & Atwater, L. E. (2008). The mediating effects of leadership and interaction style in face-to-face and virtual teams. In S. Weisband (Ed.),

Leadership at a distance: Research in technologically-supported work (pp. 127–150). Hillsdale, NJ: Lawrence Erlbaum.

166. Howell, J. M., & Shamir, B. (2005). The role of followers in the charismatic leadership process: Relationships and their consequences. *Academy of Management Review, 30*, 96–112.

167. Atwater, L. E., Dionne, S., Avolio, B. J., & Camobreco, J. F. (1999). A longitudinal study of the leadership development process: Individual differences predicting leader effectiveness. *Human Relations, 52*(12), 1543–1562.

168. Howell, J. A., & Avolio, B. J. (1992). Charismatic leadership: Submission or liberation. *Academy of Management Executive, 6,* 43–54.

169. Howell, J. M. (1988). The two faces of charisma: Socialized and personalized leadership in organizations. In J. Conger & R. Kanungo (Eds.), *Charismatic leadership: The illusive factor in organizational effectiveness.* San Francisco: Jossey-Bass.

170. Kuhnert, K. W. (1994). Developing people through delegation. In B. M. Bass & B. J. Avolio (Eds.), *Improving organizational effectiveness through transformational leadership* (pp. 10–25). Thousand Oaks, CA: Sage.

171. Miller, H. (1997). Interview with Max Depree. *Leader to Leader, 6,* 18–23.

172. Colbert, A. E., Kristof-Brown, A. L., Bradley, B. H., & Barrick, M. R. (2008). CEO transformational leadership: The role of goal importance congruence in top management teams. *Academy of Management Journal, 51,* 81–96.

173. Avolio, B. J., Avey, J. B., & Quisenberry, D. (in press). Estimating the return on leadership development. *The Leadership Quarterly.*

174. Kark, R., & Shamir, B. (2002). The dual effect of transformational leadership: Priming relational and collective selves and further effects on followers. In B. J. Avolio & F. J. Yammarino (Eds.), *Transformational and charismatic leadership: The road ahead* (Vol. 2, pp. 67–91). Oxford, UK: Elsevier Science.

175. Avolio, B. J. (2005). *Leadership development in balance: Made/Born.* Hillsdale, NJ: Lawrence Erlbaum.

176. Day, D. V., Harrison, M. M., & Halpin, S. M. (2008). *An integrative approach to leader development: Connecting adult development, identity, and expertise.* New York: Psychology Press.

177. Avolio, B. J., Rotundo, M., & Walumbwa, F. O. (2009). Early life experiences as determinants of leadership role occupancy: The role of parental influence and rule breaking behavior. *The Leadership Quarterly, 20*(3), 329–342.

178. Avolio, B. J. (2005). *Leadership development in balance: Made/Born.* Hillsdale, NJ: Lawrence Erlbaum.

179. Avolio, B. J., Walumbwa, F. O., & Weber, T. J. (2008). Integration of leadership theory, research and practice: What's next? *Annual Review of Psychology, 60,* 421–449.

180. Hannah, S. T., Woolfolk, L., & Lord, R. G. (2009). Leader self-structure: A framework for positive leadership. *Journal of Organizational Behavior, 30,* 269–290.

181. Kernis, M. H. (2003). Toward a conceptualization of optimal self-esteem. *Psychological Inquiry, 14*(1), 1–26.

182. Gardner, W. L., Avolio, B. J., Luthans, F., May, D. R., & Walumbwa, F. (2005). "Can you see the real me?" A self-based model of authentic leadership and follower development. *The Leadership Quarterly, 16*(3), 343–372.

183. Gardner et al. (2005). Ibid.

184. Ryan, R. M., & Deci, E. L. (2001). To be happy or to be self-fulfilled: A review of research on hedonic and eudaimonic well-being. In S. Fiske (Ed.), *Annual review of psychology* (Vol. 52; pp. 141–166). Palo Alto, CA: Annual Reviews.

185. Sheldon, K. M., & Elliot, A. J. (1999). Goal striving, need-satisfaction, and longitudinal well-being: The self-concordance model. *Journal of Personality and Social Psychology, 76*, 482–497.

186. Avolio, B. J., & Wernsing, T. S. (2008). Practicing authentic leadership. In S. J. Lopez (Ed.) *Positive psychology: Exploring the best in people* (pp. 147–165). Westport, CT: Greenwood.

187. Ibid.

188. Wernsing, T. S. (2010). *Leader self-awareness development: An intervention and test of a theoretical model.* Unpublished doctoral dissertation, University of Nebraska, Lincoln.

189. Avey, J. B., Avolio, B. J., Crossley, C. D., & Luthans, F. (2008). Psychological ownership: Theoretical extensions, measurement and relation to work outcomes. *Journal of Organizational Behavior, 29,* 1–19.

190. Bandura, A. (1997). *Self-efficacy: The exercise of control.* New York: Freeman.

191. Hannah, S. T., Uhl-Bien, M., Avolio, B. J., & Cabarretta, F. (2009). A framework for examining leadership in extreme contexts. *The Leadership Quarterly, 20*(6), 897–919.

192. Ibid. p. 898.

193. Bass, B. M. (1998b, March–April). Leading in the army after next. *Military Review,* 46–57.

Box and Additional Research References

Agle, B. R. (1993). *Charismatic chief executive officers: Are they more effective? An empirical test of charismatic leadership theory.* Unpublished doctoral dissertation, University of Washington, Seattle.

Agle, B. R., Nagarajan, N. J., Sonnenfeld, J. A., & Srinivasan, D. (2006). Does CEO charisma matter? An empirical analysis of the relationships among organizational performance, environmental uncertainty, and top management team perceptions of CEO charisma. *Academy of Management Journal, 49,* 161–174.

Albert Einstein. (n.d). In *Wikiquote.* Retrieved on May 21, 2010, from http://en.wikiquote.org/wiki/Albert_Einstein

American Society for Training and Development. (2007). *Managing talent key human resource challenge around the globe.* Alexandria, VA: Author.

Antonakis, J., Avolio, B. J., & Sivasubramaniam, N. (2003). Examining the contextual nature of the nine-factor, full range leadership theory using the Multi-factor Leadership Questionnaire. *The Leadership Quarterly, 14*(3), 261–295.

Arvey, R. D., Rotundo, M., Johnson, W., Zhang, Z., & McGue, M. (2006). The determinants of leadership role occupancy: Genetic and personality factors. *The Leadership Quarterly, 17*(1), 1–20.

Arvey, R. D., Zhang, Z., Avolio, B. J., & Kruger, R. F. (2007). Developmental and genetic determinants of leadership role occupancy among women. *Journal of Applied Psychology, 92,* 693–706.

Asgari, A., Silong, A., Daud, A., & Samah, A. (2008). The relationship between leader-member exchange, organizational inflexibility, perceived organizational support, interactional justice and organizational citizenship behavior. *African Journal of Business Management, 2,* 138–145.

Atkinson, R. (2002). An army at dawn: The war in North Africa, 1942-1943. New York: Henry Holt.

Atwater, L. E., Camobreco, J. F., Dionne, S. D., Avolio, B. J., & Lau, A. N. (1997). Effects of rewards and punishment on leader charisma, leader effectiveness, and follower reactions. *The Leadership Quarterly, 8*(2), 133–152.

Atwater, L. E., Dionne, S., Avolio, B. J., & Camobreco, J. F. (1999). A longitudinal study of the leadership development process: Individual differences predicting leader effectiveness. *Human Relations, 52*(12), 1543–1562.

Atwater, L. E., Lau, A., Bass, B. M., Avolio, B. J., Camobreco, J. F., & Whitmore, N. (1994). *The content, construct, and criterion-related validity of leader behavior measures*. (Research note). Washington, DC: U.S. Army Research Institute.

Atwater, L. E., Ostroff, C., Yammarino, F. J., & Fleenor, J. W. (1998). Self-other agreement: Does it really matter? *Personnel Psychology, 51,* 577–598.

Atwater, L. E., & Yammarino, F. J. (1992). Does self-other agreement on leadership perceptions moderate the validity of leadership and performance predictions? *Personnel Psychology, 45,* 141–164.

Atwater, L. E., & Yammarino, F. J. (1997). Self-other agreement: A review and model. *Research in Personnel and Human Resource Management, 15,* 121–174.

Avey, J. B., Avolio, B. J., Crossley, C. D., & Luthans, F. (2008). Psychological ownership: Theoretical extensions, measurement and relation to work outcomes. *Journal of Organizational Behavior, 29,* 1–19.

Avolio, B. J. (1995a). Integrating transformational leadership and Afrocentric thinking management. *Human Resource Management Journal, 11*(1), 17–21.

Avolio, B. J. (1995b). Leadership: Building the vital forces in highly developed teams. *Human Resource Management Journal, 11*(6), 10–15.

Avolio, B. J. (1999). *Full leadership development: Building the vital forces in organizations.* Thousand Oaks, CA: Sage.

Avolio, B. J. (2004). Examining the full range model of leadership: Looking back to transform forward. In D.V. Day, S. J. Zaccaro, & S. M. Halpin (Eds.), *Leader development for transforming organizations: Growing leaders for tomorrow* (pp. 71–98). Hillsdale, NJ: Lawrence Erlbaum.

Avolio, B. J. (2005). *Leadership development in balance: Made/Born.* Hillsdale, NJ: Lawrence Erlbaum.

Avolio, B. J. (2007). Promoting more integrative strategies for leadership theory building. *American Psychologist, 62,* 25–33.

Avolio, B. J., Avey, J. B., & Quisenberry, D. (in press). Estimating the return on leadership development. *The Leadership Quarterly.*

Avolio, B. J., & Bass, B. M. (1988). Transformational leadership, charisma, and beyond. In J. G. Hunt, B. R. Baliga, H. P. Dachler, & C. Schriesheim (Eds.), *Emerging leaders' vistas* (pp. 29–50). New York: Pergamon.

Avolio, B. J., & Bass, B. M. (1995). Individualized consideration is more than consideration for the individual when viewed at multiple levels of analysis. *The Leadership Quarterly, 6*(2), 199–218.

Avolio, B. J., Bass, B. M., Atwater, L. E., Lau, A. W., Dionne, S., Camobreco, J., & Whitmore, N. (1994). *Antecedent predictors of the full range of leadership and management styles* (Contract MDA 903–91–0131). Binghamton, NY: Binghamton University, Center for Leadership Studies.

Avolio, B. J., Bass, B. M., & Jung, D. I. (1999). Reexamining the components of transformational and transactional leadership using the Multifactor Leadership Questionnaire. *Journal of Occupational and Organizational Psychology, 72,* 441–462.

Avolio, B. J., & Gibbons, T. C. (1988). Developing transformational leaders: A lifespan approach. In J. A. Conger & R. N. Kanungo (Eds.), *Charismatic leadership: The elusive factor in organizational effectiveness* (pp. 276–308). San Francisco: Jossey-Bass.

Avolio, B. J., & Hannah, S. T. (2008). Developmental readiness: Accelerating leadership development. *Consulting Psychology Journal, 60,* 331–347.

Avolio, B. J., Howell, J. M., & Sosik, J. J. (1999). A funny thing happened on the way to the bottom-line. *Academy of Management Journal, 42,* 219–227.

Avolio, B. J., Jung, D. I., Murry, W., & Sivasubramaniam, N. (1996). Building highly developed teams: Focusing on shared leadership processes, efficacy, trust and performance. In M. M. Beyerlein, D. A. Johnson, & S. T. Beyerlein (Eds.), *Advances in interdisciplinary studies of work teams* (pp. 173–209). Greenwich, CT: JAI Press.

Avolio, B. J., Kahai, S. S., & Dodge, G. E. (2000). E-leadership: Implications for theory, research, and practice. *The Leadership Quarterly, 11*(4), 615–668.

Avolio, B. J., & Luthans, F. (2006). *High impact leader: Moments matter in authentic leadership development.* New York: McGraw-Hill.

Avolio, B. J., Mhatre, K., Norman, S., & Lester, P. (2009). The moderating effect of gender on leadership intervention impact: An exploratory review. *Journal of Leadership & Organizational Studies, 15,* 325–341.

Avolio, B. J., Reichard, R. J., Hannah, S. T., Walumbwa, F. O., & Chan, A. (2009). A meta-analytic review of leadership impact research: Experimental and quasi-experimental studies. *The Leadership Quarterly, 20*(5), 764–784.

Avolio, B. J., Rotundo, M., & Walumbwa, F. O. (2009). Early life experiences as determinants of leadership role occupancy: The role of parental influence and rule breaking behavior. *The Leadership Quarterly, 20*(3), 329–342.

Avolio, B. J., Sosik, J. J., Jung, D. I., & Berson, Y. (2003). Leadership models, methods, and applications. In I. B. Weiner (Ed.), *Handbook of psychology* (pp. 277–307). Hoboken, NJ: John Wiley.

Avolio, B. J., Waldman, D. A., & Einstein, W. O. (1988). Transformational leadership in a management game simulation: Impacting the bottom line. *Group and Organization Studies, 13,* 59–80.

Avolio, B. J., Waldman, D. A., & Yammarino, F. J. (1991). Leading in the 1990's: Towards understanding the four I's of Transformation Leadership. *Journal of European Industries Training, 175,* 571–580.

Avolio, B. J., Walumbwa, F. O., & Weber, T. J. (2008). Integration of leadership theory, research and practice: What's next? *Annual Review of Psychology, 60,* 421–449.

Avolio, B. J., & Wernsing, T. S. (2008). Practicing authentic leadership. In S. J. Lopez (Ed.) *Positive psychology: Exploring the best in people* (pp. 147–165). Westport, CT: Greenwood.

Avolio, B. J., & Yammarino, F. J. (Eds.). (2002). *Transformational and charismatic leadership: The road ahead.* Oxford, UK: Elsevier Science.

Avolio, B. J., Zhu, W., Koh, W., & Puja, B. (2004). Transformational leadership and organizational commitment: Mediating role of psychological empowerment and moderating role of structural distance. *Journal of Organizational Behavior, 25,* 951–968.

Balthazard, P. A., Waldman, D. A., & Atwater, L. E. (2008). The mediating effects of leadership and interaction style in face-to-face and virtual teams. In S. Weisband (Ed.), *Leadership at a distance: Research in technologically-supported work* (pp. 127–150). Hillsdale, NJ: Lawrence Erlbaum.

Bandura, A. (1997). *Self-efficacy: The exercise of control.* New York: Freeman.

Barling, J., Weber, T., & Kelloway, E. K. (1996). Effects of transformational leadership training on attitudinal and financial outcomes. *Journal of Applied Psychology, 81,* 827–832.

Bass, B. M. (1985). *Leadership and performance beyond expectations.* New York: Free Press.

Bass, B. M. (1990). *Bass & Stogdill's handbook of leadership.* New York: Free Press.

Bass, B. M. (1997). Does the transactional-transformational leadership paradigm transcend organizational and national boundaries? *American Psychologist, 52,* 130–139.

Bass, B. M. (1998a). *Transformational leadership: Industry, military, and educational impact.* Mahwah, NJ: Lawrence Erlbaum.

Bass, B. M. (1998b, March–April). Leading in the army after next. *Military Review,* 46–57.

Bass, B. M., & Avolio, B. J. (1993a). Transformational leadership: A response to critiques. In M. M. Chemers & R. Ayman (Eds.), *Leadership theory and research: Perspectives and directions* (pp. 49–80). New York: Academic Press.

Bass, B. M., & Avolio, B. J. (1993b). Transformational leadership and organizational culture. *International Journal of Public Administration, 17*(1), 112–122.

Bass, B. M., & Avolio, B. J. (1994). *Improving organizational effectiveness through transformational leadership.* Thousand Oaks, CA: Sage.

Bass, B. M., & Avolio, B. J. (1997a). *Manual for the Multifactor Leadership Questionnaire.* Palo Alto, CA: Mindgarden.

Bass, B. M., & Avolio, B. J. (1997b). *Platoon readiness as a function of transformational/ transactional leadership squad mores and platoon cultures* (Army Research Institute contract #DASW01-96K-008).

Bass, B. M., Avolio, B. J., & Atwater, L. (1996). The transformational and transactional leadership behavior of female and male managers as described by the men and women who directly report to them. *Applied Psychology: An International Review, 45,* 5–34.

Bass, B. M., Avolio, B. J., Jung, D. I., & Berson, Y. (2003). Predicting unit performance by assessing transformational and transactional leadership. *Journal of Applied Psychology, 88,* 207–218.

Bass, B. M., & Bass, R. (2008). *The handbook of leadership* (4th ed.). New York: Free Press.

Bass, B. M., & Riggio, R. (2006). *Transformational leadership.* Hillsdale, NJ: Lawrence Erlbaum.

Bass, B. M., Waldman, D. A., Avolio, B. J., & Bebb, M. (1987). Transformational leadership and the falling dominoes effect. *Group and Organizational Studies, 12,* 73–87.

Baum, G. J., Locke, E. A., & Kirkpatrick, S. A. (1998). A longitudinal study of the relation of vision and vision communication to venture growth in entrepreneurial firms. *Journal of Applied Psychology, 83,* 43–54.

Bennis, W. G., & Nanus, B. (1985). *Leaders: The strategies for taking charge.* New York: Harper & Row.

Berson, Y., & Avolio, B. J. (2004). Linking transformational and strategic leadership: Examining the leadership system of a high-technology organization in a turbulent environment. *The Leadership Quarterly, 15*(5), 625–646.

Berson, Y., Shamir, B., Avolio, B. J., & Popper, M. (2001). The relationship between vision strength, leadership style, and context. *The Leadership Quarterly, 12*(1), 53–74.

Berson, Y., & Yammarino, F. J. (1997). *Followership, leadership, and attachment styles: A developmental approach.* Unpublished manuscript, Binghamton University, Center for Leadership Studies, Binghamton, NY.

Bono, J. E., & Judge, T. A. (2003). Self-concordance at work: Toward understanding the motivational effects of transformational leaders. *Academy of Management Journal, 46,* 554–571.

Bowlby, J. (1969). Attachment. In *Attachment and loss: Vol 1.* London: Hogarth.

Bowlby, J. (1973). Separation: anxiety and anger. In *Attachment and loss: Vol 2.* London: Hogarth.

Brown, F. W., & Moshavi, D. E. (2002). Herding academic cats: Faculty reactions to transformational and contingent reward leadership by department chairs. *Journal of Leadership Studies, 8,* 79–93.

Brown, J. C. (1994). Leadership education through humanistic texts and traditions: The Hartwick classic leadership cases. *Journal of Leadership Studies, 1,* 104–116.

Burgess, K. A., Salas, E., Cannon-Bowers, J. A., & Hall, J. K. (1992). *Training guidelines for team leaders under stress.* Paper presented to the Human Factors Society, Atlanta, GA.

Burns, J. M. (1978). *Leadership.* New York: Free Press.

Butler, C. (1994). The magnificent seven. *Sales & Marketing Management Performance Supplement,* 41–50.

Carless, S., Mann, L., & Wearing, A. (1995). An empirical test of the transformational leadership model. In *Leadership symposium.* Symposium conducted at the Inaugural Australian Industrial and Organizational Psychology Conference, Sydney, Australia.

Carpenter, M. A., Geletkanycz, M. A., & Sanders, W. G. (2004). Upper echelons research revisited: Antecedents, elements, and consequences of top management team composition. *Journal of Management, 30,* 747–778.

Carsten, M., Uhl-Bien, M., Patera, J., West, B., & McGregor, I. (2007). *Social constructions of followership.* Presented at Academy of Management conference, Philadelphia, PA.

Cascio, W. (1995). Whether industrial and organizational psychology in a changing world of work? *American Psychologist, 50,* 928–934.

Cheverton, G. L., & Thompson, B. M. (1996). *Subordinate perceptions of transformational leadership: Relationships with organizational context, formalization, and psychological participation.* Unpublished manuscript.

Christie, P., Lessem, R., & Mbigi, L. (1994). *African management: Philosophies, concepts, and applications.* South Africa: Knowledge Resources.

Clover, W. H. (1988). *Transformational leaders: Team performance, leadership, ratings, and firsthand impressions.* Paper prepared for the Center for Creative Leadership Conference on Psychological Measures and Leadership, Colorado Springs, CO.

Cohen, S. G., Chang, L., & Ledford, G. E. (1997). A hierarchical construct of self-management leadership and its relationship to quality of work life and perceived group effectiveness. *Personnel Psychology, 50,* 275–308.

Colbert, A. E., Kristof-Brown, A. L., Bradley, B. H., & Barrick, M. R. (2008). CEO transformational leadership: The role of goal importance congruence in top management teams. *Academy of Management Journal, 51,* 81–96.

Coleman, E. P., Patterson, E., Fuller, B., Hester, K., & Stringer, D. Y. (1995). *A meta-analytic examination of leadership style and selected follower compliance outcomes.* Unpublished manuscript, University of Alabama, Tuscaloosa.

Colin Powell's thoughts on leadership. (1998). *Industry Week, 245,* 56–57.

Collins, D. B., & Holton, E. F. (2004). The effectiveness of managerial leadership development programs: A meta-analysis of studies from 1982 to 2001. *Human Resource Development Quarterly, 15*(2), 217–242.

Conger, J. A., & Kanungo, R. N. (1988). The empowerment process: Integration, theory and practice. *Academy of Management Review, 13,* 471–482.

Crookall, P. S. (1989). *Leadership in the prison industry: A study of the effect of training prison shop foremen in situational or transformational leadership on inmates' productivity and personal growth.* Unpublished doctoral dissertation, University of Western Ontario, London, Ontario, Canada.

Day, D. V. (2000). Leadership development: A review in context. *The Leadership Quarterly, 11*(4), 581–614.

Day, D. V., Harrison, M. M., & Halpin, S. M. (2008). *An integrative approach to leader development: Connecting adult development, identity, and expertise.* New York: Psychology Press.

Deming, W. E. (1986). *Drastic changes for Western management.* Madison, WI: Center for Quality and Productivity Improvement.

Den Hartog, D. N. (2000). Cultural variation of leadership prototypes across 22 European countries. *Journal of Occupational and Organizational Psychology, 73,* 1–29.

Den Hartog, D. N., Van Muijen, E. J., & Koopman, P. L. (1996). Linking transformational leadership and organizational culture. *Journal of Leadership Studies, 3,* 68–83.

Den Hartog, D. N., Van Muijen, E. J., & Koopman, P. L. (1997). Transactional versus transformational leadership: An analysis of the MLQ. *Journal of Occupational and Organizational Psychology, 70,* 19–34.

Densten, I. L., & Sarros, J. C. (1995). *Leadership and burnout in an Australian law enforcement organization.* Doctoral dissertation, Monash University, Melbourne, Australia.

Dirks, K. T., & Ferrin, D. L. (2002). Trust in leadership: Meta-analytic findings and implications for organizational research. *Journal of Applied Psychology, 87,* 611–628.

Dragoni, L., Tesluk, P. E., Russell, J. E. A., & Oh, I. (2009). Understanding managerial development: Integrating developmental assignments, learning orientation, and access to developmental opportunities in predicting managerial competencies. *Journal of Applied Psychology, 32,* 731–743.

Drucker, P. (1993). *Managing for the future: The 1990s and beyond.* New York: Truman Tally Books.

Dumdum, U. R., Lowe, K. B., & Avolio, B. J. (2002). A meta-analysis of transformational and transactional leadership correlates of effectiveness and satisfaction: An update and extension. In B. J. Avolio & F. J. Yammarino (Eds.), *Transformational and charismatic leadership: The road ahead* (pp. 35–66). Oxford, UK: Elsevier Science.

Dvir, T., Eden, D., Avolio, B. J., & Shamir, B. (2002). Impact of transformational leadership training on follower development and performance: A field experiment. *Academy of Management Journal, 45,* 735–744.

Dvir, T., & Shamir, B. (2003). Follower developmental characteristics as predicting transformational leadership: A longitudinal field study. *The Leadership Quarterly, 14*(3), 327.

Eagly, A. H. (1991, August). *Gender and leadership.* Paper presented at the national meeting of the American Psychological Association, San Francisco.

Eagly, A. H. (2005). Achieving relational authenticity in leadership: Does gender matter? *The Leadership Quarterly, 16*(3), 459–474.

Eagly, A. H., & Carli, L. L. (2003a). The female leadership advantage: An evaluation of the evidence. *The Leadership Quarterly, 14*(6), 807–834.

Eagly, A. H., & Carli, L. L. (2003b). Finding gender advantage and disadvantage: Systematic research integration is the solution. *The Leadership Quarterly, 14*(6), 851–859.

Eagly, A. H., & Johannesen-Schmidt, M. C. (2001). The leadership styles of women and men. *Journal of Social Issues, 57,* 781–797.

Eagly, A. H., Johannesen-Schmidt, M. C., & van Engen, M. L. (2003). Transformational, transactional, and laissez-faire leadership styles: A meta-analysis comparing women and men. *Psychological Bulletin, 129,* 569–591.

Eagly, A. H., & Johnson, B. T. (1990). Gender and leadership styles: A meta-analysis. *Psychological Bulletin, 108,* 233–256.

Eagly, A. H., & Karau, S. J. (2002). Role congruity theory of predjudice toward female leaders. *Psychological Review, 109,* 573–598.

Eden, D. (1990). *Pygmalion in management: Productivity as self-fulfilling prophecy.* Lexington, MA: Lexington.

Eden, D., & Shani, A. B. (1992). Pygmalion goes to boot camp: Expectancy, leadership, and trainee performance. *Journal of Applied Psychology, 67,* 194–199.

Fegley, S. (2006, September). *SHRM 2006 strategic HR management survey report.* Alexandria, VA: Society for Human Resource Management.

Follett, M. P. (1924). The creative experience. New York: Longmans Green.

Frankl, V. E. (1963). *Man's search for meaning: An introduction to logo therapy.* New York: Pocket Books.

Frost, P. J. (1997). Cross-roads. *Organizational Science, 8,* 332–347.

Fukujama, F. (1995). *Trust: The social virtues and creation of prosperity.* New York: Free Press.

Gal, R. (1981). *A portrait of an Israeli soldier.* Westport, CT: Greenwood.

Garcia, E. L. (1995). *Transformational leadership processes and salesperson performance effectiveness: A theoretical model and partial empirical examination.* Unpublished doctoral dissertation, Fielding Institute, Santa Barbara, CA.

Gardner, W. L., & Avolio, B. J. (1998). Charismatic leadership: The role of impression management. *Academy of Management Review, 23,* 32–58.

Gardner, W. L., Avolio, B. J., Luthans, F., May, D. R., & Walumbwa, F. (2005). "Can you see the real me?" A self-based model of authentic leadership and follower development. *The Leadership Quarterly, 16*(3), 343–372.

Gardner, W. L., Avolio, B. J., & Walumbwa, F. (2006). *Authentic leadership theory and practice: Origins, effects and development.* Amsterdam: Elsevier JAI Press.

Gasper, R. (1992). *Transformational leadership: An integrative review of the literature.* Unpublished doctoral dissertation, Western Michigan University, Kalamazoo.

Gelfand, M. J., Erez, M., & Aycan, Z. (2007). Cross-cultural organizational behavior. *Annual Review of Psychology, 58,* 479–514.

Gersick, C. J. G. (1988). Time and transition in work teams: Toward a new model of group development. *Academy of Management Journal, 31,* 9–41.

Geyer, A. L. J., & Steyrer, J. M. (1998). Transformational leadership and objective performance in banks. *Applied Psychology: An International Review, 47,* 397–420.

Gibbons, T. C. (1986). *Revisiting the question of born vs. made: Toward a theory of development of transformational leaders.* Unpublished doctoral dissertation, Fielding Institute, Santa Barbara, CA.

Gillis, C., Getkate, M., Robinson, D., & Porporino, F. (1995). Correctional work supervisor leadership and credibility: Their influence on offender work motivation. *Forum on Correctional Research, 7,* 15–17.

Gladstein, D. (1984). Groups in context: A model of task group effectiveness. *Administrative Science Quarterly, 29*(4)*,* 499–517.

Greenleaf, R. K., (1997). The servant as leader. In R. P. Vecchio (Ed.), *Leadership: Understanding the dynamics of power and influence in organizations* (pp. 542–562) Notre Dame, IN: University of Notre Dame Press.

Grove, A. (1996). *Only the paranoid survive: How to exploit the crisis points that challenge every company.* New York: Random House.

Gully, S. M., Incalcaterra, K. A., Joshi, A., & Beaubian, J. M. (2005). A meta-analysis of team-efficacy, potency, and performance: Interdependence and level of analysis as moderators of observed relationships. *Journal of Applied Psychology, 87,* 819–832.

Hackman, J. R. (1990). *Groups that work (and those that don't): Creating conditions for effective teamwork.* San Francisco: Jossey-Bass.

Hackman, J. R., Furnis, A. H., Hills, M. J., & Peterson, R. J. (1992). Perceptions of gender-role characteristics and transformational and transactional leadership behaviors. *Perceptual and Motor Skills, 75,* 311–319.

Hamel, G., & Prahalad, C. K. (1994). *Competing for the future: Breakthrough strategies for seizing control of your industry and creating the markets of tomorrow.* Boston: Harvard Business School Press.

Hannah, S. T., Avolio, B. J., Walumbwa, F., & Peterson, S. J. (2010). *The influence of authentic leadership on followers behavior and performance: A three study investigation.* Unpublished manuscript.

Hannah, S. T., Uhl-Bien, M., Avolio, B. J., & Cabarretta, F. (2009). A framework for examining leadership in extreme contexts. *The Leadership Quarterly, 20*(6)*, 897–919.*

Hannah, S. T., Woolfolk, L., & Lord, R. G. (2009). Leader self-structure: A framework for positive leadership. *Journal of Organizational Behavior, 30,* 269–290.

Hater, J. J., & Bass, B. M. (1988). Superiors' evaluations and subordinates' perceptions of transformational and transactional leadership. *Journal of Applied Psychology, 73,* 695–702.

Heifetz, R. (1994). *Leadership without any easy answers.* Boston: Harvard Business Press.

Hesketh, M. (1997). Dilemmas in transfer of training. *Applied Psychology: An International Review, 46,* 317–386.

Hicks, R. S. (1990). *Effectiveness of transactional and transformational leadership in turbulent and stable conditions.* Unpublished doctoral dissertation, Claremont Graduate School, Claremont, CA.

Hofstede, G. H. (1991). *Cultures and organizations: Software of the mind.* New York: McGraw-Hill.

Hofstede, G. H. (2001). *Culture's consequences: Comparing values, behaviors, institutions, and organizations across nations.* Thousand Oaks, CA: Sage.

Holladay, S. J., & Coombs, W. T. (1994). Speaking of visions and visions being spoken. *Management Communication Quarterly, 8*(2), 165–189.

Horine, J., & Bass, B. M. (1993). *Transformational leadership: The cornerstone of quality* (Report No. 933). Binghamton, NY: Binghamton University, Center for Leadership Studies.

House, R. J., Hanges, P. J., Javidan, M., Dorfman, P.W., & Gupta, V. (2004). *Culture, leadership, and organizations: The GLOBE study of 62 societies.* Thousand Oaks, CA: Sage.

Howell, J. A., & Avolio, B. J. (1993). Predicting consolidated unit performance: Leadership behavior, locus of control, and support for innovation. *Journal of Applied Psychology, 78,* 891–902.

Howell, J. A., & Avolio, B. J. (1992). Charismatic leadership: Submission or liberation. *Academy of Management Executive, 6,* 43–54.

Howell, J. J., & Higgins, C. A. (1992). Leadership behaviors influence tactics and career experience of champions of technical innovation. *The Leadership Quarterly, 1*(4), 249–264.

Howell, J. M., & Boies, K. (2004). Champions of technological innovation: The influence of contextual knowledge, role orientation, idea generation, and idea promotion on champion emergence. *The Leadership Quarterly, 15*(1), 123–143.

Howell, J. M., & Higgins, C. A. (1990). Champions of technological innovations. *Administrative Science Quarterly, 35*(2), 317–341.

Howell, J. M., Neufeld, D. J., & Avolio, B. J. (1998). *Leadership at a distance: The effects of physical distance, charismatic leadership, and communication style on predicting business unit performance.* Unpublished manuscript, University of Western Ontario, London, Ontario, Canada.

Howell, J. M., Neufeld, D. J., & Avolio, B. J. (2005). Leadership at a distance: The effects of physical distance, charismatic leadership, and communication style on predicting business unit performance. *The Leadership Quarterly, 16,* 273–286.

Howell, J. M., & Shamir, B. (2005). The role of followers in the charismatic leadership process: Relationships and their consequences. *Academy of Management Review, 30,* 96–112.

Howell, J. M., & Shea, M. C. (1998). *The effects of champion strengths, boundary activities, and support for innovation on team potency and product innovation.* Unpublished manuscript, University of Western Ontario, London, Ontario, Canada.

HR News. (1997, August). The importance of trust in organizations. *SHRM Newsletter,* 1–5.

Hyatt, D. E., & Ruddy, Y. M. (1997). An examination of the relationship between work group characteristics and performance: Once more into the breech. *Personnel Psychology, 50,* 553–585.

Ilies, R., Gerhardt, M. W., & Le, H. (2004). Individual differences in leadership emergence: Integrating meta-analytic findings and behavioral genetics estimates. *International Journal of Selection and Assessment, 12,* 207–219.

Jack's men. (1977, July 7). *Industry Week,* pp. 12–17.

Jehn, K. A. (1997). A qualitative analysis of conflict types and dimensions in organizational groups. *Administrative Science Quarterly, 42,* 530–557.

Johnson, A., & Beyerlein, S. T. (1996). *Advances in interdisciplinary studies of work teams* (pp. 173–209). Greenwich, CT: JAI Press.

Johnson, A. M., Vernon, P. A., Molson, M., Harris, J. A., & Jang, K. L. (1998). *Born to lead: A behavior genetic investigation of leadership ability.* Paper presented at the national meeting of the Society for Industrial Organizational Psychology, Dallas, TX.

Judge, T. A., & Piccolo, R. (2004). Transformational and transactional leadership: A meta-analytic test of their relative validity. *Journal of Applied Psychology, 89,* 755–768.

Kahai, S. S., & Avolio, B. J. (2008). Effects of leadership style and anonymity on the discussion of an ethical issue in an electronic meeting system context. In S. Weisband (Ed.), *Leadership at a distance: Research in technologically-supported work* (pp. 97–126). Hillsdale, NJ: Lawrence Erlbaum.

Kahai, S. S., Avolio, B. J., & Sosik, J. J. (1998). Effects of source, participant anonymity, and initial difference in opinion in an EMS context. *Decision Sciences, 29,* 427–460.

Kahai, S. S., Sosik, J. J., & Avolio, B. J. (1997). Effects of leadership style and problem structure on work group process and outcomes in an electronic meeting system environment. *Personnel Psychology, 50,* 121–146.

Kark, R., & Shamir, B. (2002). The dual effect of transformational leadership: Priming relational and collective selves and further effects on followers. In B. J. Avolio & F. J. Yammarino (Eds.), *Transformational and charismatic leadership: The road ahead* (Vol. 2, pp. 67–91). Oxford, UK: Elsevier Science.

Kark, R., Shamir, B., & Chen, G. (2003). The two faces of transformational leadership: Empowerment and dependency. *Journal of Applied Psychology, 88,* 246–255.

Kazenbach, J. R., & Smith, D. K. (1993). *The wisdom of teams: Creating the high-performing organization.* Boston: Harvard Business School Press.

Kazenbach, J. R. (1998). *Teams at the top.* Boston: Harvard Business School Press.

Kegan, R., & Lahey, L. L. (2009). *Immunity to change. How to overcome it and unlock the potential in yourself and your organization.* Boston: Harvard Business School Press.

Keller, R. T. (1992). Transformational leadership and the performance of research and development project groups. *Journal of Management, 18,* 489–501.

Keller, R. T. (2006). Transformational leadership, initiating structure, and substitutes for leadership: A longitudinal study of research and development project team performance. *Journal of Applied Psychology, 91,* 202–210.

Kelley, R. E. (1992). *The power of followership: How to create leaders people want to follow, and followers who lead themselves.* New York: Doubleday/Currency.

Kelloway, E. K., & Barling, J. (1993). Members' participation in local union activities: Measurement, prediction, and replication. *Journal of Applied Psychology, 78,* 262–279.

Kernis, M. H. (2003). Toward a conceptualization of optimal self-esteem. *Psychological Inquiry, 14*(1), 1–26.

Kirkman, B. L., Lowe, K. B., & Gibson, C. B. (2006). A quarter century of culture's consequences: A review of empirical research incorporating Hofstede's cultural values framework. *Journal of International Business Studies, 37,* 285–320.

Koh, W. L. K. (1990). *An empirical validation of the theory of transformational leadership in secondary schools in Singapore.* Unpublished doctoral dissertation, University of Oregon, Eugene.

Koh, W., Terburg, J. R., & Steers, R. M. (1992). *The impact of transformational leadership on organizational commitment, organizational citizenship behavior, teacher satisfaction, and student performance in Singapore.* Paper presented at the Academy of Management, Miami Beach, FL.

Kotter, J. L. (1992). *Corporate culture and performance.* New York: Free Press.

Kouzes, J. M., & Posner, B. Z. (1991). *Credibility: How leaders gain and lose it. Why people demand it.* San Francisco: Jossey-Bass.

Kozlowski, S. W. J., Gully, S. M., Salas, E., & Canon-Bowers, J. A. (1996). Team leadership and development: Theories, principles, and guidelines for training leaders and teams. In M. M. Beyerlein, D. A. Johnson, & S. T. Beyerlein (Eds.), *Advances in interdisciplinary studies of work teams* (pp. 253–291). Greenwich, CT: JAI Press.

Kuhnert, K. W. (1994). Developing people through delegation. In B. M. Bass & B. J. Avolio (Eds.), *Improving organizational effectiveness through transformational leadership* (pp. 10–25). Thousand Oaks, CA: Sage.

Kuhnert, K. W., & Lewis, P. (1987). Transactional and transformational leadership: A constructive developmental analysis. *Academy of Management Review, 12,* 648–657.

Kumpfer, K. L., Turner, C., Hopkins, R., & Librett, J. (1993). Leadership and team effectiveness in community coalitions for the presentation of alcohol and other drug abuse. *Health Education Research, 9,* 359–374.

Lahey, L., Souvaine, E., Kegan, R., Goodman, R., & Felix, S. (1991). *A guide to the subject-object interview: Administration and interpretation.* Unpublished manuscript, Harvard University, Graduate School of Education, Boston.

Laing, R. D. (1981). *Dialogue with R. D. Laing: The man and his ideas.* New York: Praeger.

Lehnen, L. P., Ayman, R., & Korabik, K. (1995). *The effects of transformational leadership and conflict management styles on subordinates' satisfaction with supervision.* Paper presented at the annual conference of the Society for Industrial Organizational Psychology, Orlando, FL.

Leithwood, K., & Jantzi, D. (1990). Transformational leadership: How principals can help reform cultures. *School Effectiveness and School Improvement, 1,* 249–280.

Leithwood, K., Jantzi, D., Silins, H., & Dart, B. (1990). *Using the appraisal of school leaders as an instrument for school restructuring.* Unpublished manuscript.

Leithwood, K., & Steinbach, R. (1991). Indicators of transformational leadership in everyday problem solving of school administrators. *Journal of Personnel Evaluation in Education, 4,* 221–243.

Lerner, J. S., & Tetlock, P. E. (1994). Accountability and social cognition. In V. S. Ramachandra (Ed.), *Encyclopedia of human behavior* (Vol. 1, pp. 3098–3121). San Diego, CA: Academic Press.

Leung, K., Bhagat, R. S., Buchan, N. R., Erez, M., & Gibson, C. B. (2005). Culture and international business: Recent advances and their implications for future research. *Journal of International Business Studies 36,* 357–378.

Levy, S. R., Stroessner, S. J., & Dweck, C. S. (1998). Stereotype formation and endorsement: The role of implicit theories. *Journal of Personality and Social Psychology, 74,* 1421–1436.

Liao, H., & Chuang, A. (2007). Transforming service employees and climate: A multilevel, multisource examination of transformational leadership in building long-term service relationships. *Journal of Applied Psychology, 92,* 1006–1019.

Lord, R. G., & Brown, D. J. (2004). *Leadership processes and follower self-identity.* Hillsdale, NJ: Lawrence Erlbaum.

Lord, R. G., & Hall, R. J. (2005). Identity, deep structure and the development of leadership skills. *The Leadership Quarterly, 16,* 591–615.

Lord, R. G., & Maher, K. J. (1991). *Leadership and information processing: Linking perceptions and performance.* Boston: Routledge.

Lowe, K., Kroeck, K. G., & Sivasubramaniam, N. (1996). Effectiveness correlates of transformational and transactional leadership: A meta-analytic review. *The Leadership Quarterly, 7*(3), 385–425.

Lucius, R., & Kuhnert, K. (1997). *Adult development and leadership: Examining tomorrow's leaders today.* Unpublished manuscript, University of Georgia, Athens.

Luthans, F., Avey, J. B., Avolio, B. J., & Peterson, S. J. (in press). Impact of micro intervention training on psychological capital and development. *Human Resource Development Quarterly.*

Luthans, F., Norman, S. M., Avolio, B. J., & Avey, J. B. (2008). The mediating role of psychological capital in the supportive organizational climate: Employee performance relationship. *Journal of Organizational Behavior, 29,* 219–238.

Luthans, F. L., Youssef, C., & Avolio, B. J. (2007). *Psychological capital: Developing the human capital edge.* Oxford, UK: Oxford University Press.

Manz. C. M. (1986). Self-leadership: Toward an expanded theory of self-influence process in organizations. *Academy of Management Review, 11,* 585–600.

Manz, C. M., & Sims, H. P., Jr. (1991). *Super leadership: Leading others to lead themselves.* Upper Saddle River, NJ: Prentice Hall.

Martin, M. M. (1996). *Leadership in a cultural trust chasm: An analysis of trust-directed behaviors and vision-directed behaviors that lead to positive follower attitude responses.* Unpublished doctoral dissertation, Virginia Commonwealth University, Richmond.

Masi, R. J. (1994). *Transformational leadership and its roles in empowerment, productivity, and commitment to quality.* Unpublished doctoral dissertation, University of Illinois, Chicago.

Matusek, L. R. (1997). *Finding your voice: Learning to lead anywhere you want to make a difference.* San Francisco: Jossey-Bass.

McKenzie, G. (1998). *Orbiting the giant hairball.* Harmondsworth, UK: Penguin.

Meindle, J. R., Ehrlich, S. B., & Dukerich, J. M. (1985). The romance of leadership. *Administrative Sciences Quarterly, 30,* 78–102.

Miller, D. (1990). *The Icarus Paradox: How exceptional companies bring about their downfall.* New York: Harper Business.

Miller, H. (1997). Interview with Max Depree. *Leader to Leader, 6,* 18–23.

Most, R., & Avolio, B. J. (1997). Utilizing Web-site technology in developing the full potential of organizations. *Industrial Psychologist, 34*(4), 11–13.

Mumford, M., Stokes, G. S., & Owens, W. A. (1990). *Patterns of life history: The* ecology *of human development.* Hillsdale, NJ: Lawrence Erlbaum.

Niehoff, B. F., Eng, C. A., & Grover, R. A. (1990). The impact of top management actions on employee attitudes and perceptions. *Group and Organizational Studies, 15,* 337–352.

O'Connor, J., Mumford, M. D., Clifton, T. C., Gessner, T. L., & Connelly, M. S. (1995). Charismatic leaders and destructiveness: An historiometric study. *The Leadership Quarterly, 6*(4), 529–558.

O'Connor P. M. G., & Quinn L. (2004). Organizational capacity for leadership. In C. D. McCauley & E. Van Velsor (Eds.), *The Center for Creative Leadership handbook of leadership development.* San Francisco: Jossey-Bass.

Onnen, M. K. (1987). *The relationship of clergy leadership characteristics to growing or declining churches.* Unpublished doctoral dissertation, University of Louisville, Louisville, KY.

Pearce, C. L. (2004). The future of leadership: Combining vertical and shared leadership to transform knowledge work. *Academy of Management Executive 18,* 47–57.

Pearce, C. L., & Conger, J. A. (2003). *Shared leadership: Reframing the hows and whys of leadership.* Thousand Oaks, CA: Sage.

Peck, M. S. (1993). *A world waiting to be born: Civility rediscovered.* New York: Bantam.

Pereira, D. F. (1986). *Factors associated with transformational leadership in an Indian engineering firm.* Unpublished manuscript.

Peterson, S. J., & Zhang, Z. (in press). Examining the relationships between top management team psychological characteristics, transformational leadership, and business unit performance. In M. A. Carpenter (Ed.), *Handbook of top management research.* New York: Edward Elgar.

Philbin, L. P. (1997). *Transformational leadership and the secondary school principal.* Unpublished doctoral dissertation, Purdue University, Lafayette, IN.

Pillai, R. (1993). *The role of structural, contextual, and cultural factors in the emergence of charismatic leadership in organizations.* Unpublished doctoral dissertation, State University of New York at Buffalo.

Pillai, R. (1996). Crisis and the emergence of charismatic leadership in groups: An experimental investigation. *Journal of Applied Social Psychology, 26,* 543–562.

Pillai, R., Schriesheim, C. A., & Williams, E. S. (1999). Fairness perceptions and trust as mediators for transformational and transactional leadership: A two-sample study. *Journal of Management, 25,* 897–933.

Pitman, B., III. (1993). *The relationship between charismatic leadership behaviors and organizational commitment among white-collar workers.* Unpublished doctoral dissertation, Georgia State University, Atlanta.

Plomin, R., & Daniels, D. (1987). Why are children in the same family so different from each other? *Behavioral and Brain Sciences, 10,* 1–16.

Podsakoff, P. M., Todor, W. D., Grover, R A., & Huber, V. L. (1984). Situational indicators of leader reward and punishment behaviors: Fact or fiction? *Organizational Behavior and Human Performance, 34,* 21–63.

Popper, M., & Liphshitz, R. (n.d.). *Organizational teaming: Mechanisms and feasibility.* Unpublished manuscript, University of Haifa, Haifa, Israel.

Popper, M., Mayseless, O., & Castelnovo, O. (1998). *Transformational leadership attachment.* Unpublished manuscript, University of Haifa, Haifa, Israel.

Quinn, J. B. (1997). *Innovation explosion: Using intellect and software to revolutionize growth strategies.* New York: Free Press.

Quinn, J. B., Anderson, P., & Finkelstein, R. (1996). Managing professional intellect: Making the most of the best. *Harvard Business Review, 20,* 72–80.

Rest, J. R. (1986). *Moral development: Advances in research and theory.* New York: Prayer.

Rivera, J. B. (1994). *Visionary versus crisis-induced charismatic leadership: An experimental test.* Unpublished doctoral dissertation, Texas Tech University, Lubbock.

Rose, R. J. (1995). Genes and human behavior. *Annual Review of Psychology, 46,* 625–654.

Ryan, R. M., & Deci, E. L. (2001). To be happy or to be self-fulfilled: A review of research on hedonic and eudaimonic well-being. In S. Fiske (Ed.), *Annual Review of Psychology* (Vol. 52, pp. 141–166). Palo Alto, CA: Annual Reviews, Inc.

Salas, E., Mullen, B., Rozell, D., & Driskell, J. E. (1997, April). *The effects of team building on performance: An integration.* Paper presented at the national meeting of the Society for Industrial and Organizational Psychology, St. Louis, MO.

Schein, V. E. (2001). A global look at psychological barriers to women's progress in management. *Journal of Social Issues, 57,* 675–688.

Seltzer, J., Numerof, R. E., & Bass, B. M. (1989). Transformational leadership: Is it a source of more burnout and stress? *Journal of Health and Human Resources Administration, 12,* 174–185.

Sergiovanni, T. J. (1990). *Value-added leadership: How to get extraordinary results in schools.* Orlando, FL: Harcourt Brace.

Shamir, B., House, R. J., & Arthur, M. B. (1993). The motivational effects of charismatic leadership: A self-concept based theory. *Organizational Science, 4,* 577–594.

Shamir, B. (1995). Social distance and charisma. *The Leadership Quarterly, 6*(1), 19–47.

Shamir, B., Zakay, E., Breinin, E., & Popper, M. (1998a). *Diversity and homogeneity of charisma within groups.* Unpublished manuscript, Hebrew University, Jerusalem, Israel.

Shamir, B., Zakay, E., Breinin, E., & Popper, M. (1998b). *Leadership and social identification in military units: Direct and indirect relationships.* Unpublished manuscript, Hebrew University, Jerusalem, Israel.

Shea, C., & Howell, J. H. (1995). *The effects of charismatic leadership and task feedback on self-efficacy, performance quality, and attributes.* Doctoral dissertation, Richard Ivey School of Business, Western Ontario, Canada.

Sheff, D. (1996, June/July). Levi's changes everything. *Fast Company,* p. 65.

Sheldon, K. M., & Elliot, A. J. (1999). Goal striving, need-satisfaction, and longitudinal well-being: The self-concordance model. *Journal of Personality and Social Psychology, 76,* 482–497.

Silins, H. C. (1992). Effective leadership for school reform. *Alberta Journal of Educational Research, 38,* 317–334.

Sinclair, A. (1992). The tyranny of team idealogy. *Organizational Studies, 13,* 611–626.

Sivasubramaniam, N., Murry, W. D., Avolio, B. J., & Jung, D. I. (2002). A longitudinal model of the effects of team leadership and group potency on group performance. *Group and Organization Management, 27,* 66–96.

Sosik, J. J., Avolio, B. J., & Kahai, S. S. (1997). The impact of leadership style and anonymity on group potency and effectiveness in a GDSS environment. *Journal of Applied Psychology, 82,* 89–103.

Stewart, G., & Manz, C. C. (1994). *Leadership for self-managing work teams: A theoretical integration.* Paper presented at the national conference of the Society for Industrial and Organizational Psychology, Nashville, TN.

Storm, H. (1994). *Lightning bolt.* New York: Ballantine.

Tapscott, D. (1995). *The Digital economy: Promise and peril in the age of networked intelligence.* New York: McGraw-Hill.

Team. (2008). In *Concise Oxford English dictionary.* Oxford, UK: Oxford Univerity Press.

Tepper, B. J. (1993). *Patterns of downward influence and follower conformity in transactional and transformational leadership.* Unpublished doctoral dissertation, University of Kentucky, Lexington.

Thite, M. (1997). *Relationship between leadership and information technology project sources.* Unpublished doctoral dissertation, Swinburne University of Technology, Melbourne, Australia.

Three-block war. (n.d.). In *Wikipedia.* Retrieved on May 12, 2010, from http://en.wikipedia.org/wiki/Three_block_war

Turner, N., & Barling, J. (1998). *Moral reasoning and transformational leadership.* Kingston, Ontario, Canada: Queen's University.

Turner, N., Barling, J., & Epitropski, O. (2002). Transformational leadership and moral reasoning. *Journal of Applied Psychology, 87,* 304–310.

Vernon, T. (1996). Personal communication on results concerning the heritability of self-ratings of leadership using the Multifactor Leadership Questionnaire (MLQ).

Waldman, D. A., Bass, B. M., & Yammarino, F. J. (1990). Adding to the contingent-reward behavior: The augmenting effect of charismatic leadership. *Group and Organizational Studies, 15,* 381–394.

Waldman, D. A., Javidan, M., & Varella, P. (2004). Charismatic leadership at the strategic level: A new application of upper echelons theory. *The Leadership Quarterly, 15*(3), 355–380.

Waldman, D. A., Ramirez, G. G., House, R. J., & Puranam, P. (2001). Does leadership matter? CEO leadership attributes and profitability under conditions of perceived environmental uncertainty. *Academy of Management Journal, 44*(1), 134–143.

Walumbwa, F. O., Avolio, B. J., Gardner, W. L., Wernsing, T. S., & Peterson, S. J. (2008). Authentic leadership: Development and validation of a theory-based measure. *Journal of Management, 34,* 89–126.

Walumbwa, F. O., Avolio, B. J., & Zhu, W. (2008). How transformational leadership weaves its influence on individual job performance: The role of identification and efficacy beliefs. *Personnel Psychology, 61,* 793–825.

Walumbwa, F. O., Lawler, J. J., & Avolio, B. J. (2007). Leadership, individual differences, and work-related attitudes: A cross-culture investigation. *Applied Psychology–An International Review–Psychologie Appliquee–Revue Internationale, 56,* 212–230.

Wang, H., Law, K. S., Hackett, R. D., Wang, D., & Chen, Z. X. (2005). Leader-member exchange as a mediator of the relationship between transformational leadership and followers' performance and organizational citizenship behavior. *Academy of Management Journal, 48,* 420–432.

Watson, W. (2002). *Weathering the storm: A study of employee attitudes and opinions.* Retrieved November 29, 2007, from www.watsonwyatt.com

Weber, M. (1947). *The theory of social and economic organizations* (T. Parsons, Trans.). New York: Free Press. (Original work published 1927)

Weber, T. J., Carsten, M. K., Harms, P. D., & Avolio, B. J. (2009). *Transformational leadership and follower outcomes: A meta-analysis of direct and mediating links.* Paper presented at the Academy of Management Meetings, August 7–11, Chicago.

Weick, K. (1991). Educational organizations as loosely coupled systems. *Administrative Sciences Quarterly, 21,* 1–19.

Weierter, S. (1994). *Substitutes for transactional leadership: The impact of transactional leader behaviors on workgroup perceptions at the first line supervisor level.* Unpublished doctoral dissertation, Griffith University, Brisbane, Australia.

Weisband, A. (2008). Research challenges for studying leadership at a distance. In S. Weisband (Ed.). *Leadership at a distance: Research in technologically-supported work* (pp. 3–12). Hillsdale, NJ: Lawrence Erlbaum.

Wernsing, T. S. (2010). *Leader self-awareness development: An intervention and test of a theoretical model.* Unpublished doctoral dissertation, University of Nebraska, Lincoln.

Westley, F., & Mintzberg, H. (1991). Visionary leadership and strategic management. In J. Henry & D. Walker (Eds.), *Managing innovation.* Thousand Oaks, CA: Sage.

Wofford, J. C., Goodwin, V. L., & Whittington, J. L. (1998). A field study of a cognitive approach to understanding transformational and transactional leadership. *The Leadership Quarterly, 9*(1), 55–84.

Xiao, Y., Seagull, F. J., Mackenzie, C. F., Klein, K. J., & Ziegert, J. (2008). Adaption of team communication patterns: Exploring the effects of leadership at a distance: Task urgency, and shared team experience. In S. Weisband (Ed.), *Leadership at a distance: Research in technologically-supported work* (pp. 71–96). Hillsdale, NJ: Lawrence Erlbaum.

Yagil, D. (1998). *Charismatic leadership and organizational hierarchy: Attribution of charisma to close and distant leaders.* Unpublished manuscript, University of Haifa, Haifa, Israel.

Yammarino, F. J., & Bass, B. M. (1990). Long-term forecasting of transformational leadership. In *Measures of leadership* (pp. 151–169). West Orange, NJ: Leadership Library of America.

Zhu, W., Chew, I., & Spangler, W. D. (2005). The effect of CEO transformational leadership on organizational outcomes: Mediating role of human capital enhancing HRM. *The Leadership Quarterly, 16,* 39–52.

INDEX

ABOUT THE AUTHOR

Bruce J. Avolio

Marion B. Ingersoll Professor, Executive Director, Center for Leadership and Strategic Thinking

Michael G. Foster School of Business, University of Washington

Dr. Avolio has an international reputation as a researcher and practitioner in leadership. He has consulted with public and private organizations in North and South America, Africa, Europe, and Southeast Asia, as well as in Australia, New Zealand, Saudi Arabia, and Israel. His research and consulting includes work with the militaries of the United States of America, Singapore, Sweden, Finland, Israel, and South Africa.

Dr. Avolio is a fellow of the Academy of Management, American Psychological Society, American Psychological Association, and the Gerontological Society. He is the former president of both the Society for Human Resource Management Foundation and the Organizational Behavior Division of the Academy of Management.

Dr. Avolio has published 10 books and over 125 articles on leadership and related areas. His books include *Transformational and Charismatic Leadership: The Road Ahead* (Elsevier Science, 2002), *Full Leadership Development: Building the Vital Forces in Organizations* (Sage, 1999), and *Developing Potential Across a Full Range of Leadership: Cases on Transactional and Transformational Leadership* (Lawrence Erlbaum, 2000). His newest books are *Leadership Development in Balance: Made/Born* (Lawrence Erlbaum, 2005), *The High Impact Leader: Moments Matter in Authentic Leadership Development* (McGraw-Hill, 2006), and *Psychological Capital: Developing the Human Competitive Edge* (Oxford Press, 2007) with Fred Luthans and Carolyn Youssef.

Dr. Avolio has worked with government agencies on national leadership development projects and with governments at the state and local levels. His current projects include

- working with public healthcare leaders to design a leadership institute for healthcare providers and educators,
- working on a 4-year project with the U.S. Veteran's Administration (VA) on strategic leadership development and ownership, and
- working on several contracts, including a $300K contract with the U.S. Military Academy at West Point to investigate ethical leadership development; a $730K contract to conduct a longitudinal investigation of leadership development with military officers, and a $186K contract with the VA to examine how taking ownership and developing leadership produce better healthcare results.

Dr. Avolio's latest interest and presentations focus on the following:

- How do we accelerate authentic leadership development for maximum impact on performance?
- How do we use the positive psychological capacities of leaders to accelerate change?
- How do we show decision makers the return on development investment in leadership?
- How can we develop leaders and leadership to effectively operate in extreme contexts?

Supporting researchers for more than 40 years

Research methods have always been at the core of SAGE's publishing program. Founder Sara Miller McCune published SAGE's first methods book, *Public Policy Evaluation*, in 1970. Soon after, she launched the *Quantitative Applications in the Social Sciences* series—affectionately known as the "little green books."

Always at the forefront of developing and supporting new approaches in methods, SAGE published early groundbreaking texts and journals in the fields of qualitative methods and evaluation.

Today, more than 40 years and two million little green books later, SAGE continues to push the boundaries with a growing list of more than 1,200 research methods books, journals, and reference works across the social, behavioral, and health sciences. Its imprints—Pine Forge Press, home of innovative textbooks in sociology, and Corwin, publisher of PreK–12 resources for teachers and administrators—broaden SAGE's range of offerings in methods. SAGE further extended its impact in 2008 when it acquired CQ Press and its best-selling and highly respected political science research methods list.

From qualitative, quantitative, and mixed methods to evaluation, SAGE is the essential resource for academics and practitioners looking for the latest methods by leading scholars.

For more information, visit **www.sagepub.com**.